Postcard History Series

Delray Beach

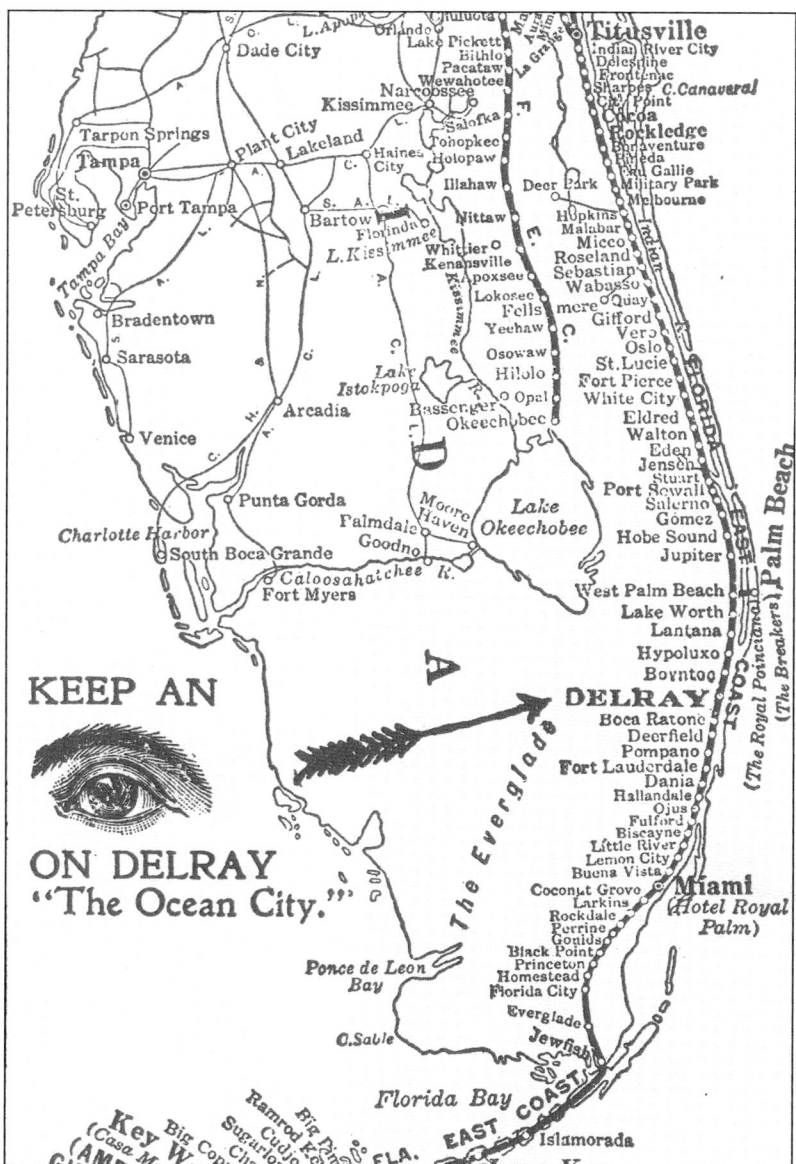

EYE ON DELRAY. This 1920 map is from the inside cover of a local promotional brochure, "Rays of Delray," in the Delray Beach Historical Society archives. The importance of the Florida East Coast Railway is apparent.

ON THE FRONT COVER: In 1911, the town of Delray was incorporated. That same year, the first bridge was built over the canal at the Atlantic Avenue crossing. It was a hand-cranked swing bridge. Boys enjoyed climbing up the pulley wires and diving from the pole tops. Here townspeople are gathered, perhaps for an evening stroll across the new bridge. A tourist boat rests at the dock. At the boathouse, a lifesaving ring reads, "USS Osceola." (Henry Higgins.)

ON THE BACK COVER: "Sunny Greetings from Delray Beach." This 1950s street scene reveals a sunny, palm-lined Atlantic Avenue in front of the Colony Hotel.

Postcard History Series

Delray Beach

Dorothy W. Patterson and Janet M. DeVries

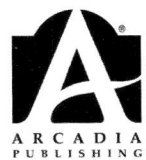

ARCADIA
PUBLISHING

Copyright © 2008 by Dorothy W. Patterson and Janet M. DeVries
ISBN 978-0-7385-5330-6

Published by Arcadia Publishing
Charleston, South Carolina

Printed in the United States of America

Library of Congress Catalog Card Number: 2007934720

For all general information contact Arcadia Publishing at:
Telephone 843-853-2070
Fax 843-853-0044
E-mail sales@arcadiapublishing.com
For customer service and orders:
Toll-Free 1-888-313-2665

Visit us on the Internet at www.arcadiapublishing.com

To the memory of my mother, Jennie Wynnelle Taylor Patterson, an excellent correspondent and a creator of artistic, handmade postcards
—Dorothy W. Patterson

To the savers and collectors who have stowed away all these tiny treasures called postcards for future generations to admire, discover, and glimpse a bit of history
—Janet M. DeVries

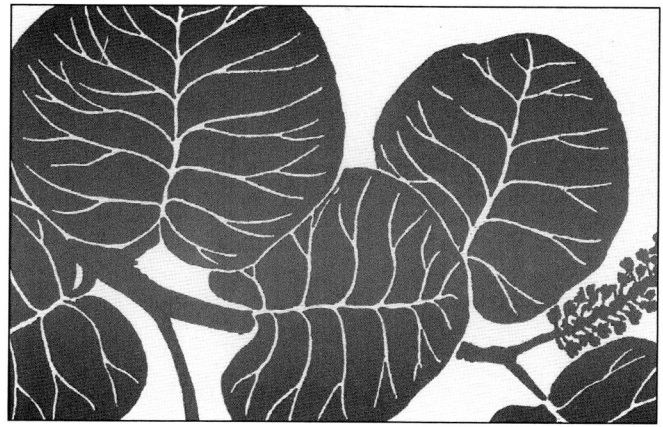

SEA GRAPE LEAVES. This Delray Beach Historical Society exhibit announcement showcases an illustration of sea grape leaves.

Contents

Acknowledgments		6
Introduction		7
A Postcard History		10
1.	Settlement by the Sea	11
2.	Banner Town of Palm Beach County	21
3.	Resort Life Begins with a Boom	33
4.	Anchors of Small-town Life	49
5.	Shimmering Waterways	69
6.	Always Atlantic Avenue	81
7.	Mile-long Municipal Beach	103
8.	Mid-century Years: 1941–1971	117

ACKNOWLEDGMENTS

We are indebted to the many people who, since 1964, have remembered the archives and have donated their postcards to the Delray Beach Historical Society. We want to thank the collectors who kindly lent their postcards for this book. Henry Higgins, who grew up in town, is a collector specializing in Delray Beach postcards. He graciously offered access to his entire collection. Karen Wiita Van Wormer, former executive director of the Delray Beach Historical Society, and Expanding and Preserving our Cultural Heritage (EPOCH) at the Spady Cultural Arts Museum also made their postcards available. All postcards without credit are from the Delray Beach Historical Society's collection.

We are grateful for our time working in the archives of the Delray Beach Historical Society and the Boynton Beach City Library. This learning experience has taught us the importance of collections documenting life in the United States. Appreciation is extended to the members of the Delray Beach Historical Society, Boynton Beach City Library, and Boynton Beach Historical Society.

Local Arcadia authors Susan Gillis, McCall Credle Rosenthal, and Sharon Koskoff were always willing to provide advice. Thank you to Vera Farrington, Dwight Bradshaw, and Mary Swinford for reading the text. We greatly appreciate the editing help from Charles Hofman, grandson of Delray pioneers Adolf and Anna Hofman.

In lieu of a bibliography, we have chosen to use the room for additional images and text. However, all research for this book was performed using the records, files, and collections in the Delray Beach Historical Society archives.

Introduction

Postcards caught my interest in 2006 while designing an archives gallery exhibit titled Florida Collectibles. When focusing on the collection of Henry Higgins, I became more aware of the charming bits of Florida history contained in the postcards. And when I read the messages, I was fascinated by the immediacy of the scraps of human history written there—not to mention that all this communication cost only 1¢ for a period of over 50 years. The following summary of Delray Beach history puts the postcards from the Delray Beach Historical Society's collection—as well as the collections of others—into a framework. This information covers the first 70 years of the 20th century.

The land where Delray Beach now exists seems a place lightly used by humans until about 1895. We have no knowledge of early Spanish settlement, although the 1894–1895 settlers found an old sour orange grove and the remains of a rock wall near the beach. The indigenous people that Jonathan Dickinson met in 1696 when his ship wrecked north of Delray were gone by the time the Lower Creeks (Seminoles) advanced into Florida in the 18th century. An 1841–1842 military map drawn during the Second Seminole War shows a Seminole camp at the site of a spread-out swampy lake now known as Lake Ida. These were temporary camps of small Seminole groups. On some 19th-century maps, a place in the area that is now east Delray was designated the Orange Grove Haul-over.

The U.S. Life Saving Service built the Orange Grove House of Refuge No. 3 (one of five constructed on Florida's southeast coast) in 1876. At that time, between Lake Worth and Biscayne Bay were 60 miles of practically uninhabited tropical wilderness. West of a wide beach was a coastal ridge covered with saw palmetto and cooled by the prevailing southeast breeze. The great river in the ocean, the Gulf Stream, swung in close to land here. Some days the roll and pitch of huge waves scalloped the horizon line. The muck land around the present Intracoastal Waterway was a swampy morass, and a creek called the Spanish River meandered along the coast from present Boca Raton to Delray Beach. Mosquitoes loved it. Caves existed in the ridge along the beach in the area to the north. The old coastline of a previous age can be recognized by a crest of higher land about a mile inland. This second ridge and the land to the west consist of white sandy soil. Settlers from the North thought it looked like snow. Prior to and at the beginning of settlement days, it was covered with scrub pine and palmetto.

Upon Florida's state incorporation in 1845, Section 16 of each township (one square mile) was to be used to support public schools. In 1871, the east half of Section 16 was conveyed for $1.25 an acre to William H. Hunt and Sara G. Gleason, the business partner and wife of William Gleason, who served a two-year term as lieutenant governor of Florida. Gleason had lived in Florida such a short time that he was later ruled ineligible to hold the office. By 1895, the Florida East Coast Line Canal had been made navigable to the House of Refuge. When Henry Flagler's company, the Florida East Coast Railway, began laying track, speculators took note. Anticipating settlers as the railroad pushed south, the Gleason family advertised the land for $25 an acre. Former Saginaw postmaster and U.S. Congressman William S. Linton saw the advertisement and bought a half-section in the beach area from Gleason and Hunt. The settlers purchased other parcels from Flagler's Model Land Company, as well as from Georgia land speculators Simeon Brinson and John Herring. W. S. Linton named the fledgling town for himself.

When the Linton party arrived with a civil engineer, a railroad clerk, a railroad supply agent, and about five farmers, a few African American families were already settled west of the canal, now known as the Intracoastal Waterway. They were working as farmers and fishermen. Many of the first houses were built on Atlantic Avenue and on Swinton Avenue west of the beach area, near the higher land of the old coastal ridge. The people in Linton held high financial hopes for the winter crops sent north on the Florida East Coast Railway, completed through Delray in 1896. This true pioneer experience included hunger, discomfort, suicides, and fears of epidemics like yellow fever. The hardest times were comparatively short, however, because the 20th century and its rapidly compounding technology were fast approaching. Clearing the deep palmetto roots from the land and enduring the heat and stinging insects was difficult, dirty work. No machines were available, and there were only a few horses and mules to help with the work. Moreover, the high hopes were smashed when the hard-won first crop was killed by a freeze. Some of the settlers left amid financial ruin. William Linton defaulted on his land payments, and those who stayed had to pay for their land again. W. W. Blackmer, the former railroad clerk, brought townspeople together in the schoolhouse and proposed a new beginning and a new name. "Delray" was chosen because Blackmer, a Detroit native, liked a section near his old city called del Rey, later anglicized to Delray. The name had come from Mexico. A veteran of the Mexican War, Belgrade resident Anthony Burdeno, had successfully petitioned the town of Belgrade, Michigan, to change its name to del Rey.

African American families stayed when many others left and gave the young community an anchor. Residents of the African American neighborhoods had established a school, two churches, and a Masonic lodge before the end of the 19th century.

For some reason, the census skipped the small settlement in 1900. After 1905, newspaper articles and photographs of Delray events reveal that Japanese settlers from the Yamato farming colony south of town began participating in Delray activities such as attending parades, going to the movies, and shopping. A look at the 1910 census shows a town of 904 citizens from various states around the country, including the Southern states and Michigan; Germany; and a significant number (157) from the Bahamas. Although small, Delray was a fully formed town interested in education and cultural pursuits. Dramatic performances, music clubs, and bands were popular from the beginning. Later a community theater would flourish. Major occupations continued to be farming and fishing. Incorporation of the town of Delray came in 1911, with John Shaw Sundy serving as the first mayor for seven terms.

With the coming of the 1920s Florida real estate boom, Delray shed its homespun pioneer garb and took on the more sophisticated attire of a pretty resort town. Especially during 1924 and 1925, stuccoed Spanish-style homes and buildings were going up at a rapid pace, and remodeling was popular. The mood in South Florida was high; people were making quick profits in real estate and buying new cars.

The effect of the sudden bust and depression in Delray after 1926 was softened by the seasonal visitors who had started a winter colony in Delray and the nearby town of Gulf Stream. During the 1920s and for many years afterward, Delray became known for its artists and authors, especially famous cartoonists. Two nationally syndicated cartoonists—H. T. Webster (creator of *Casper Milquetoast, the Time Soul*) and Fontaine Fox of *Toonerville Trolley* fame—had offices upstairs in the Arcade Building, over the Arcade Tap Room. Other well-known cartoonists came to town, such as Herb Roth, W. J. "Pat" Enright, Wood Cowan, and Denys Wortman. The Arcade Tap Room on East Atlantic Avenue was a relaxing gathering place for the artists and writers who stayed in Delray during the winter season. Among them were illustrators Charles Williams and Herb Niblick and writers Hugh McNair Kahler, Clarence B. Kelland, Nina Wilcox Putnam, and Edna St. Vincent Millay. They were joined by titled aristocrats, famous politicians, entertainers, and sports figures.

During the Depression, not much money was available since the two banks had failed, but progress continued, and the town still looked prosperous because of the previous burst of new building in the boom years. In 1927, the city of Delray merged with the beach area and became the city of Delray Beach. Some have called the 1930s Delray Beach's "golden age of architecture," when the city ranked 50th in population and 10th in building permits in Florida. In the 20th century, homes and buildings in Delray were never very large or pretentious, although several high-rise condominiums appeared along the Intracoastal Waterway in the 1960s. The cityscape was primarily low rise, low density, understated, and filled with palm trees.

For the four years of World War II, the citizens of Delray Beach volunteered to watch the beach and ocean 24 hours a day from the faux bell tower atop the Seacrest Hotel. Nearby, military personnel patrolled the beach on horseback. All of Florida, especially those towns that had been used as military training bases, began changing even more rapidly after World War II. Some of the veterans who had trained at Boca Raton's close-by airfield returned to settle in Delray Beach after the war.

This growth and change persisted through the 1950s and 1960s and to the present. The vibrant social life of the winter months continued, as well as the basic conservatism of the town. Famous people came to see the polo games at Gulf Stream and attend the Polo Ball in Boca Raton. Prominent figures in many fields patronized the restaurants on Atlantic Avenue.

African American citizens organized the Delray Beach Civic League and the Naciremas Club (American spelled backward with an "s" added), founded in 1946 as a base for civil rights actions. Conflict and political turmoil continued into the 1960s over the use of the municipal beach, city pool, and city golf course, among other issues. By 1970, the schools had been integrated.

Delray Beach grew in population by a significant percentage every decade, but because the town was so small in the beginning, it was 1980 before the population passed the 30,000 mark. During the 1970s, the city started to spread west. Land used for farming and hunting was being developed for housing, and the city experienced what some newspaper accounts called "the second boom."

A Postcard History

Postcards are more than souvenirs. They are small pieces of history chronicling everyday events and heralding important occasions. Many postcards, especially those with messages and postmarks, leave important clues to our past. Postcards are collected for a variety of reasons, including sentimental value, historic nature, and in some cases financial investment.

The study and collection of postcards is called deltiology, and collectors are deltiologists. The word derives from the Greek *deltion*, which means "small writing tablet." Worldwide, deltiology is the third largest hobby after stamp collecting and money collecting. Consequently, there are hundreds of postcard clubs in the country and around the world. These clubs—along with historical societies, libraries, museums, and related organizations—host postcard shows on a regular basis.

Postcard history in this country can be traced back to the 1860s, when William Henry Jackson, an artist and photographer, drew pictures of Civil War battlefields on cards and used them for correspondence with his family. The private postal card was developed by John P. Charlton of Philadelphia in 1861, for which he obtained the copyright, and that was later transferred to H. L. Lipman. These cards were adorned with a small border and labeled "Lipman's Postal Card, Patent Applied For." They were on the market until 1873, when the first government postcards appeared.

Plain postcards, which were used prior to the Lipman cards, were issued by individual countries with that nation's stamp affixed upon them. These cards were referred to as postals. The first non-postal card—meaning a privately made postcard where postage had to be affixed—was introduced in Austria in 1869, and by 1870, picture postcards were all the rage.

The first marketing of picture postcards in the United States occurred at the Columbian Exposition in Chicago in 1893. These "pioneer cards" were limited to larger cities, mostly on the eastern seaboard, and required 2¢ for postage. The Private Mailing Card Act of 1898, however, allowed privately printed cards to be mailed for a 1¢ rate. These cards bear the words "Private Mailing Card" and are known to collectors as PMCs.

Beginning in 1901, use of the term "postcard" was allowed by nongovernment printers. Only the name and address of the recipient were allowed on the reverse of the cards, though some companies added white space on the face for messages. The Golden Age of postcards began in 1907. Congress allowed the reverse of the cards to be divided into the name/address section and message section. More creative uses for postcards were born, and thus a collecting explosion soon followed.

Real photo postcards, also known as RPs, or postcards on film stock, were first used around 1900. These early images were mainly advertising pieces. The real photo postcards of the 1900s to the 1950s were very limited productions of small-town views.

In the 1930s, cards with white borders and poorer-quality printing were produced. High-quality, hand-colored, sepia-toned postcards published from the 1920s to the 1940s are known as Albertype cards. The use of new processes and brighter printing dyes on textured or linen paper in the 1930s and 1940s brought about advertising and roadside images with vivid colors.

Americans loved the brightly colored images. A new type of postcard—the color photochrome, or chrome—appeared around 1939. The Union Oil Company started a series of "scenes of the west" chrome postcards advertising its Union 76 service stations. Chromes are still being produced today. The 1¢ mailing rate continued for over 50 years until January 1, 1952, when the U.S. Post Office raised the rate to 2¢.

Postcards have the ability to bear witness to past events, to provoke memories, to promote cultural awareness, and to richly illustrate our history.

One

SETTLEMENT BY THE SEA

The close proximity of the ocean has always been a strong part of Delray Beach's identity. A poem spelling out ENVIRONMENT in a 1914 promotional brochure begins, "Eastward the broad Atlantic rolls upon her coast." Settlers saw the beach as a place of recreation for swimming, fishing, shell collecting, and picnicking. In addition, the beach was a wide-open space in which to enjoy the ocean breeze and seek relief from the mosquitoes—valued activities in the days before air-conditioning. Early on, the ocean provided an important source of food, income, and transportation.

The citizens of Delray Beach have labeled the town for promotional purposes with a variety of names through the years: Delray-by-the-Sea, Picturesque Delray: Coast Line City of Florida, Delray: The Ocean City, and currently Village-by-the-Sea. Residents have always been proud of the beautiful beach and of the human scale that makes Delray Beach a walkable town. In past promotional advertisements, Delray claimed a main street "closest to the ocean" and to be the town "closest to the Gulf Stream," although we know that the Gulf Stream is nearer land a little farther north. Another early publication called it "the only farming city in Florida that is located on the Atlantic Ocean."

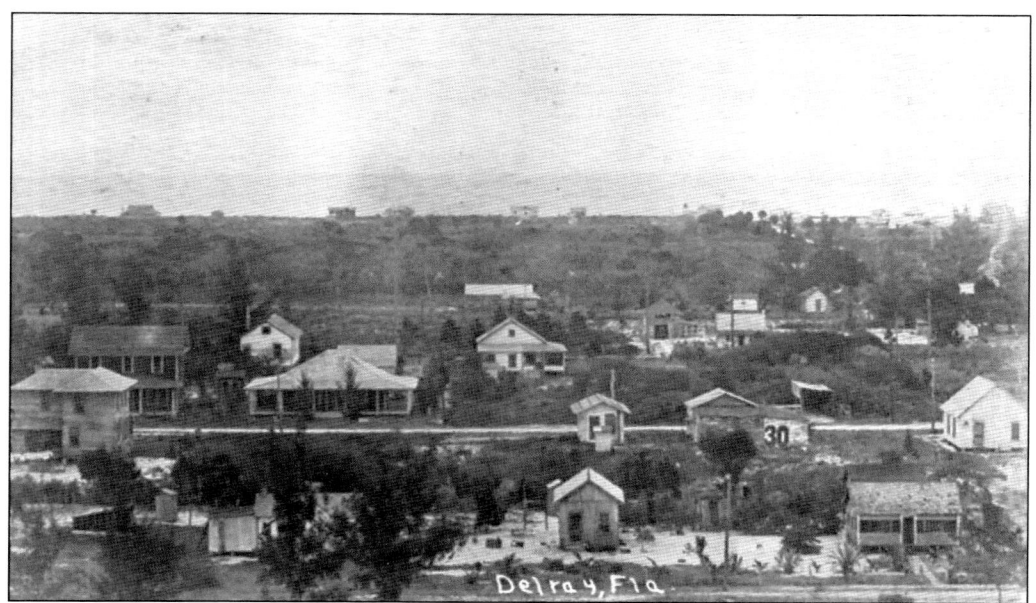

DELRAY VIEW. This early-20th-century view was perhaps photographed from a second story or water tower. Under magnification, the number 30 is visible in the middle ground, along with JAN and lines that suggest an event advertisement. Some homes include outhouses for bathrooms. Atlantic Avenue stretches to the beach area in a thin ribbon of white sand at the upper right corner. A pale horizon line crosses the top.

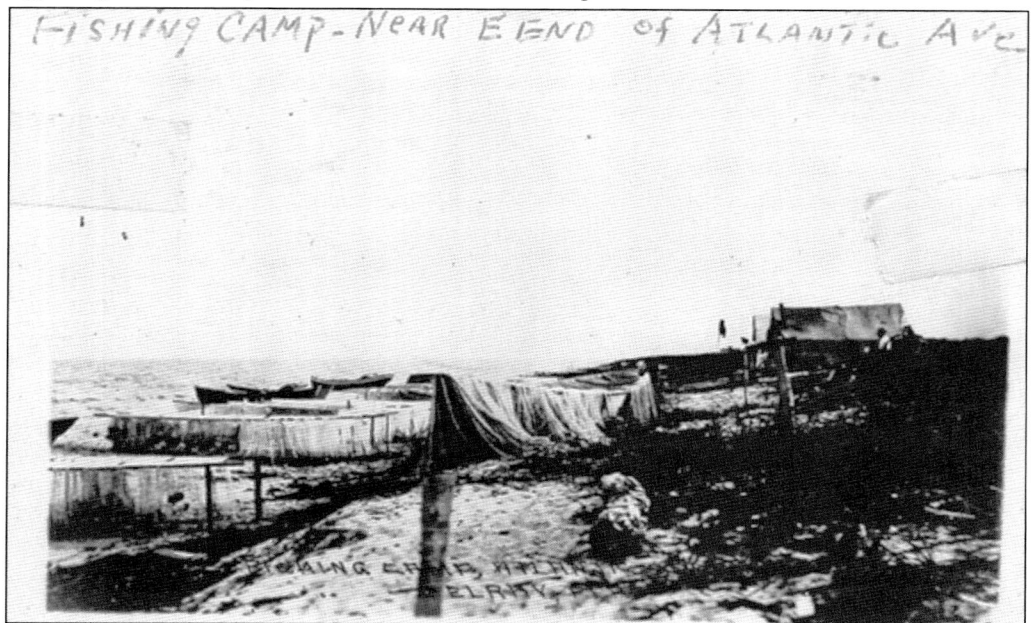

FISHING CAMP. A fishing camp existed on the beach at the end of Atlantic Avenue in settlement days. The 1910 census of Delray lists over 150 men with the occupation of "ocean fisherman." However, agriculturalists far outnumbered those in the fishing industry. Most of the ocean fishermen had emigrated from the Bahamas. In this scene, nets are laid out to dry while wooden fishing boats wait on the beach.

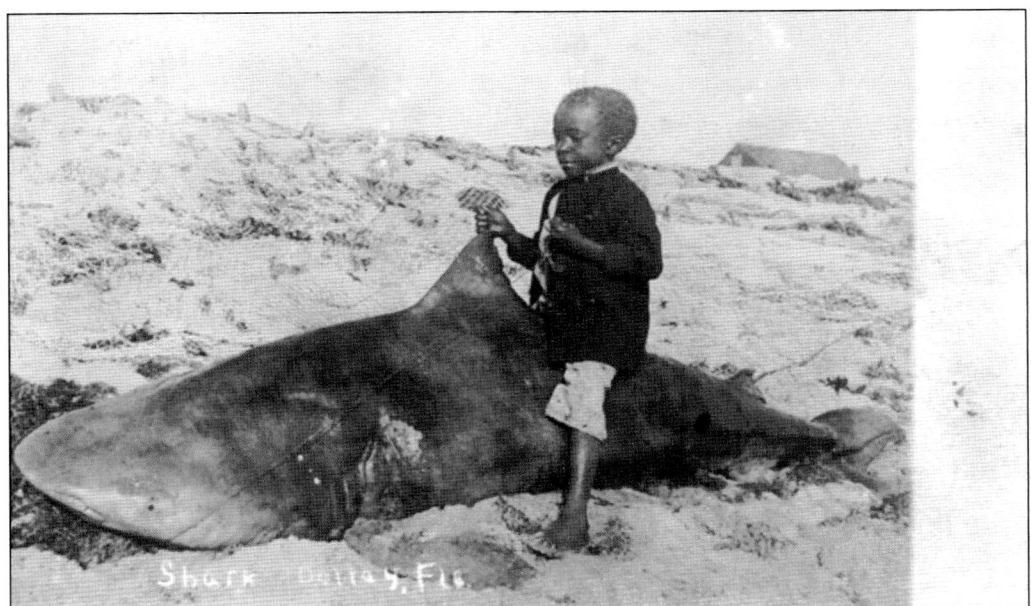

SHARK! The shark is surrounded by a net. A boy holds string "reins," pretending to ride— a common photographic convention then. A Detroit grandson received this well-chosen postcard with a smeared Delray postmark that may read 1911. The grandfather wrote, "Dear Jim, Grandpa almost caught a shark yesterday. Two came so close to my row boat that I tried to hit it with the oar—and only about two miles from shore." (Henry Higgins.)

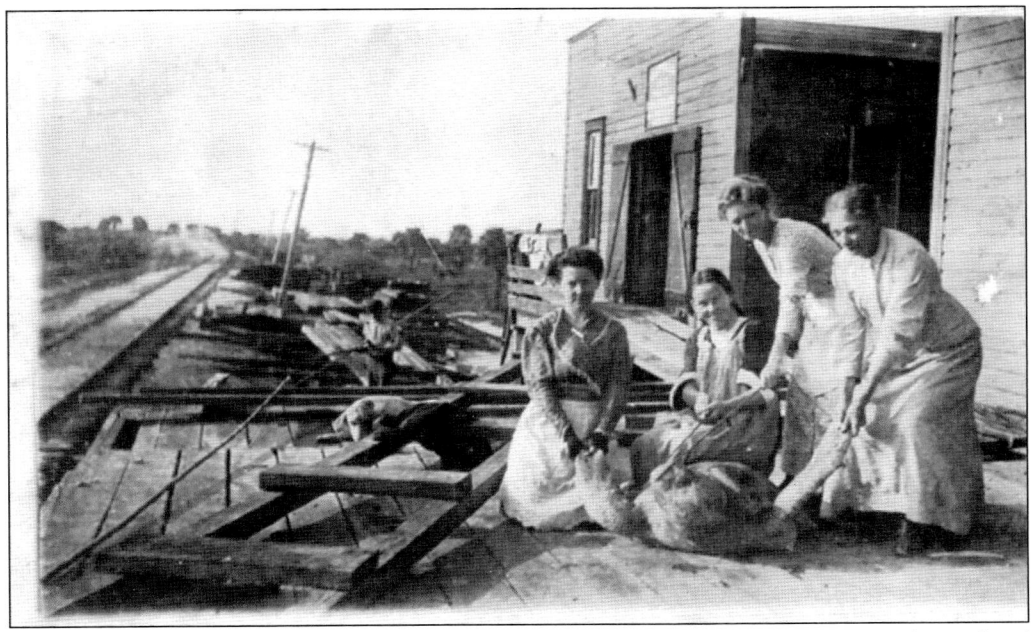

FOUR WOMEN AND A TURTLE. In this undated postcard view, a woman "rides" a loggerhead sea turtle at a loading platform next to the Florida East Coast Railway tracks in South Florida. This card and several others were found in an old potato chip can at a local storage company. An area family is pictured in these images, from the late 19th century through World War II.

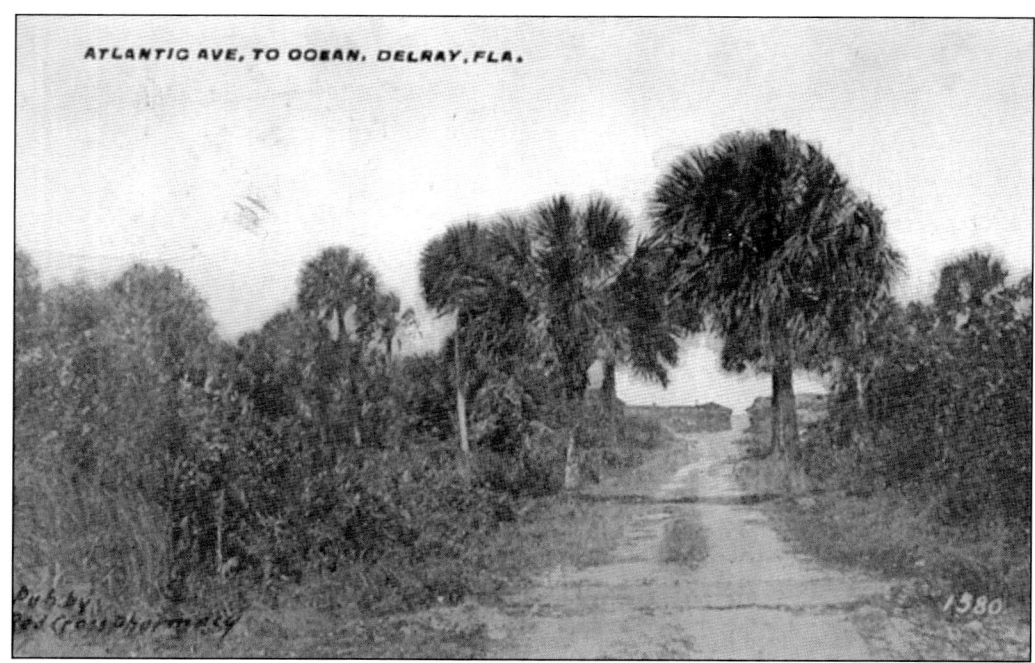

ATLANTIC AVENUE TO OCEAN. This ocean road at one time could be called the "lonesome road." In the foreground, boards cover the Spanish River, a beachside creek flowing from Boca Raton to Boynton Beach. In the distance, the road rises over the coastal ridge. Another Higgins collection postcard of the same scene, postmarked 1919, is part of a hand-tinted series published by Red Cross Pharmacy. (Henry Higgins.)

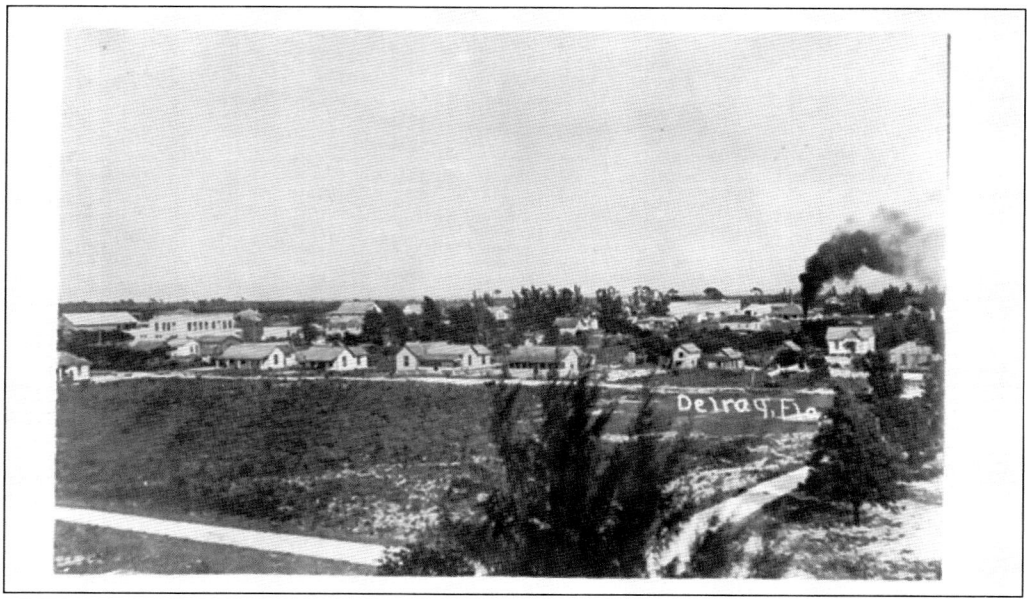

A BIRD'S-EYE VIEW OF DELRAY. A Florida East Coast train steams into town puffing smoke. Pictured is another one of the scenes published as a hand-tinted postcard by the local Red Cross Pharmacy. Delray's train station was constructed at the crossroads of Southeast Third Street and Atlantic Avenue about 1896. (Henry Higgins.)

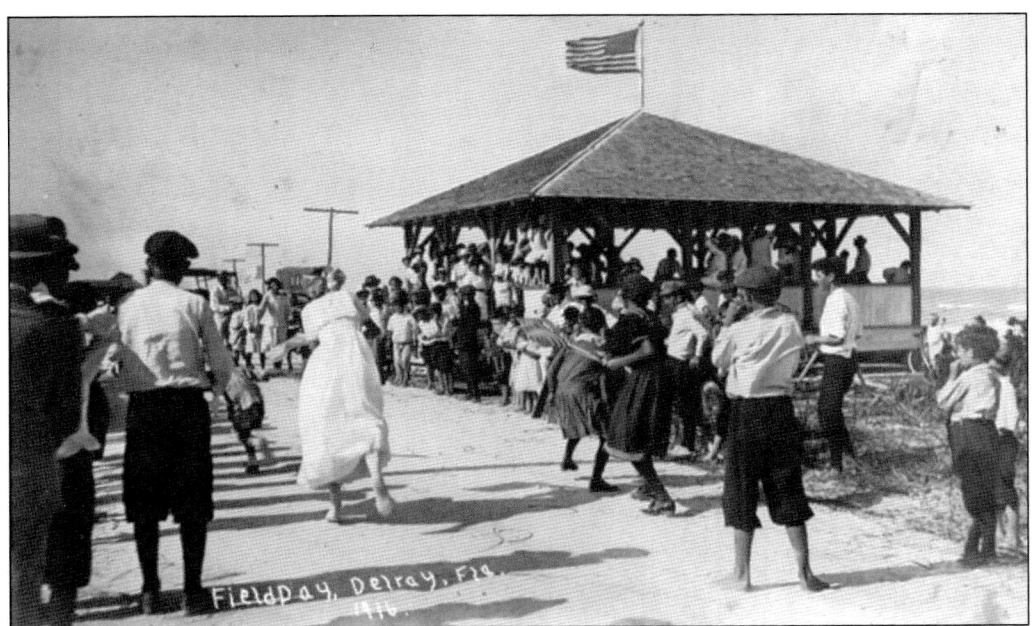

FIELD DAY, DELRAY, FLA. Schoolchildren watch a relay race at the beach pavilion in 1916. The event may be in celebration of the Fourth of July, since small American flags are being used as batons. The pavilion and two bathhouses were built soon after settlement. This first pavilion existed until the two destructive hurricanes of 1926 and 1928.

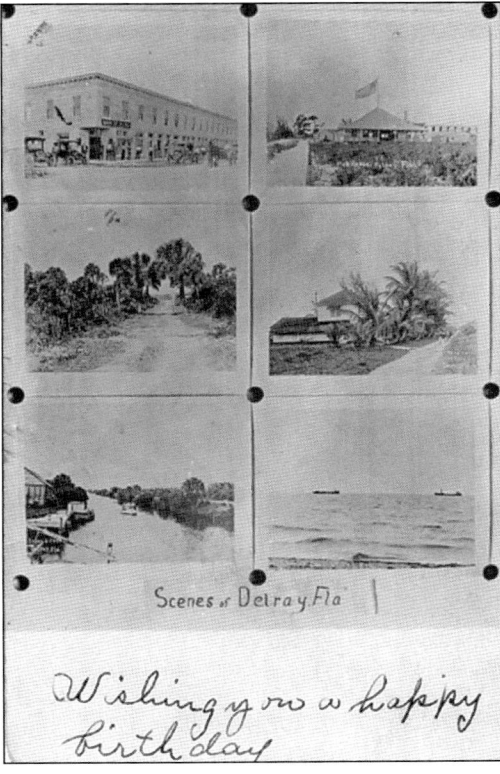

SCENES OF DELRAY, FLA. This c. 1915 postcard, sent locally as a birthday greeting, was probably delivered by hand. The six scenes depict, from left to right, the Bank of Delray, the Booster Club, the ocean road (Atlantic Avenue), Atlantic Avenue farther west, the canal crossing at Atlantic Avenue, and ships at sea. The message reads, "Wishing you a happy birthday" on the face, and on the reverse, "From Lottie to Ethel."

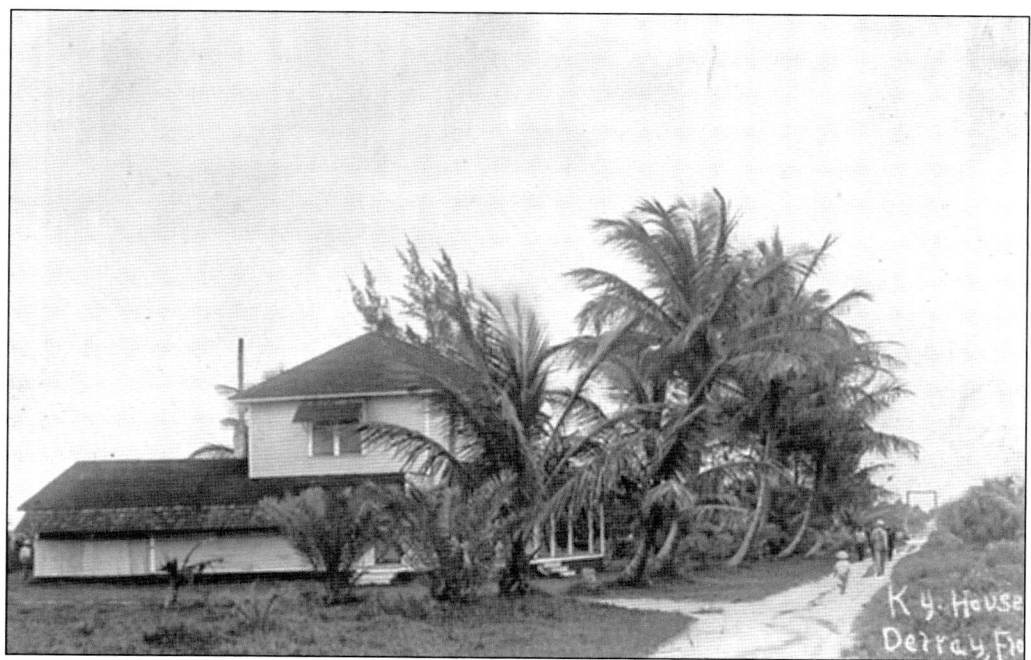

KENTUCKY HOUSE, DELRAY, FLA. A group walks on the white sand road past the Kentucky House. The Bradshaws established a boardinghouse in the two-story frame house—a spacious home at that time in Delray—when they arrived from Kentucky in 1911. In the background, the supports of the Atlantic Avenue bridge are visible. The donor of the postcard wrote "circa 1914" on the front.

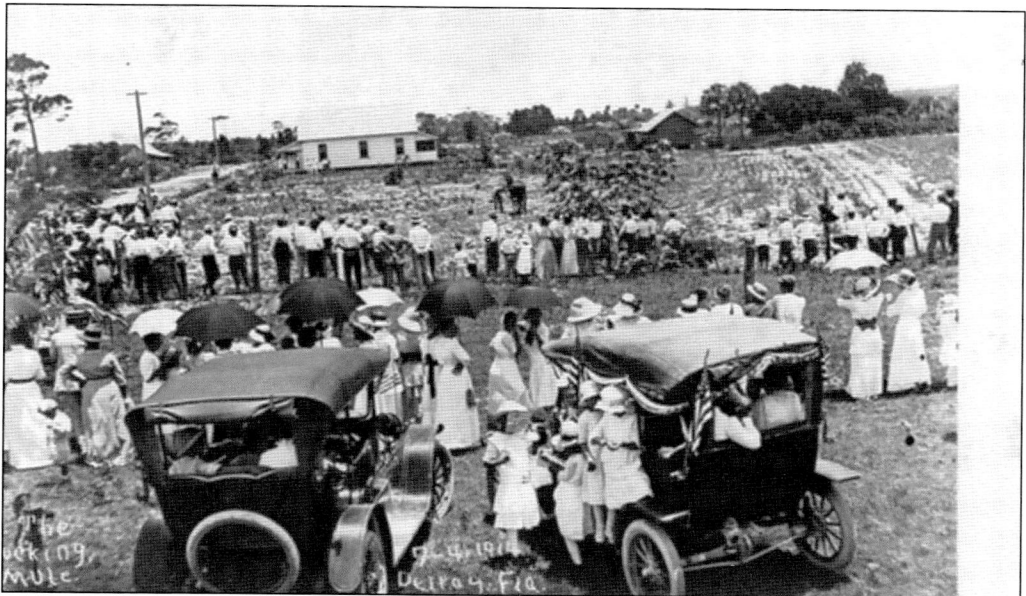

THE BUCKING MULE CONTEST. Women and girls are all dressed up for July 4, 1914, when this contest took place in a field on the outskirts of town. Note the native pines and sabal palms in the background. The mule appears in the distance, in the middle of the field. A parade held the same day can be seen in the next chapter.

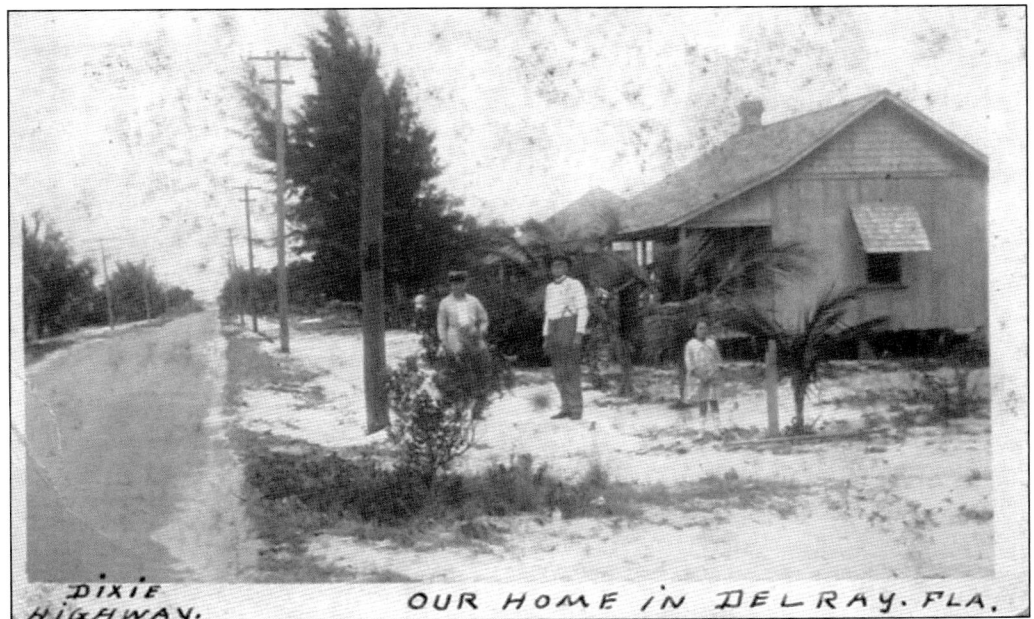

OUR HOME IN DELRAY, FLA. This message, written to "Lillie" in Ohio during March 1920, explains that bus fare to Palm Beach is 60¢ and to Miami, $1.68. Further, "there are no cellars in houses here and chimneys are not used." The writer describes the larger trees, which are "cocoanuts," and the "smaller bushes, which are hibiscus, all in bloom." (Henry Higgins.)

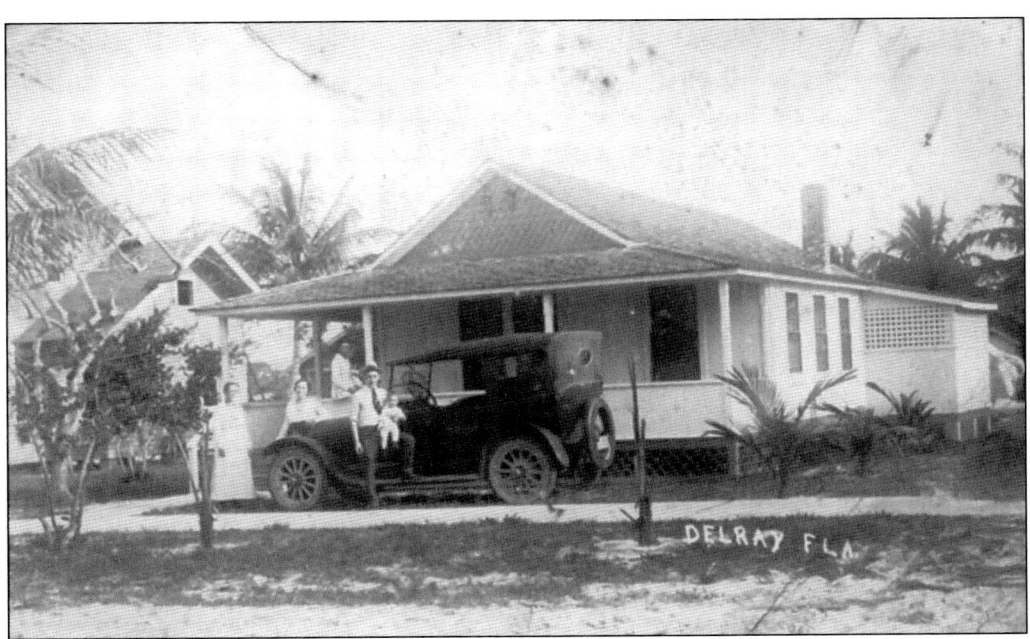

FAMILY WITH CAR. Howard and Dorothy Rex and family, pictured here, were written up in the *Rays of Delray* newspaper in June 1920. Howard Rex, a telegraph operator, was hired by the Florida East Coast Railway and assigned to Delray. The Atlantic Avenue house stood about 600 feet east of the business section and about 900 feet west of the ocean beach. (Henry Higgins.)

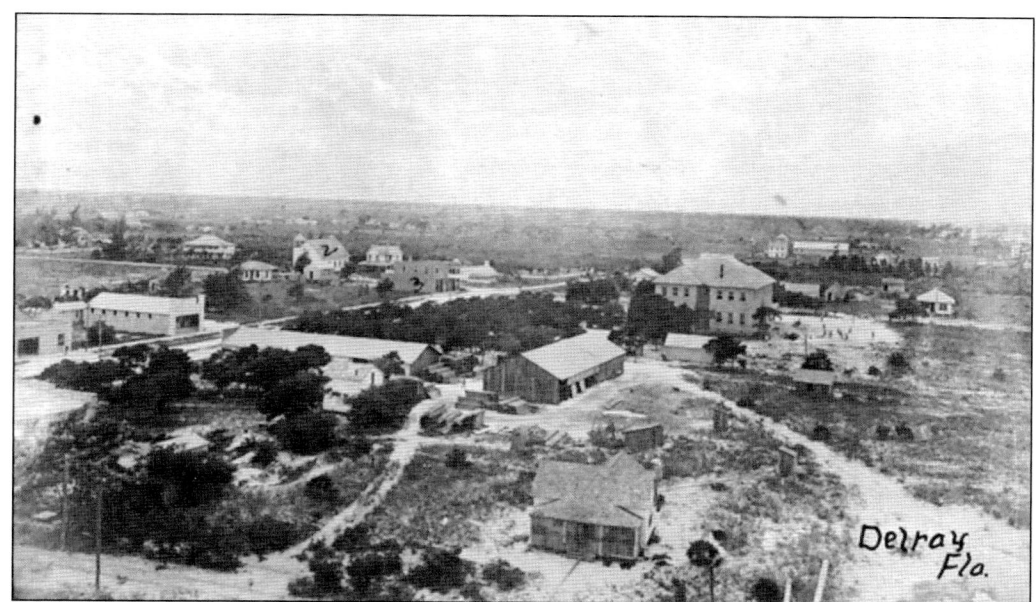

VIEW OF DELRAY, 1915. The donor of this postcard identified three sites: the Delray School (1), the Methodist church (2), and the Rhoden Building (3). Easily recognized as well are the Bijou Theater, on the south side of Atlantic; and the Methodist parsonage, behind the church at the intersection of Atlantic and Swinton Avenues. The Bahamian-style Cathcart House is located south of the church. The 1913 school now serves as the Cornell Museum, with the historical society archives currently contained upstairs.

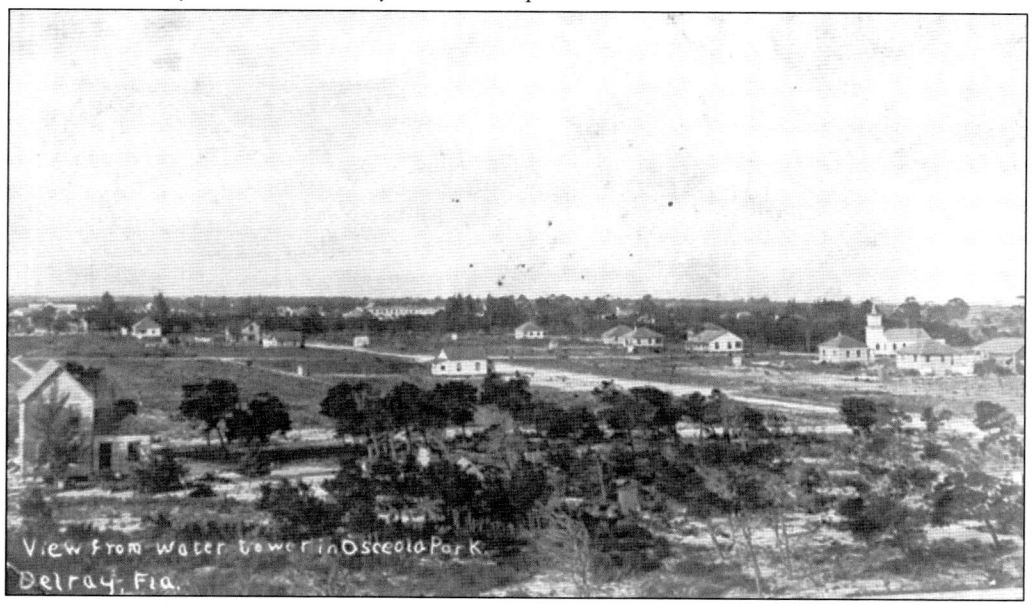

VIEW FROM WATER TOWER. The first subdivision in Delray Beach, Osceola Park, was developed in the southeast section of town, between the Florida East Coast tracks and the canal. George G. Currie and F. J. Lewis of the Currie Investment and Title Guaranty Company recorded the plat in January 1913. Two parks—Currie Commons and a ball field—were set aside. Currie Commons, the large grassy area, is a city park today.

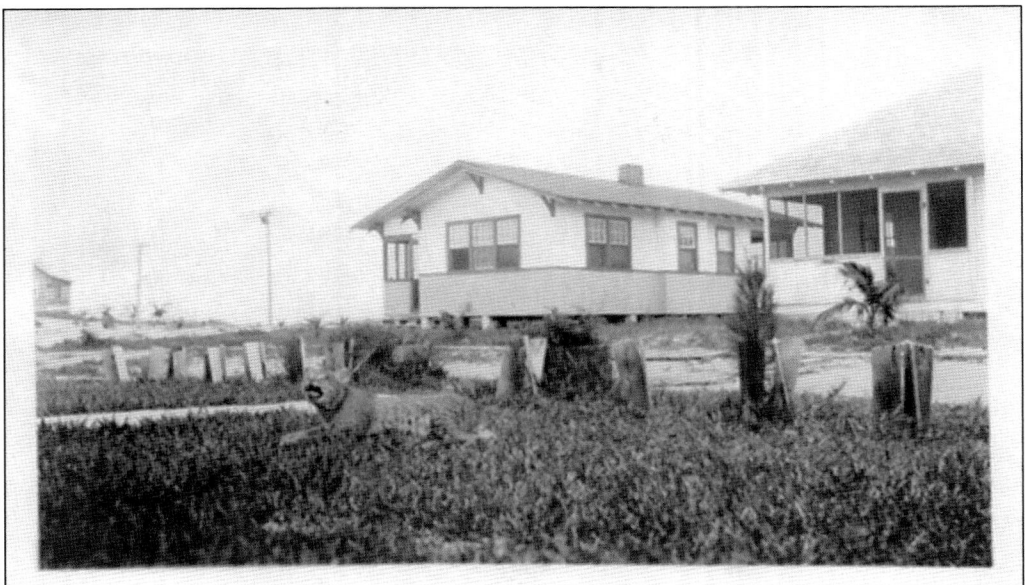

DR. ZERNO'S BEACH HOME. Though not a postcard, this image reveals important historical information regarding the Arvilla Tea Room. Its donor wrote, "Dr. Zerno's home became the Arvilla Tea Room. The mounted wildcat in the front yard is laying in Mr. Davis' front yard circa 1917. D. J. Davis shot the wildcat in Mrs. Fish's hen house."

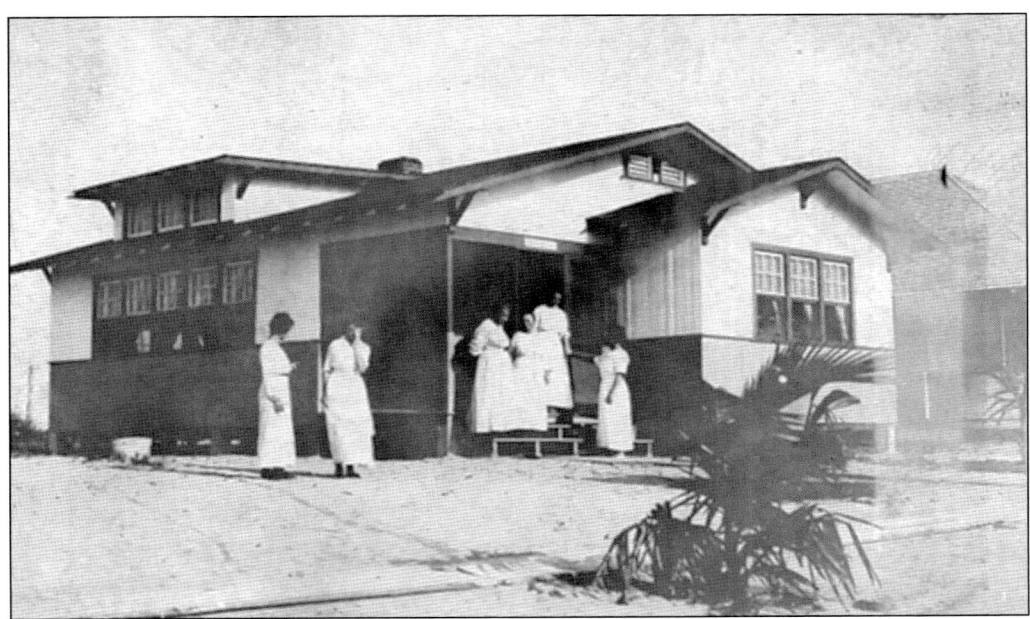

THE ARVILLA TEA ROOM. It appears that the Zerno cottage was enlarged before becoming the tearoom, but it is still recognizable. A Delray Beach institution for many years, the Arvilla was listed in a 1935 directory under "Refreshments & Lunches." The telephone number was 15. Local directories recorded the tearoom through the 1940s.

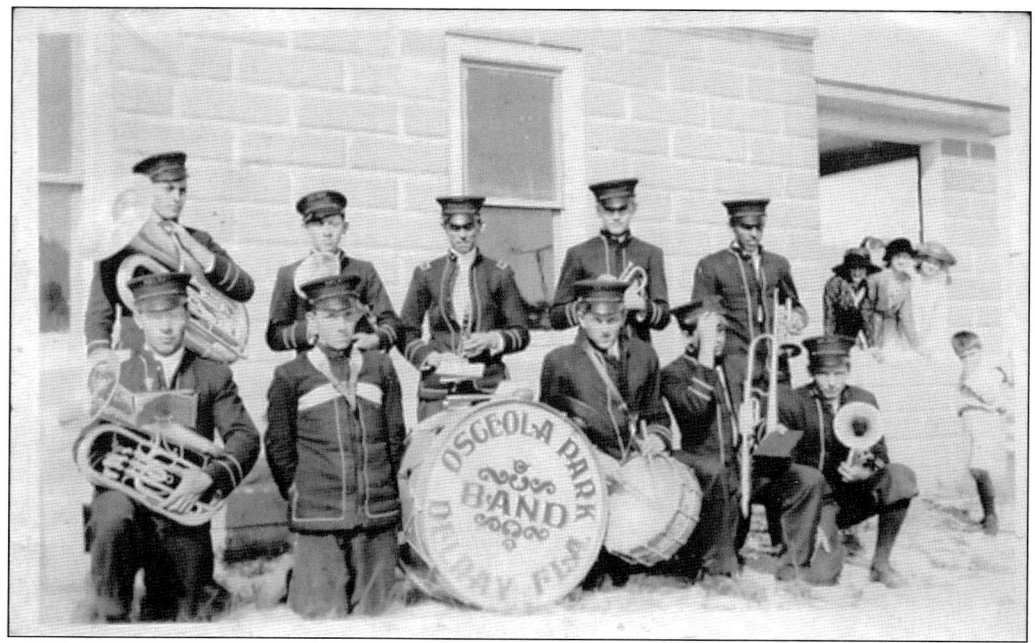

THE OSCEOLA PARK BAND. Shown here are the following: (first row) two unidentified people, Charlie Nelson, Haild Zeder, and Ben Sundy; (second row) Albert Carrington, Rudolph Wuepper, director Albert Miller, John Wackerman, and John Miller. Al Miller was associated with band music in town for many years. After World War II, he directed an all-women group that played every Friday night at the bandstand.

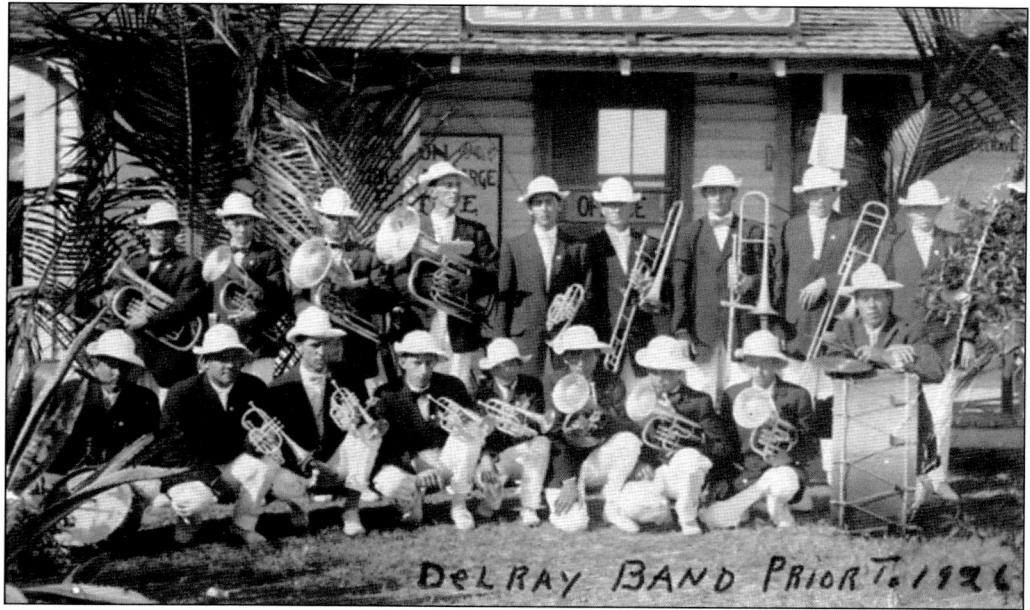

THE DELRAY BAND. The Delray Band, posing in front of the Delray Land Company, played at land sales and promotions as well as town celebrations. It appears that some of the men were also in the Osceola Park Band. In addition to organizing and training a town band, Al Miller established the first Boy Scout troop in 1910 and served as Delray's first volunteer fire chief.

Two

Banner Town of Palm Beach County

Along with Delray: City of Destiny, another promotional appellation for the town of Delray was Banner Town of Palm Beach County. The idea for the nickname, with "banner" meaning superior, came from Delray's prowess in garnering blue ribbons at fairs in Palm Beach County.

A majority of the townspeople were engaged in farming or related businesses; thus, agriculture was the focus of expectations and the basis of the early economy. Delray was known for its large shipments of pineapples and tomatoes, with most of this produce transported north on the Florida East Coast Railway. In the 1930s, gladiolus became a major crop, and the city was surrounded by fields of flowers. In the late 1940s, townspeople started the beautiful and ambitious Gladioli Festival, which continued through the early 1950s. Cattle ranching was also important. Agricultural pursuits remained a significant part of the economy into the 1970s.

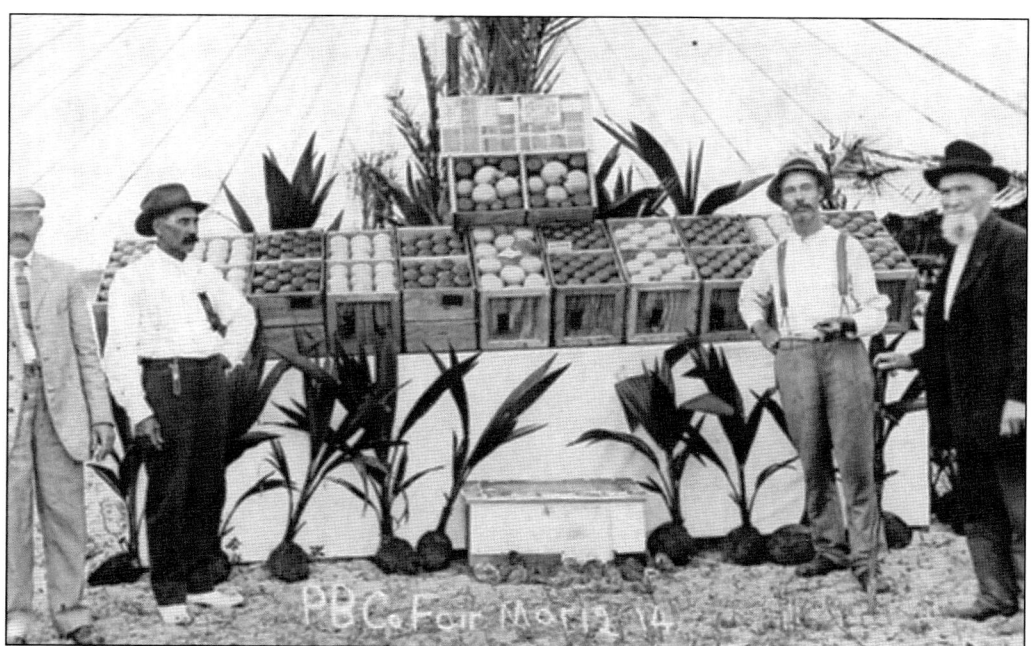

COUNTY FAIR. Delray seemed in a whirl of community pride during 1913 and 1914. There is a discrepancy in dates: 1913 is written on the reverse of the county fair postcards, while the photographer has made a notation of 1914. Citrus fruit and tomatoes are displayed behind the four men, possibly two local growers and two judges. The white-shirted man on the left may be wearing a prize ribbon.

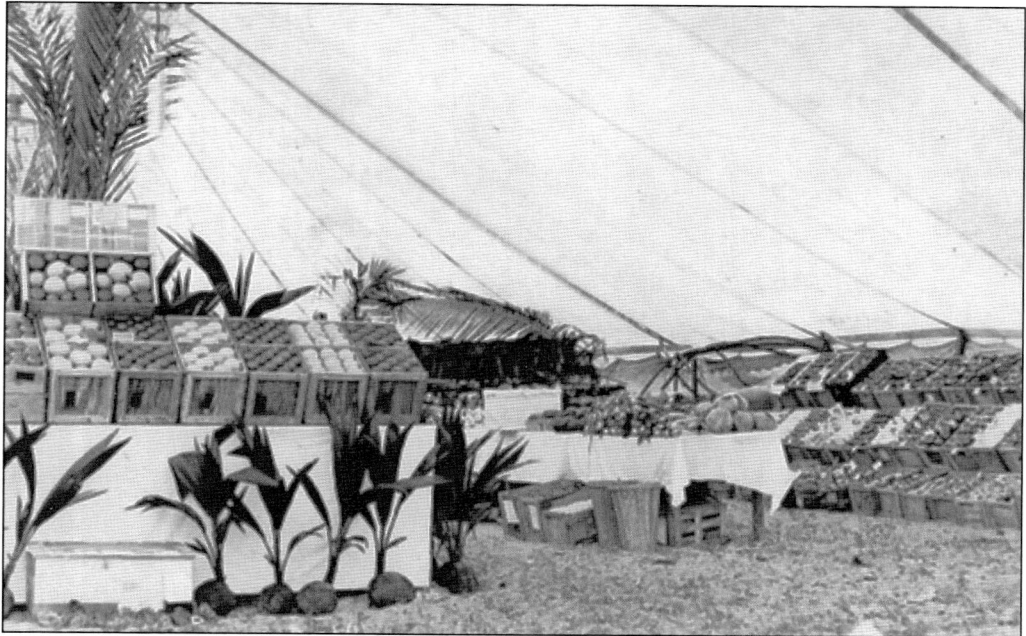

DELRAY PRODUCE AT THE PALM BEACH COUNTY FAIR. Another view of the same display shows additional Delray produce under the tent. The entrants took pains to make their exhibits attractive, thus decorating their booth with sprouted coconuts.

COUNTY FAIR, DELRAY, FLA. On the reverse, the donor of this card has written, "Mr. Nichols, Delray, 1913 County Fair." However, it appears that the photographer has written March 12, 1914, on the negative—the same date on all of the cards in this series. The entire banana tree was moved into the tent and replanted for display.

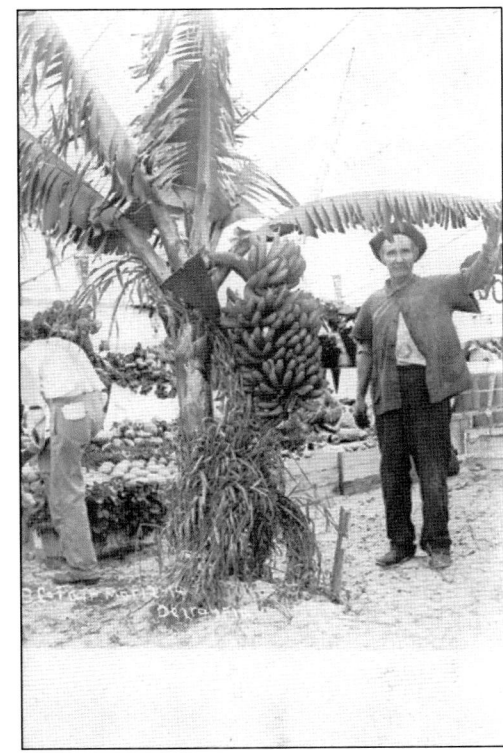

PINEAPPLE DISPLAY. Prominent pioneer H. J. Sterling said, "In the development of the pineapple industry along the east coast, Delray took precedence over all other towns as we had the largest acreage, shipping as high as eighteen to twenty car loads a day during the height of the shipping season, and having established the first canning plant on the Florida east coast."

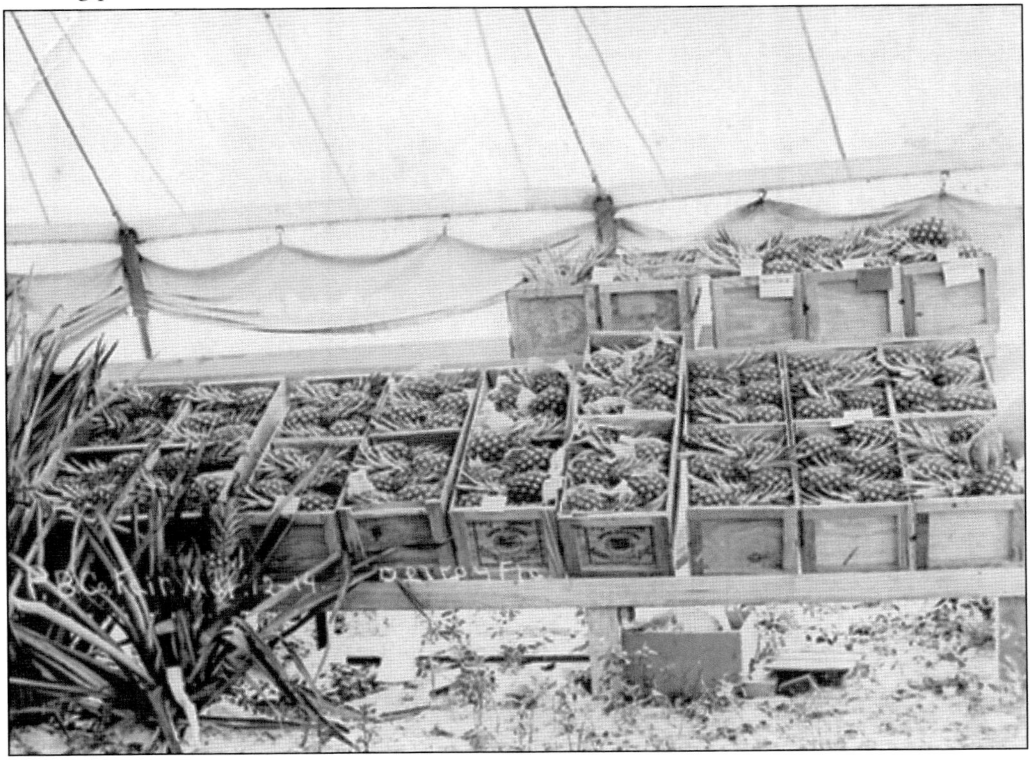

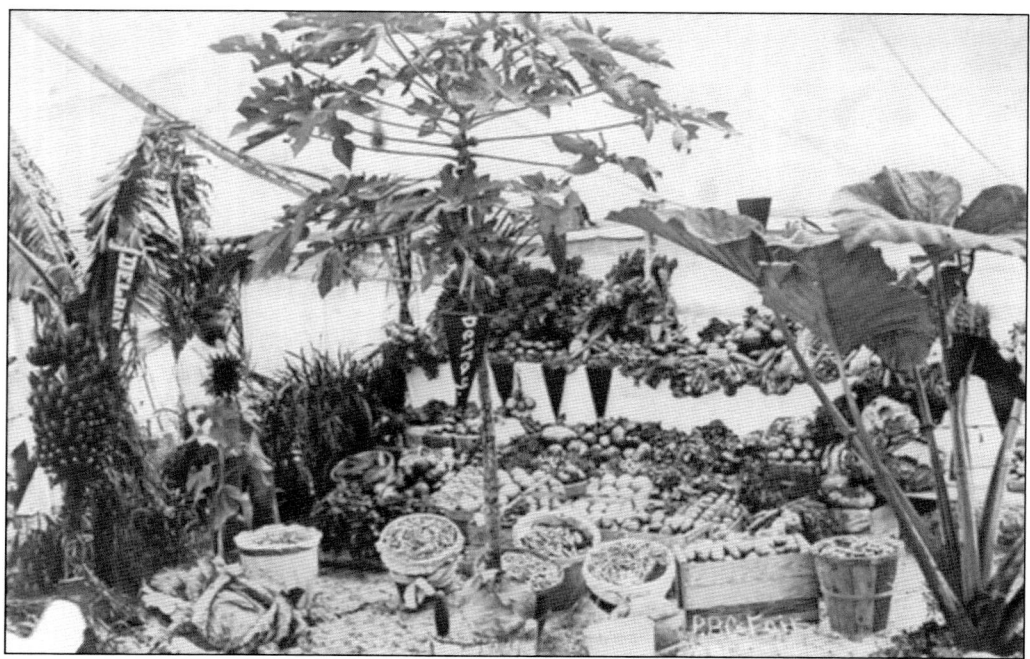

DELRAY'S BOUNTY. In addition to a banana plant, a papaya tree and other growing plants are included in the display. Seen in the foreground are hampers of beans, giant cabbages, and a cucumber stuck on its end in a bucket. This card was postmarked in Delray on September 4, 1913. (Henry Higgins.)

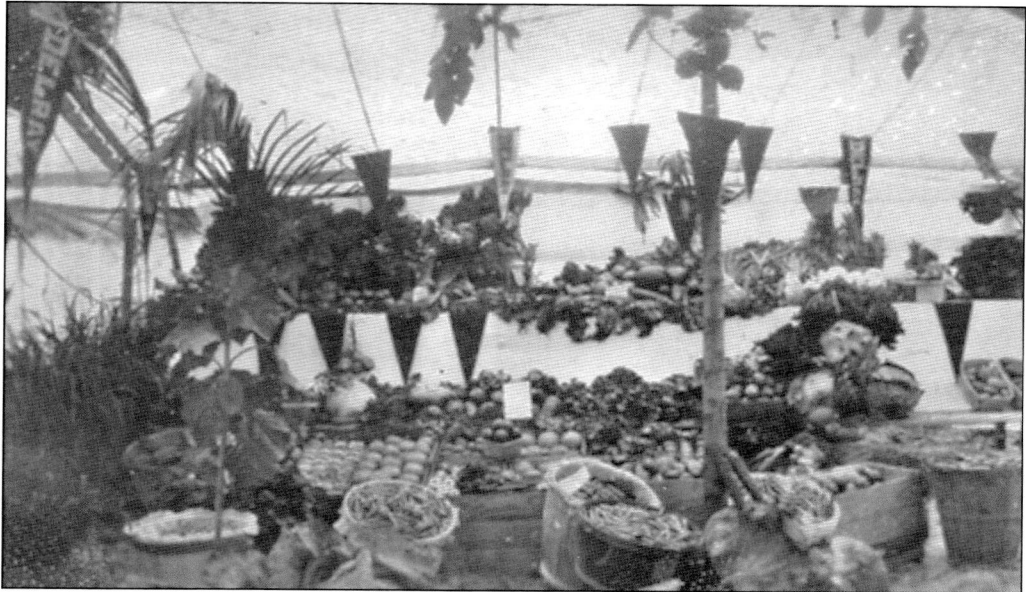

FAIR SCENE. The donor wrote, "County Fair, 1913," on this card as well. It is similar to the one above. While many vegetables were grown on the rich muck land on both sides of the canal, pineapples were grown on the high, sandy soil west of the waterway. Pioneer Delray farmer Adolf Hofman stated that he and others set out the first pineapple fields while they were still living in tents.

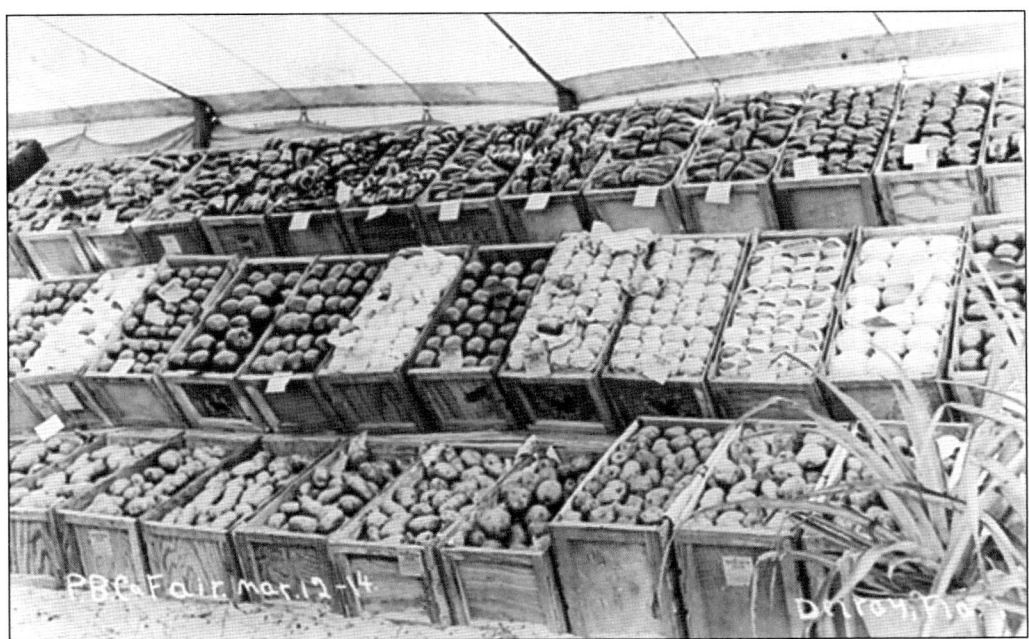

CRATES OF PRODUCE. Speaking of this period, local businessman Henry Sterling said, "During those years Delray was known as the banner town of Palm Beach County, taking more blue ribbons for its products than any other section. For several years the County Fair was held at Delray." Crates in the first row contain potatoes; the second, tomatoes; and the third, peppers.

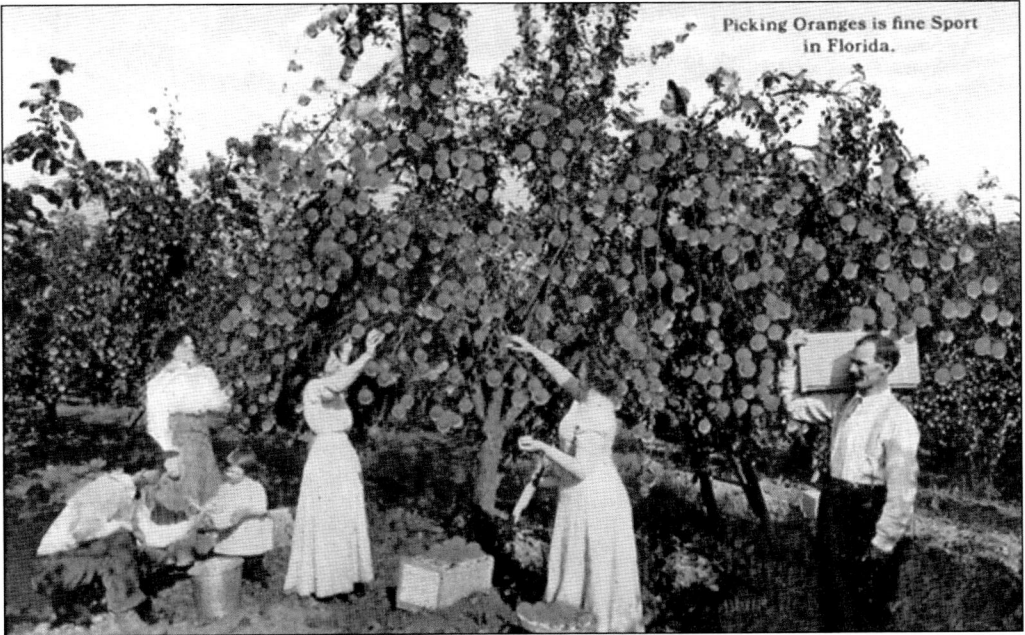

PICKING ORANGES IS FINE SPORT. Women dressed in early-20th-century styles pick oranges from trees loaded with fruit. During Delray's pioneer days, citrus fruit harvests were boasted in local publications. In regard to the scene pictured here, one might suspect some staging.

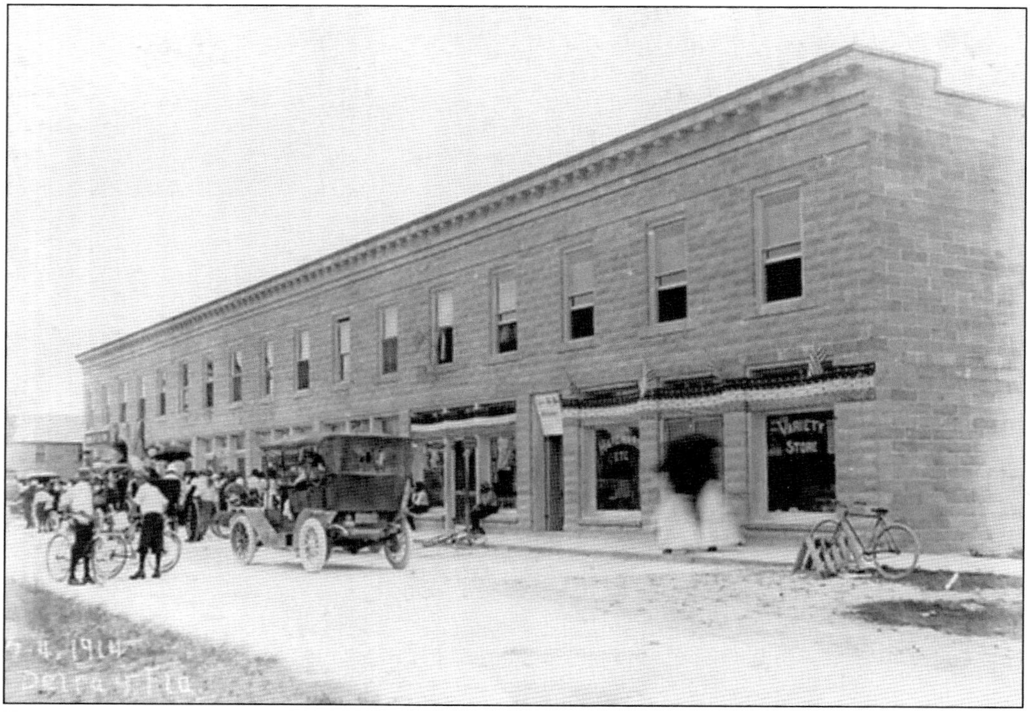

FOURTH OF JULY, 1914. The next eight images depict the progression of the 1914 Fourth of July parade. Here the crowd waits in front of the Cromer Block, which has been decorated for Independence Day. Two of the business signs are visible: "Hardware, Etc." and "The Variety Store."

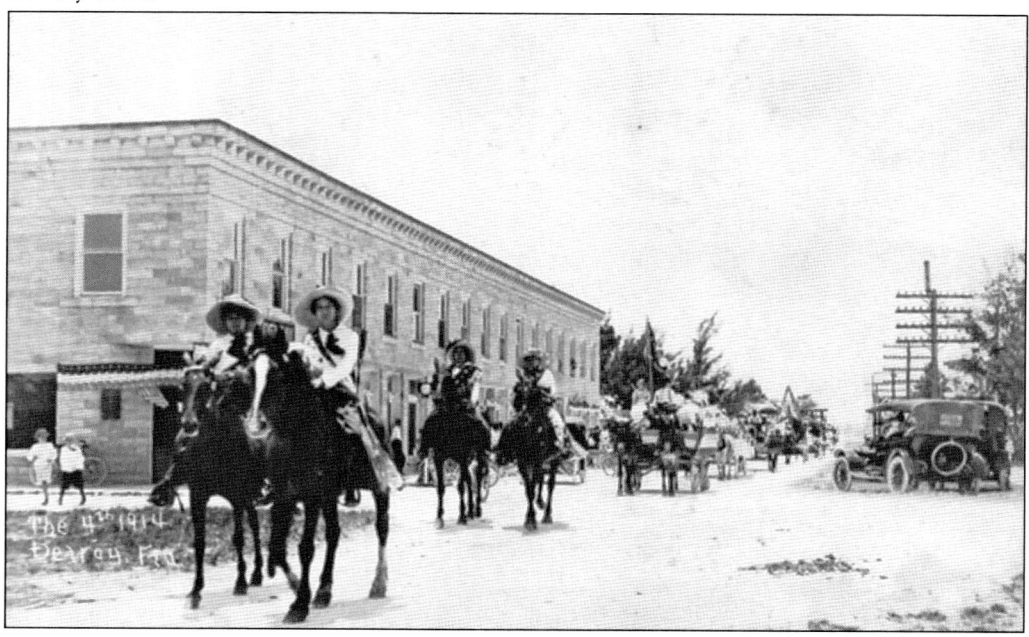

THE PARADE BEGINS. Four women on horseback lead the parade, while the floats are drawn by horses and mules. A star is visible in the background.

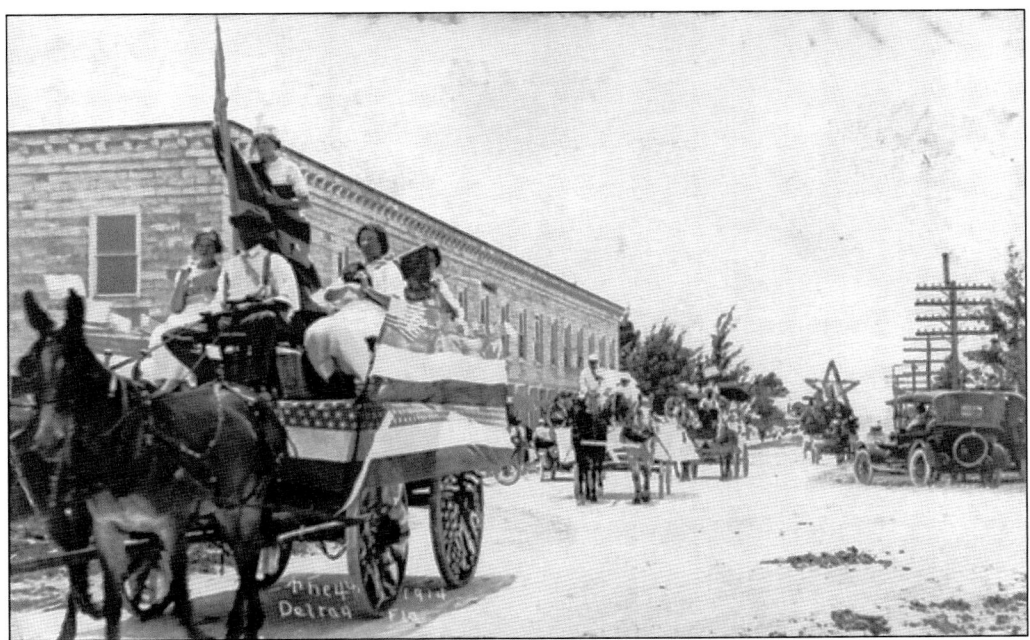

LIBERTY. A woman in a mule-drawn wagon evidently represents the sculpture *Lady Liberty* or *Lady Freedom* atop the U.S. Capitol dome. The woman standing bears the sword, shield, and helmet of the dome version and is surrounded by her court. The man driving the float is dressed in a white shirt, tie, suspenders, and dark trousers in the July heat.

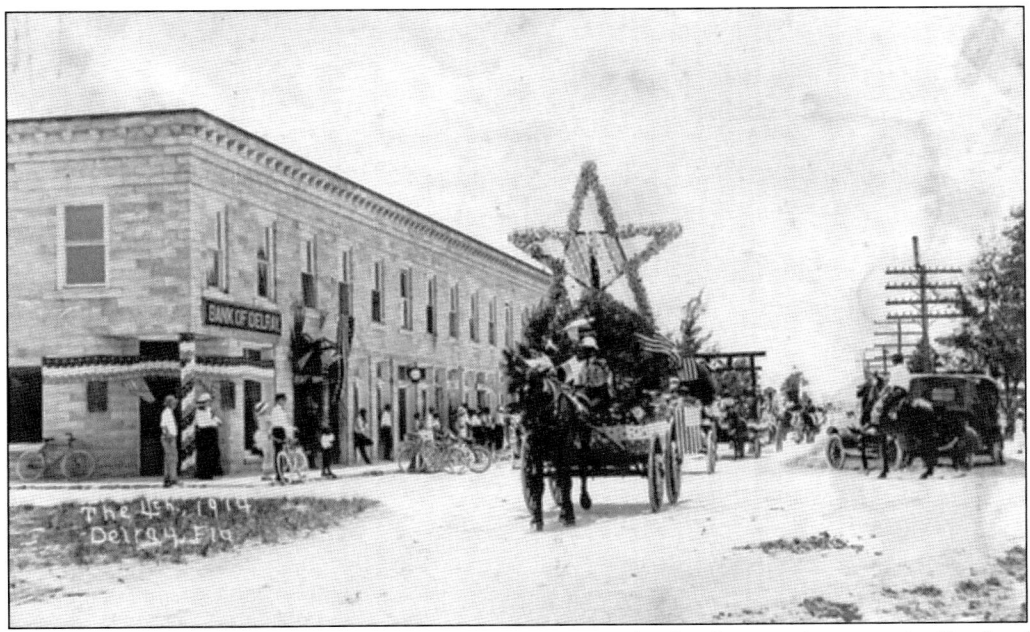

THE STAR FLOAT. The float with the big star rolls to the forefront as it passes the Bank of Delray on the corner. Two floats from the Japanese Yamato Colony will pass next.

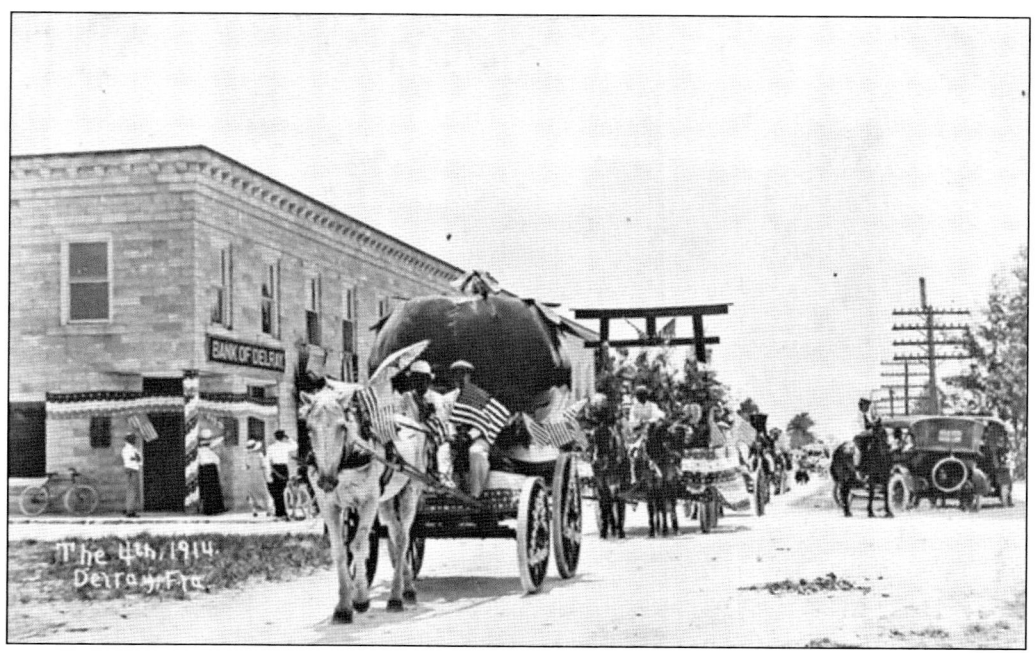

HOMAGE TO THE TOMATO. This float is built around a giant tomato, a leading crop rivaling the pineapple. Behind it is another well-designed entry from the Japanese Yamato Colony featuring a Shinto Temple entrance.

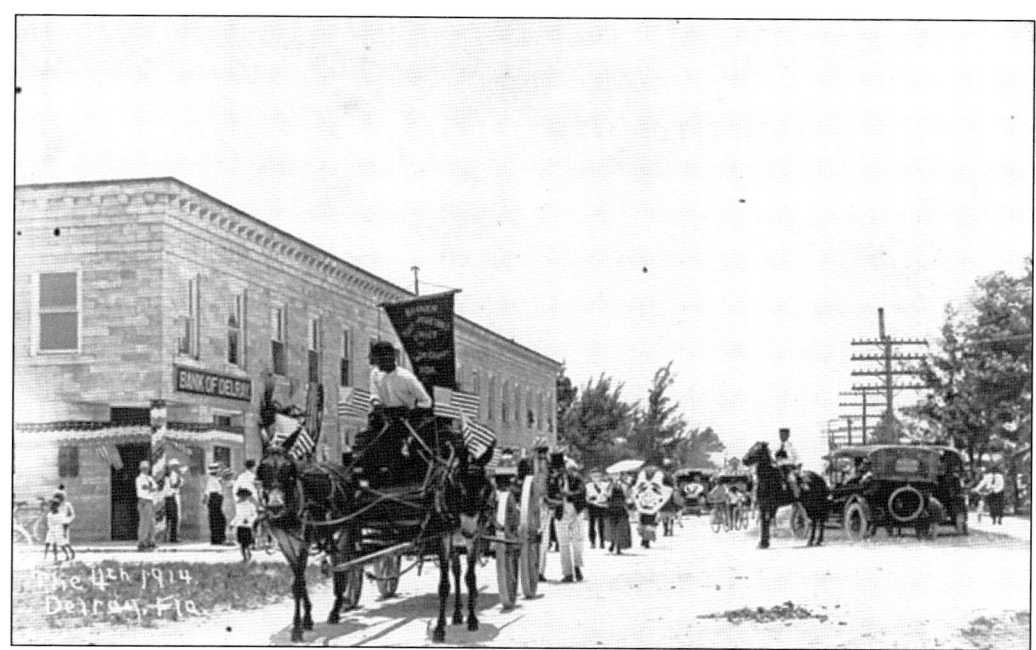

BANNER TOWN OF PALM BEACH COUNTY. Serendipitously, this float displays a large banner reading, "Banner Fruit and Vegetable District, Palm Beach County, Fla." Behind it are people dressed as characters—one with a giant mask—followed by decorated cars.

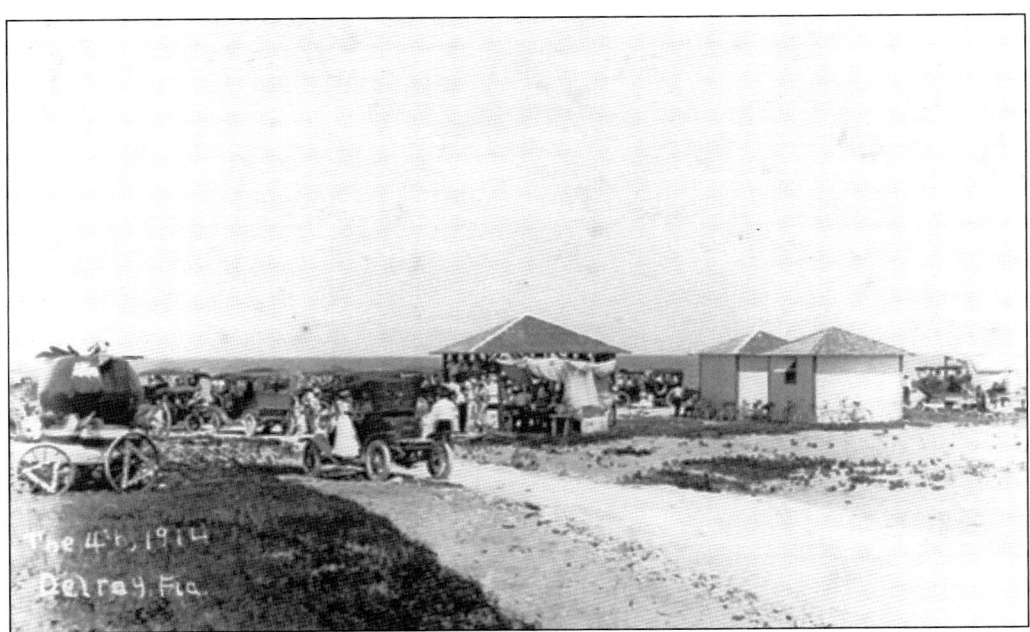

END OF THE PARADE. The parade has ended at the beach. The tomato float is parked to the side while participants enjoy themselves. A woman wearing a long white dress stands on the running board of a car while speaking to the driver. The buildings pictured are the Delray Beach pavilion and two bathhouses.

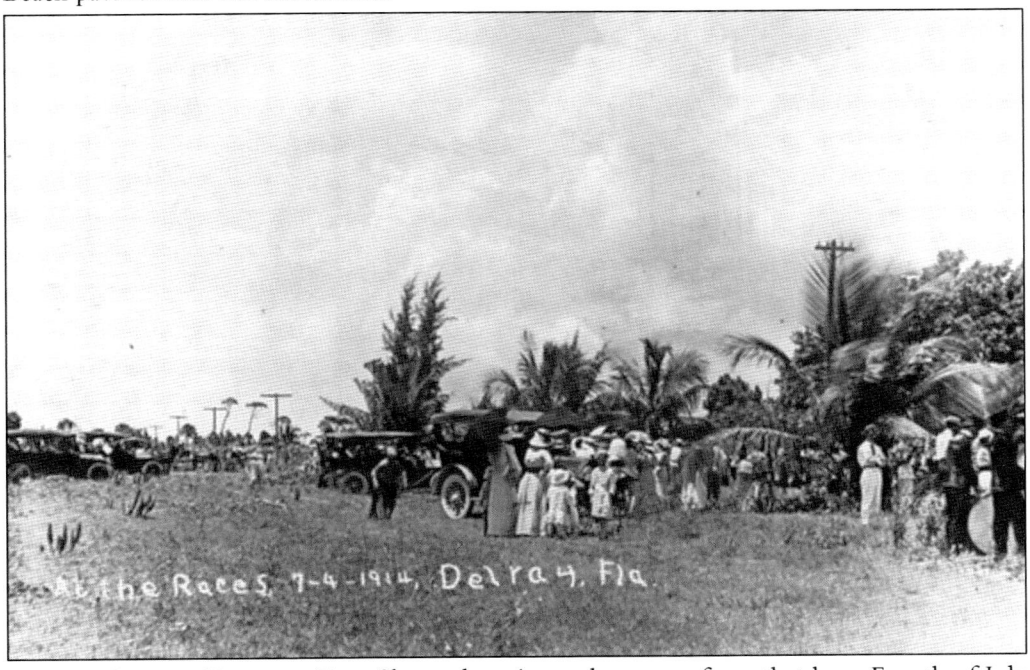

AT THE RACES, DELRAY, FLA. Shown here is another event from that busy Fourth of July day. Although the trees are hiding the activity beyond, we know that it is a horse race because horses and riders can be seen in another photograph of the occasion. Band members—one with a bass drum—are present in the far right corner.

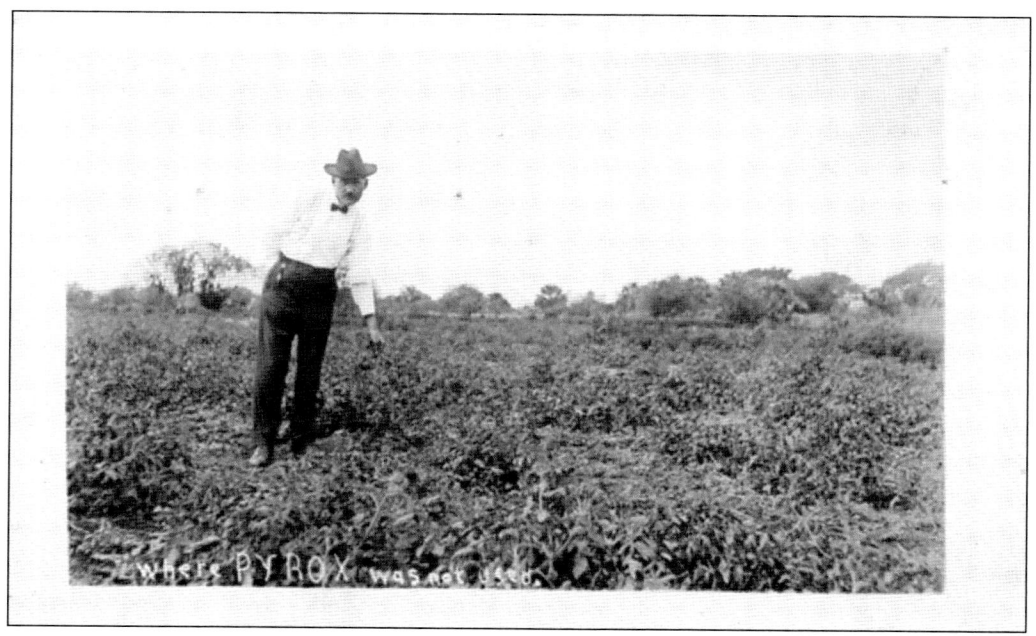

WHERE PYROX WAS NOT USED. John Wuepper demonstrates growth in a field where "Pryox was not used." Since the economy of Delray was based on agriculture, this kind of demonstration was important. The card was dated 1913 by the donor.

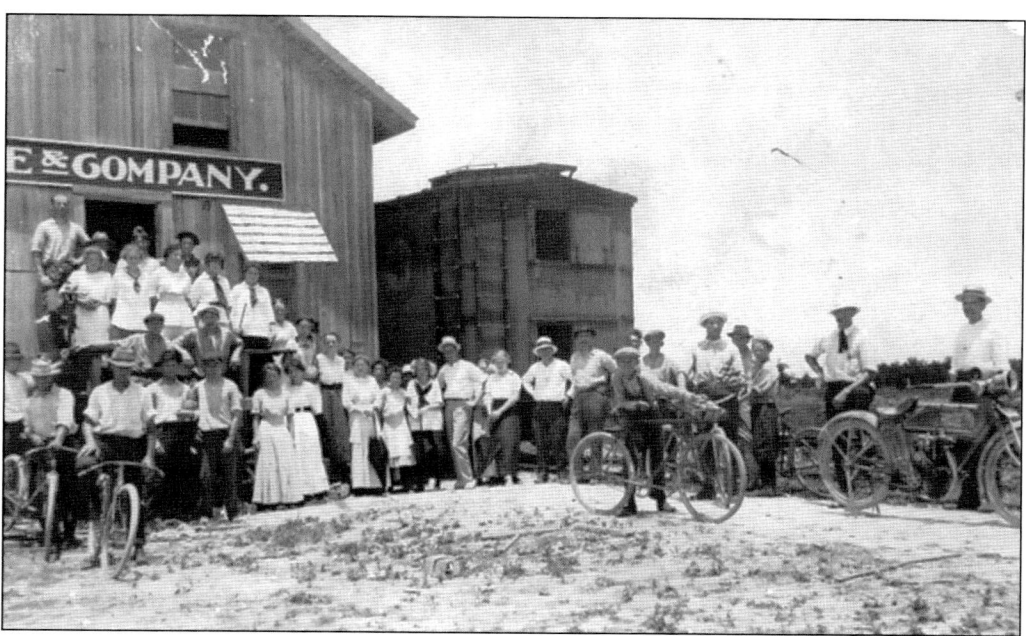

CHASE AND COMPANY. The Chase and Company packinghouse stood opposite the Sundy Feed Store along the railroad tracks. If they were fast, girls packing tomatoes could make as much as $5 a day. Boys made about the same amount building crates. These teenage employees worked after school and on Saturdays. The donor wrote on the reverse, "Chase Packing House about 1916."

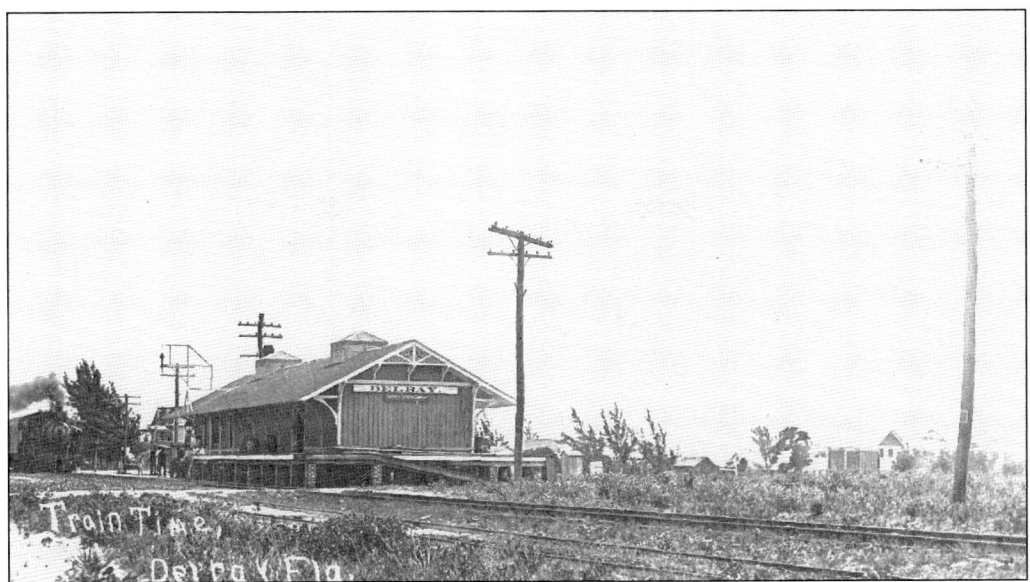

TRAIN TIME, 1911. This postcard was sent to the chamber of commerce from Orlando in 1957. On the reverse is this message: "Sirs, I came across this picture so thought would send it to you. W. W. Glasgow. We worked at Chase & Company there in 1911." The bright yellow train station depicted here in a faded black-and-white photograph was built by Henry Flagler's Florida East Coast Railway in the late 1890s.

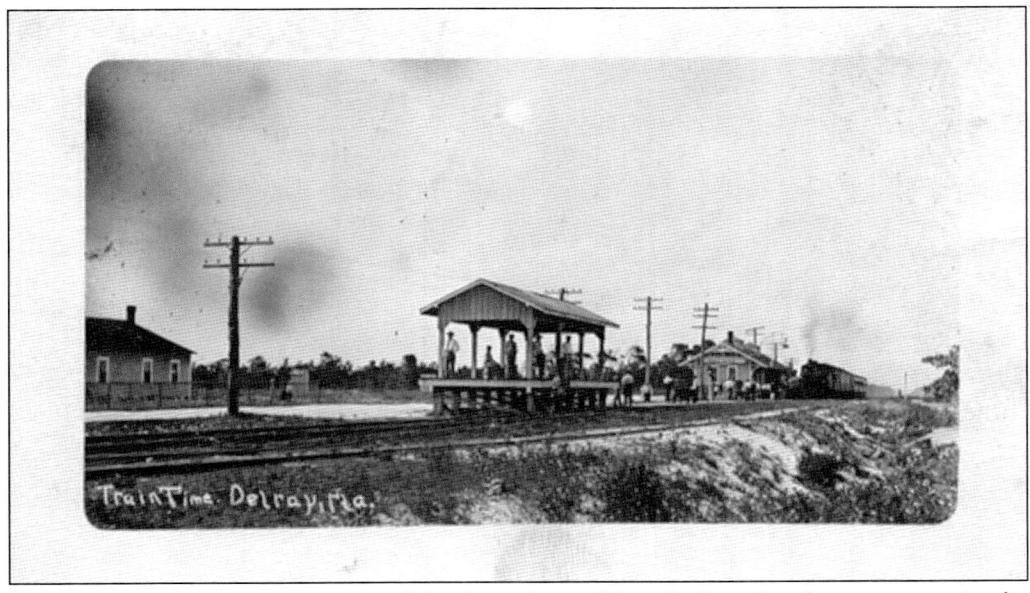

TRAIN TIME, DELRAY, FLA. In this view, the packing shed at the depot appears in the foreground. Delray's banner harvests of winter crop fruits and vegetables were shipped north to New York, Boston, and Chicago from this point. Transporting the produce quickly by rail was absolutely essential to the success of the town's agriculture-based economy and to the growth and development of Delray. (Henry Higgins.)

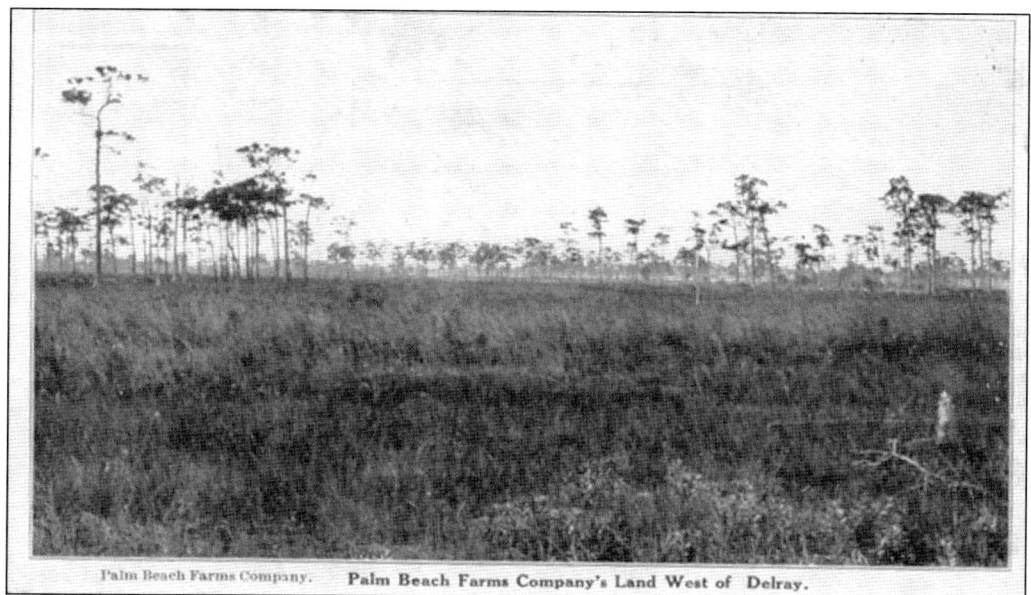

PALM BEACH FARMS. The postcard advertisement on the reverse asks, "Five Acres Enough? Yes. In Palm Beach County, Florida 'the garden spot of the world.' Set aside 34 cents a day and own a beautiful semi-tropical home. $250.00, $10 down—$10 a Month buys one of our contracts. We give a town lot FREE to each purchaser." Palm Beach Farms Company. Bryant and Greenwood, Republic Building, Chicago, is the return address. (Henry Higgins.)

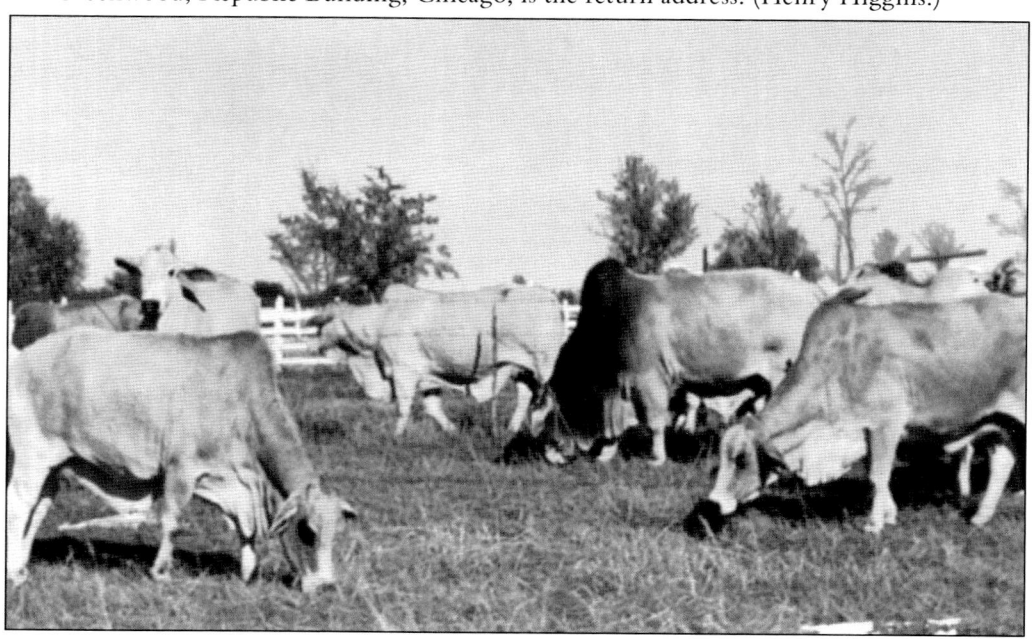

BRAHMAN CATTLE. Along with others, this card was used to illustrate a comprehensive 1961 Florida State University class project about Delray Beach by Robert Paul Miller. At the time, cattle ranching was important to the local economy. In Palm Beach County, beef and dairy cattle tied for third place in income produced from farming. Government tables quoted the rapid expansion of the Florida cattle industry during the 1950s.

Three

RESORT LIFE BEGINS WITH A BOOM

As the famous Florida real estate boom of the 1920s gathered steam, the town began its transition to a resort town with an economy partially based on tourism with the added bonus of a lively winter colony of prominent people in business, industry, entertainment, sports, and the arts. The most popular style of architecture changed from vernacular frame cottages and bungalows to the stuccoed Mediterranean Revival style that was sweeping Florida. When the population grew to about 2,000, a new, separate high school was needed. People were extremely optimistic as new businesses were opened, new homes were built, and many of the old homes and buildings were remodeled. Seven resort hotels, such as the Kentucky House, Alterep, Seacrest, and Casa Del Rey, were available to visitors.

This resort life was maintained by the labor of the townspeople. A hotel for the traveling waiters and chauffeurs was built in the African American neighborhood called the Sands in 1949. The La France was the only hotel serving guests of color between West Palm Beach and Fort Lauderdale. This book does not include a chapter on the bust or the long depression following, because there are no images of that time that look any different from the boom years. Although local people and the city had little money during this period, the many new buildings, new cars, and the profusion of palm trees left the town looking good for a long time. In addition, the winter colony was busy building cottages in various Revival styles such as Colonial, Bermuda, Creole, and Monterey, making Delray the 50th in population and 10th in permits for new construction and renovation in the state. The resort life has continued to expand and change through the years.

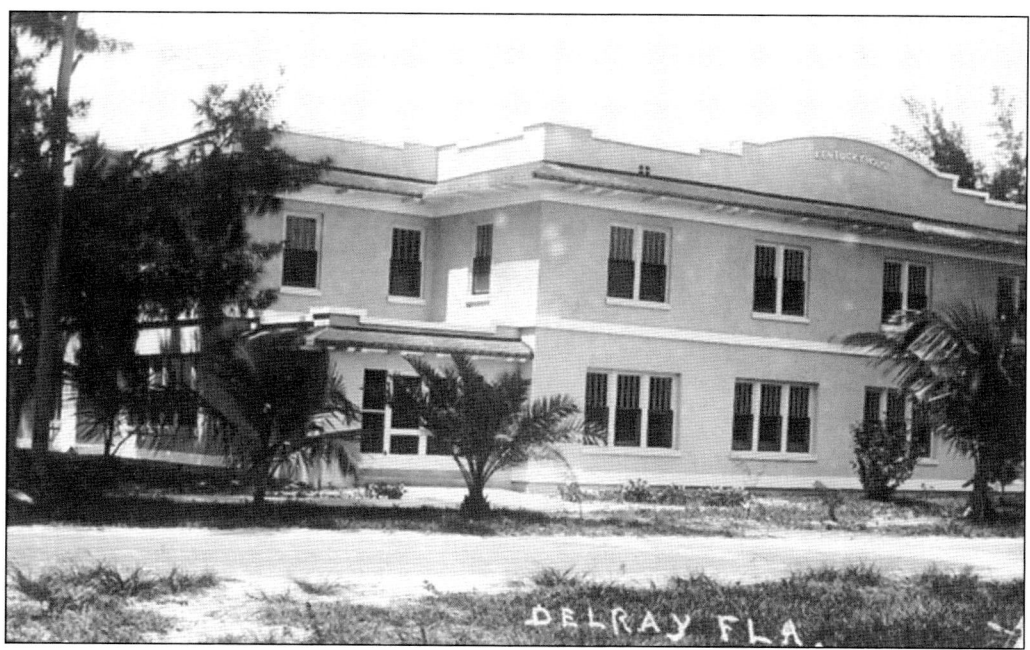

THE NEW KENTUCKY HOUSE. This substantial hotel was the first of the resort hotels built during the boom. L. H. Bradshaw actually constructed it in 1921, when there was not much of a boom, but it set the trend in town.

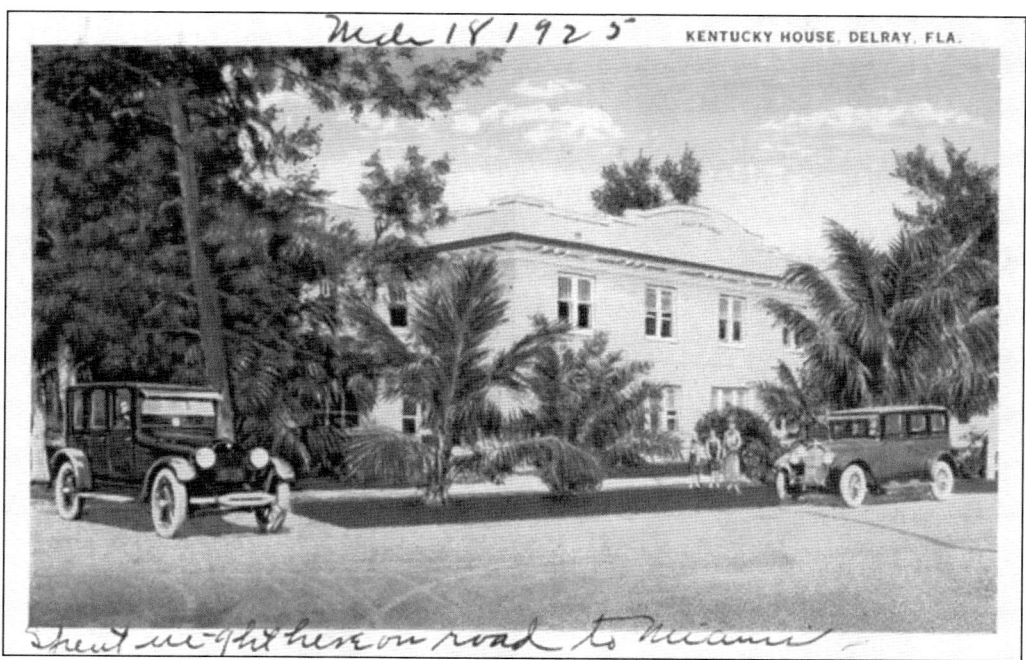

KENTUCKY HOUSE. The Beautiful Florida Series was published by the Ashville Post Card Company. The hotel is pictured here a few years after construction at the height of the boom period. Someone has written the date of 1925 and below, "Spent night here on the road to Miami."

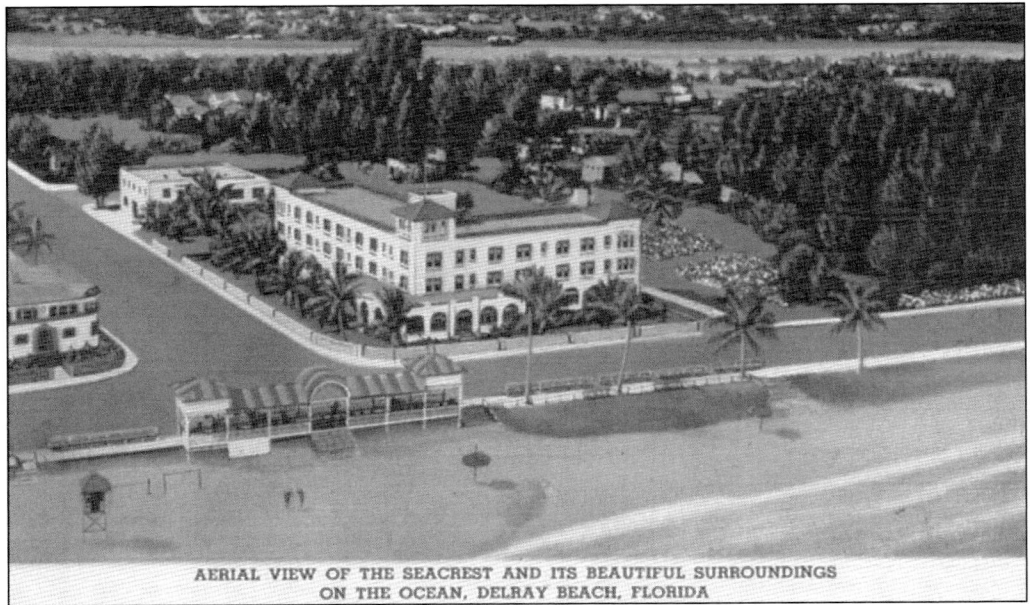

AERIAL VIEW OF THE SEACREST AND ITS BEAUTIFUL SURROUNDINGS ON THE OCEAN, DELRAY BEACH, FLORIDA

THE SEACREST. In 1924, railroad agent E. H. Scott built the Seacrest on the ocean. This genuine Curteich-Chicago C. T. Photo-Colorit postcard shows the hotel's beautiful setting on the barrier island. From Thanksgiving to Easter, the Seacrest catered to upscale seasonal guests from the North. On the beach is the whimsical pavilion, which was enjoyed for a time between hurricanes in 1928 and 1947.

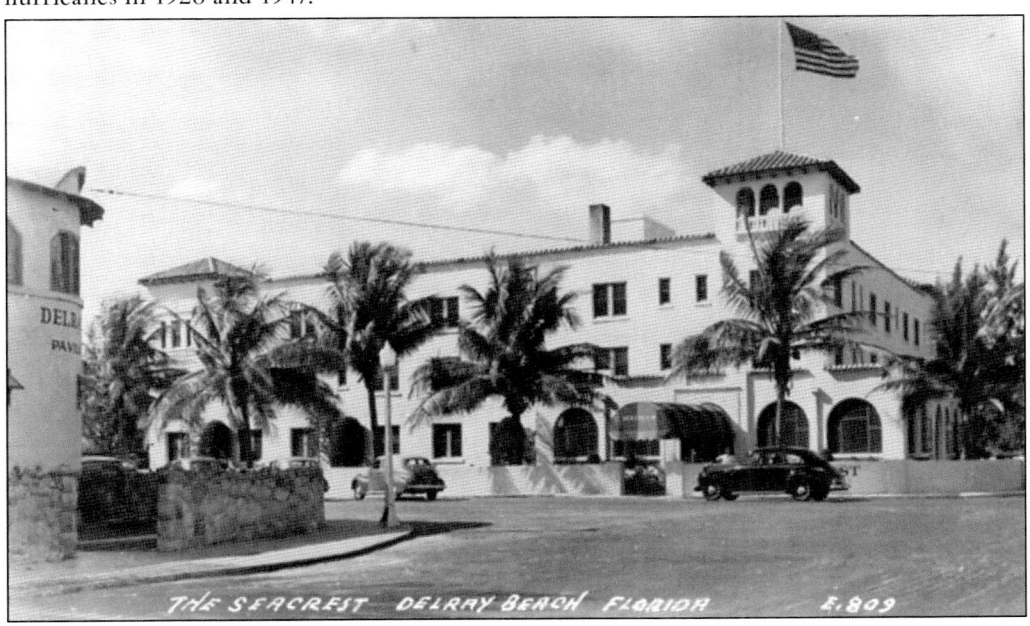

THE SEACREST IN THE 1940s. Such notables as Pulitzer Prize–winning poet Edna St. Vincent Millay spent a winter season at the Seacrest during the 1930s. In the World War II years, civilians volunteered 24 hours a day to man the air watch atop the hotel. The faux bell tower, flying the American flag, was the site where the volunteers recorded airplanes overhead and ships at sea.

The "Garden

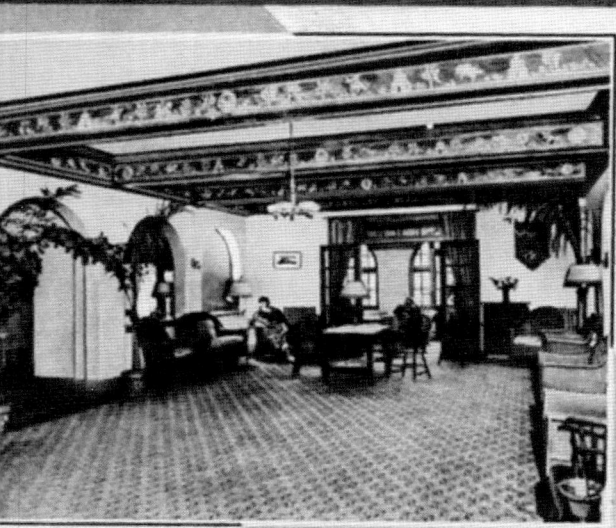

★ Delray Beach, the locale of the Se
It is unsurpassed in the abundance of
the almost constantly blowing trade w

★ Operated on the American Plan,
nature. The area surrounding Delray
United States. So the freshest and fin
An able and experienced chef prepar
supervision of the management.

★ A discriminating clientele chooses
compounded of the benificient sunshin
to living. Ocean bathing, the comforts
ideal place to spend the Winter. It is t
every member of the family feel at ho

★ As the Summer climate of Delray Beach is just as enjoyable as that of Winter, the Seacrest is open the year 'round. Service is somewhat modified during the Summer months and rates are correspondingly lower.

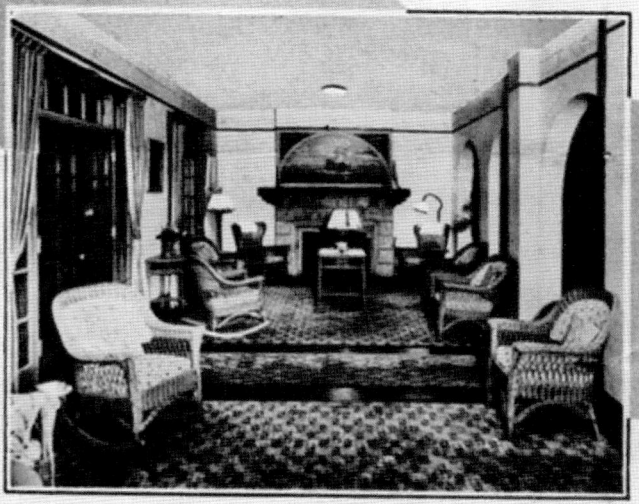

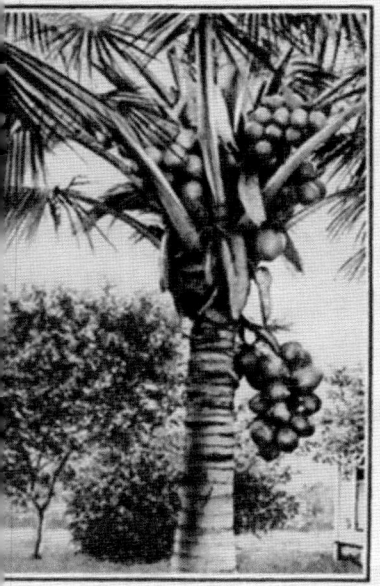

★ The Seacrest's lobby, lounge, dining room, on the ocean side of the hotel. From these v ships majestically sailing the Southern waters front of the hotel.

SEACREST BROCHURE. Images of the hotel's interior are shown on this side of the brochure, which was printed by the same company as the above card on page 35. The text is enthusiastic. On the reverse are a rendering of the exterior and a photograph of a palm-lined Atlantic Avenue. A partial floor plan reveals a typical sample of the 64 rooms, "the greater number of them commanding an unobstructed view of the Ocean and Beach." According to hotel

...pot" of Florida

...s been called the "garden spot" of Florida.
... A delightful temperature is maintained by
...g from the Gulf Stream.

...rest is fortunately situated and favored by
...known as the "Winter Market Basket" of the
...ts and vegetables are available at all times.
...acrest's delightful meals, under the personal

...crest year after year. The tropical climate
...ezes and health-giving atmosphere adds zest
... and the finest of surroundings make this an
... desire of the owners and the management that
...times. Make the Seacrest your Winter home.

★ For those who enjoy sports, every facility is available. Located about three miles from the hotel is the Delray Beach Golf Club—with a nine-hole course in excellent condition.

★ Exciting polo games may be watched twice a week at nearby privately owned fields. Surf fishing delights the adventuresome fisherman. Disciples of Isaac Walton find Kingfish, Pompano, Bluefish and Spanish Mackerel close to shore. Arrangements for deep-sea fishing can be made through the management—who have access to guides and boats that go out from nearby inlets.

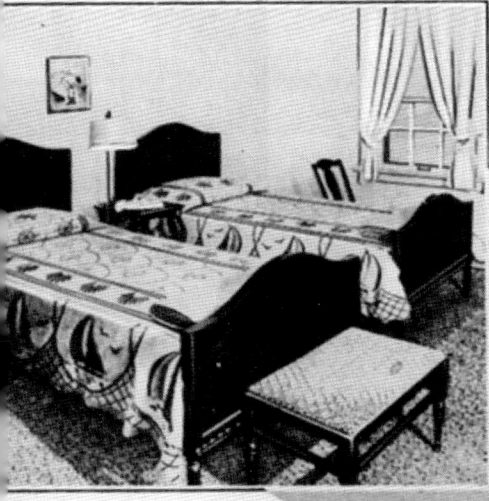

and writing room are
...ints one can watch the
...ean lane is directly in

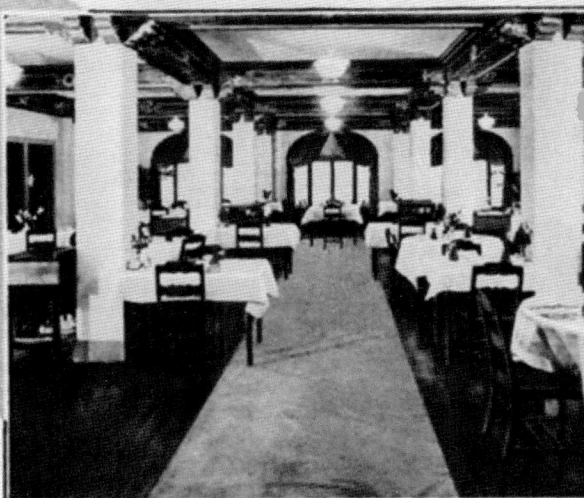

literature, guests had the option of arriving by train—either the Florida East Coast or the Seaboard Airline. Other options were Florida Bus Lines with an arrangement to be met by a car from the Seacrest, or by personal car along U.S. Highway No. 1 and Florida Route No. 4. Robert H. Tyler is listed as manager and E. H. Scott as owner.

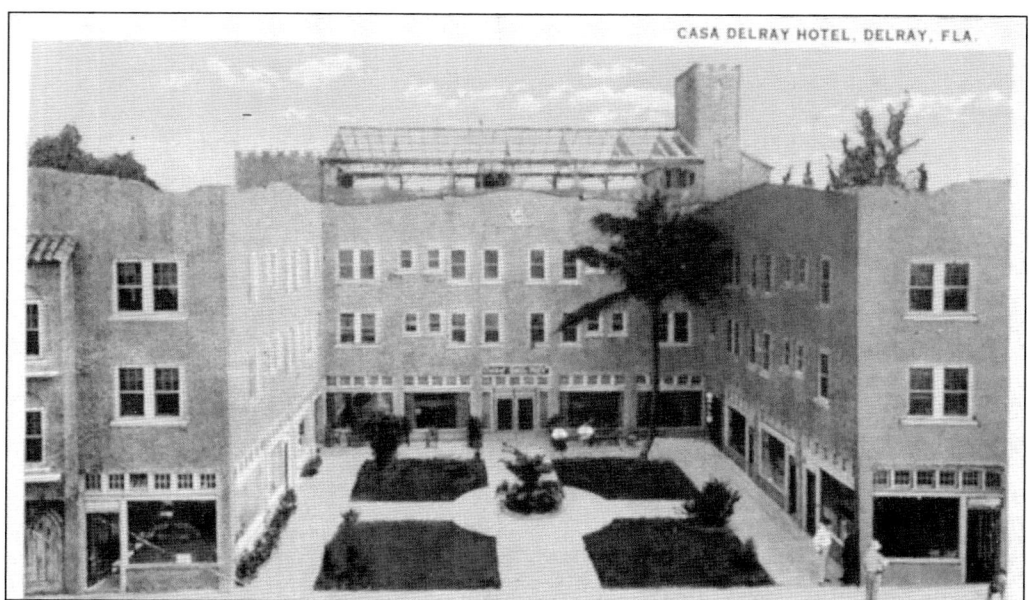

CASA DEL REY. The three-story Casa Delray Hotel was featured on another of the Beautiful Florida Series postcards. On hotel silverware, the name was written "Hotel Casa Del Rey." Built in the Mediterranean Revival Style by pioneer Henry J. Sterling in 1925, the hotel was an impressive addition to the East Atlantic Avenue streetscape. Delray builder James Sinks served as the contractor. Guests enjoyed a top-floor restaurant with a retractable roof.

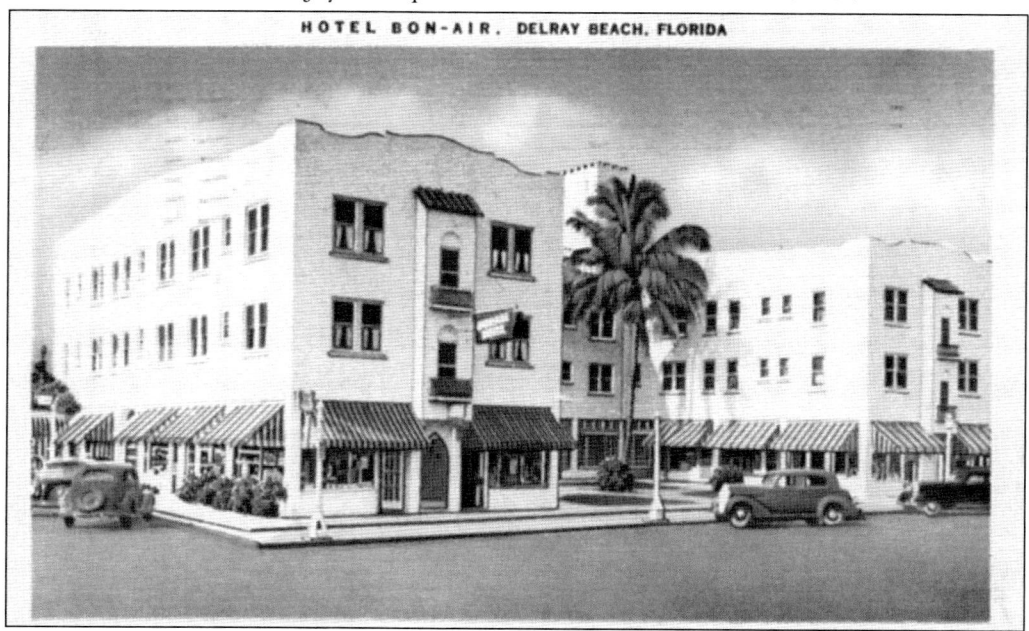

HOTEL BON-AIR. This Cook Company postcard was sent as a Decoration Day greeting in 1945. As happened with most hotels in town after the 1926 real estate bust, the original owners lost control, and banks or new owners changed the name. World War II brought more visitors, and more than one described the hotel as a "tropical wonderland." The Bon-Air was demolished in 1968. (Karen Wiita Van Wormer.)

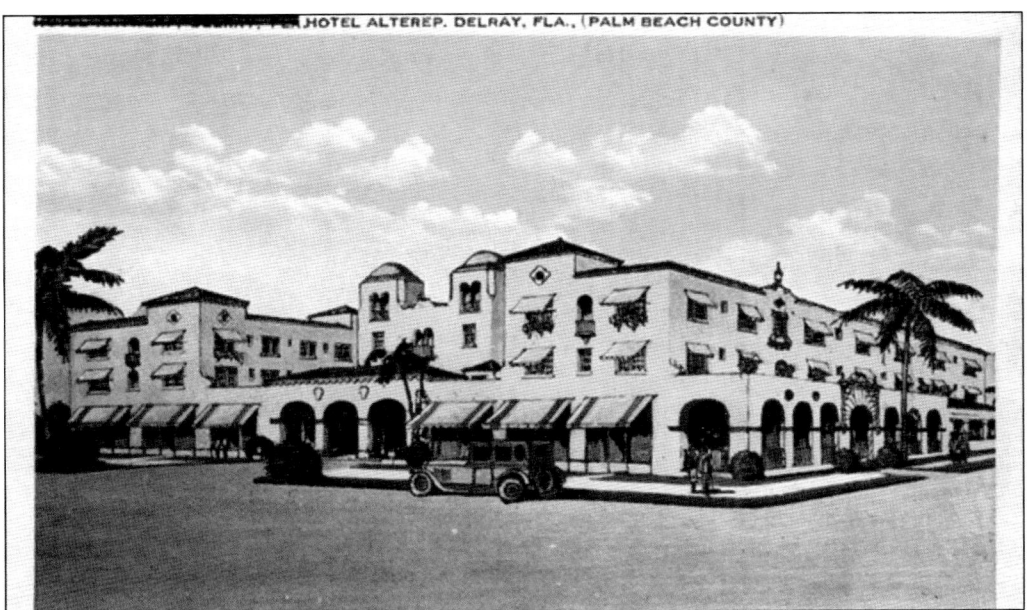

HOTEL ALTEREP. The Alterep was the last big hotel built on Atlantic Avenue during the 1920s boom. Designed in the Mediterranean Revival style by architect Martin Luther Hampton and furnished by John Wanamaker of Philadelphia, the building opened in January 1926, a few months before the real estate market crashed. Alterep was an abbreviation of the owner's name: Albert T. Repp. This postcard was published by C. A. Stead of Jacksonville, Florida.

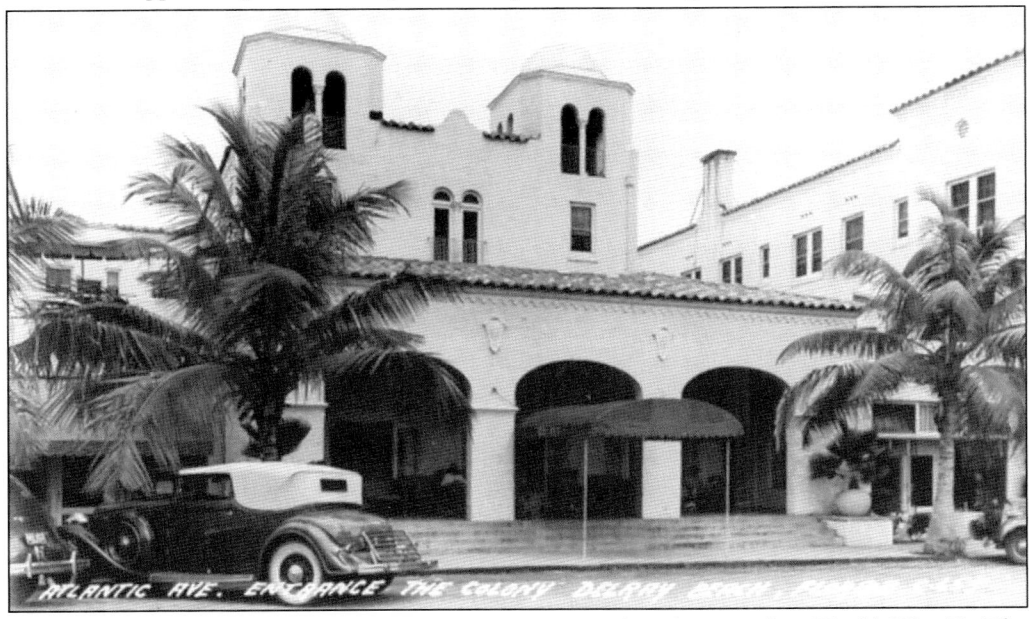

THE COLONY HOTEL. This iconic postcard was purchased soon after World War II. The message on the reverse is a question: "Does this picture remind you of anything?" Pictured is the Colony, the only survivor of Delray's old hotels on Atlantic Avenue. The hotel was purchased by its second and present owner, the Boughton family, in 1935. Most of its historical features remain intact.

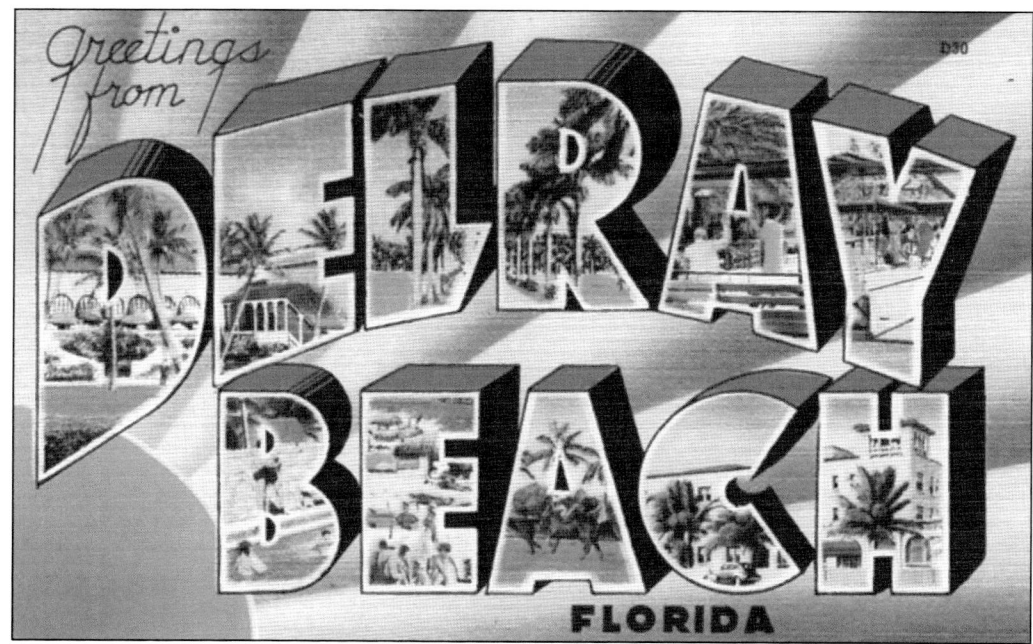

DELRAY BEACH. A popular postcard purchased in the mid-1940s and published by the Eli Witt Tobacco Company of West Palm Beach read, "Greetings from DELRAY BEACH, Florida." Displayed in the large letters are well-known resort scenes in Delray Beach and its vicinity: (left to right) the Gulf Stream Golf Club, the palms on Atlantic Avenue, shuffleboard at the city park, the casino pool, polo at Gulf Stream, and the Seacrest Hotel.

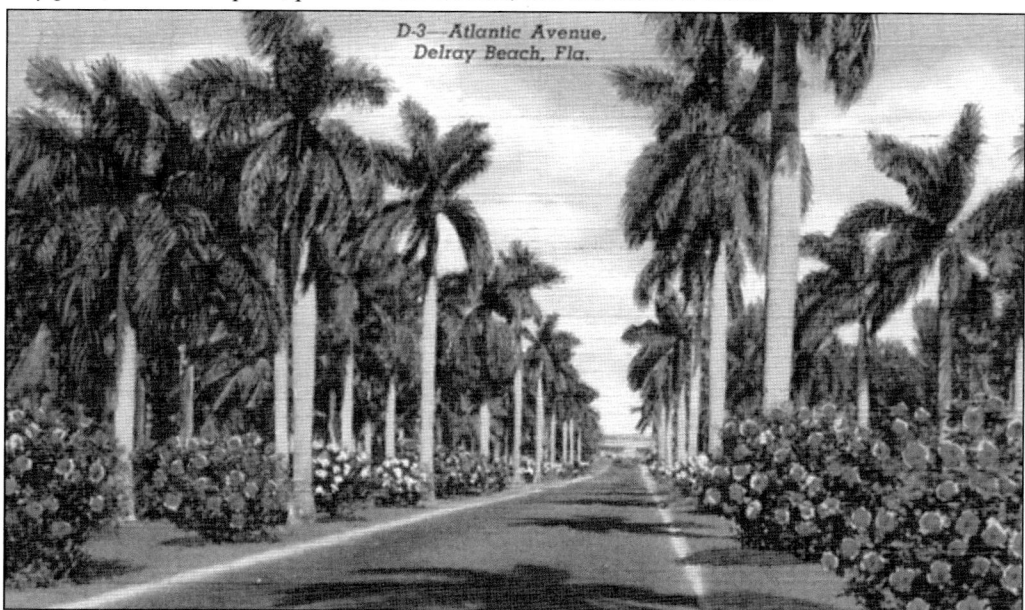

EAST ATLANTIC AVENUE. Mailed in 1951 from Pompano Beach, Florida, this card depicts the beloved view of Atlantic Avenue east of the bridge, lined with blooming hibiscus and a double row of royal and coconut palms. Framed within the photograph is the beach pavilion at the end of the avenue. At the time of mailing, this image no longer existed.

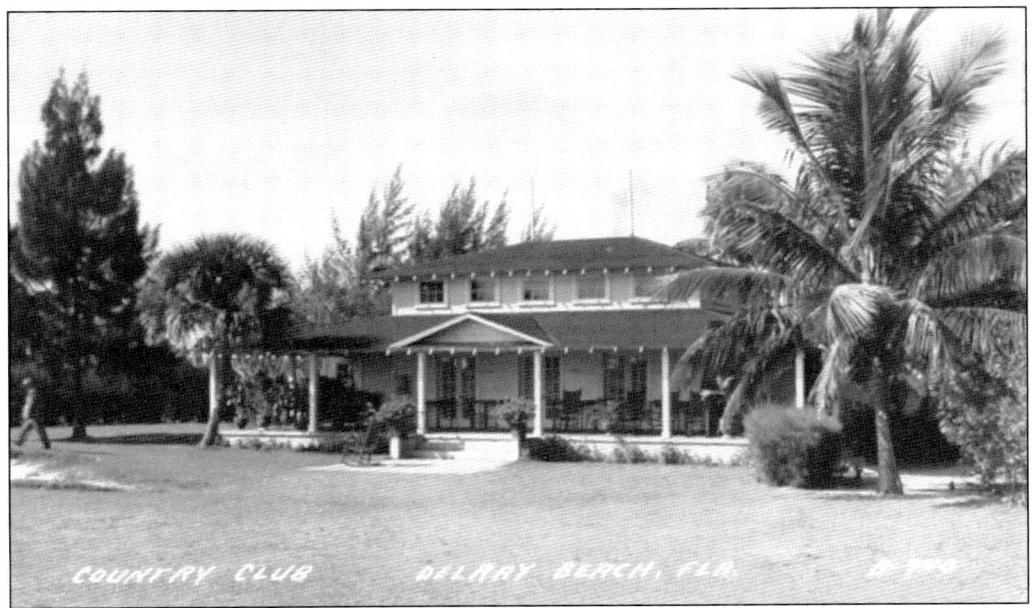

COUNTRY CLUB, DELRAY BEACH, FLA. Delray's first city golf course was established in the 1920s. The front porch of the homey clubhouse was lined with rocking chairs and potted plants, and the building was surrounded by tropical vegetation. Golf became popular in Delray in that decade, and the city course proved an attraction for winter colony tourists.

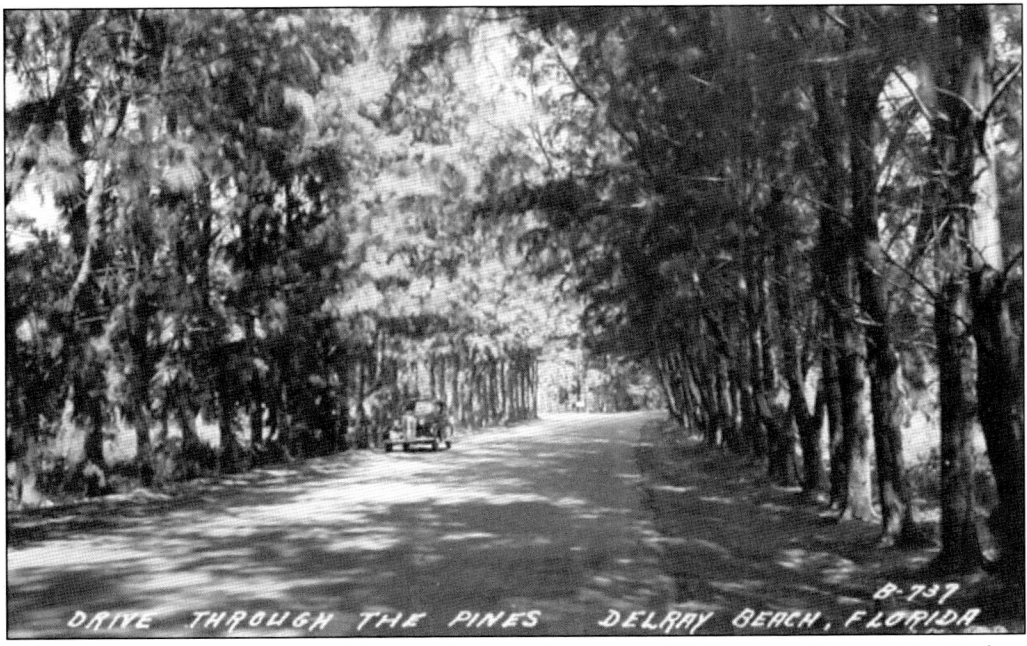

DRIVE THROUGH THE PINES. The heavily shaded canopy of Highway A1A connecting Delray Beach and Gulf Stream was a popular photographic subject. When Gulf Stream was established in the mid-1920s, the pines planted there grew rapidly, giving the road a tunnel effect. Years later, the state proclaimed Australian pine an invasive species, but the town petitioned to have those along A1A in Gulf Stream declared historic.

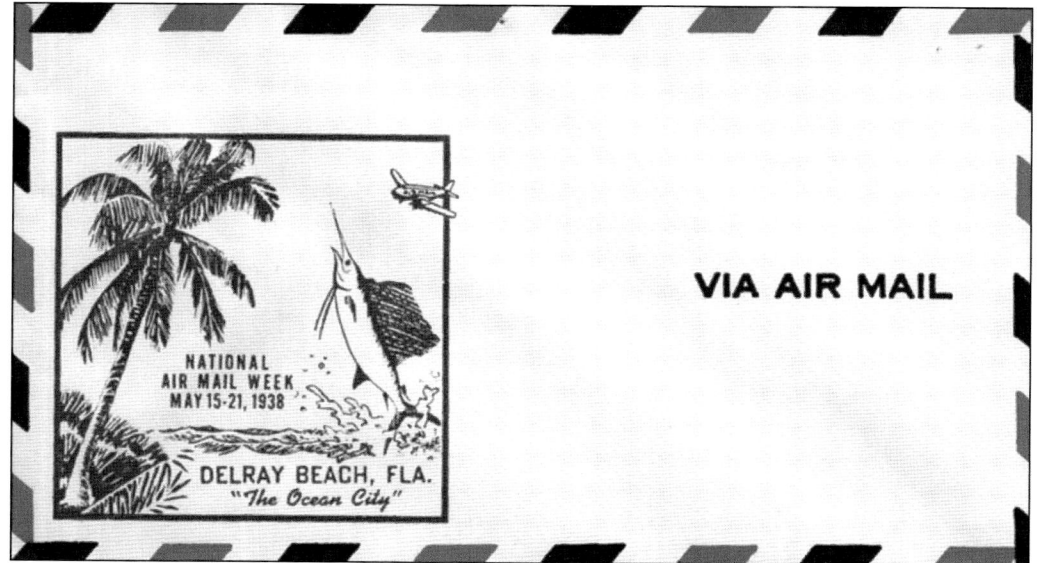

AIR MAIL WEEK, 1938. This 1938 Air Mail envelope celebrates National Air Mail Week and promotes the city of Delray Beach. "The Ocean City" is evoked with a palm tree and a sailfish leaping out of the sea. (Henry Higgins.)

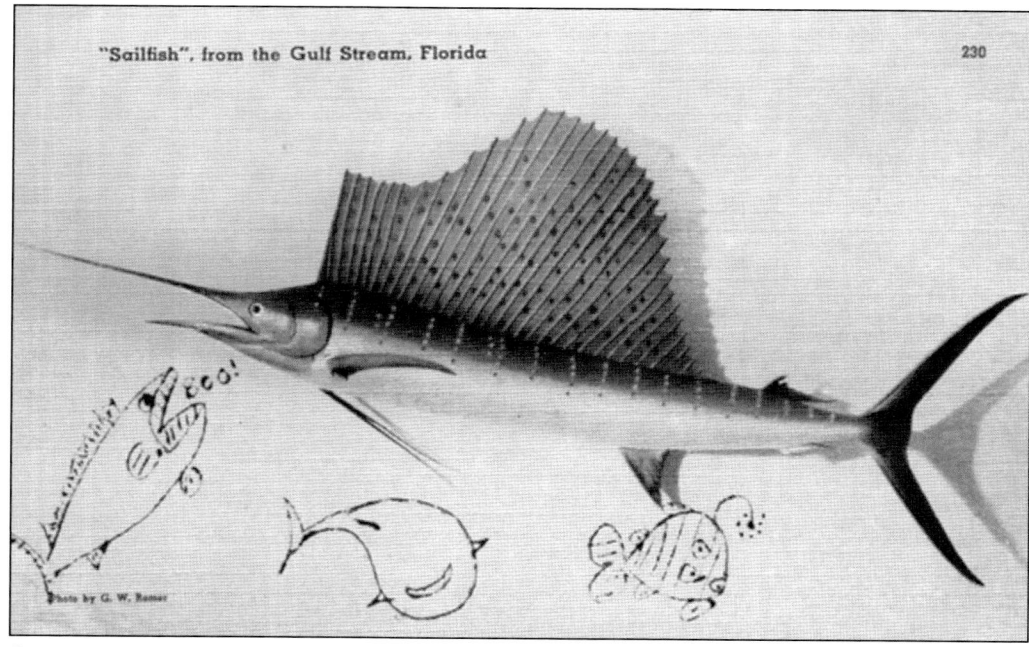

SAILFISH FROM THE GULF STREAM. Featuring a sailfish, this card was part of a 1930s fishing scrapbook donated to the historical society by Randall Davis. Davis drew several other fish underneath the sailfish. The Tichnor Quality View postcard includes text printed on the reverse: "Sailfish is a name given to the basking shark, *Selache maximus*, which swims with its dorsal fins exposed something like the sail of a ship."

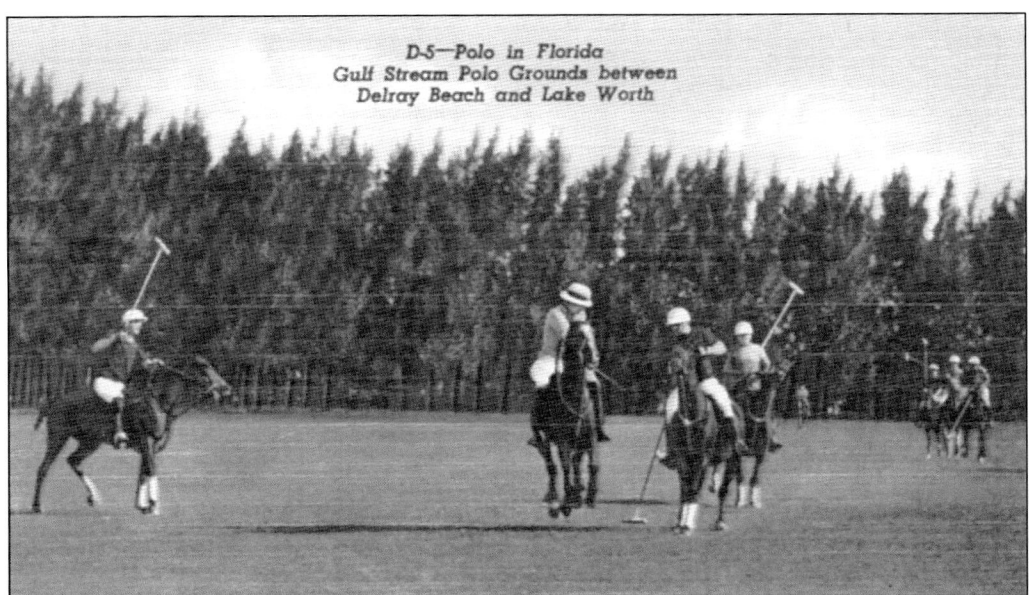

GULF STREAM POLO FIELD. The town of Gulf Stream was established during the 1920s boom with sports in mind, especially polo and golf. The fields were advertised as "the only polo fields south of Aiken, South Carolina." Chamber of commerce literature often referred to polo and called Delray Beach the "Winter Polo Capitol." Local newspapers covered games, famous players, and visitors, as well as related social events. (Karen Wiita Van Wormer.)

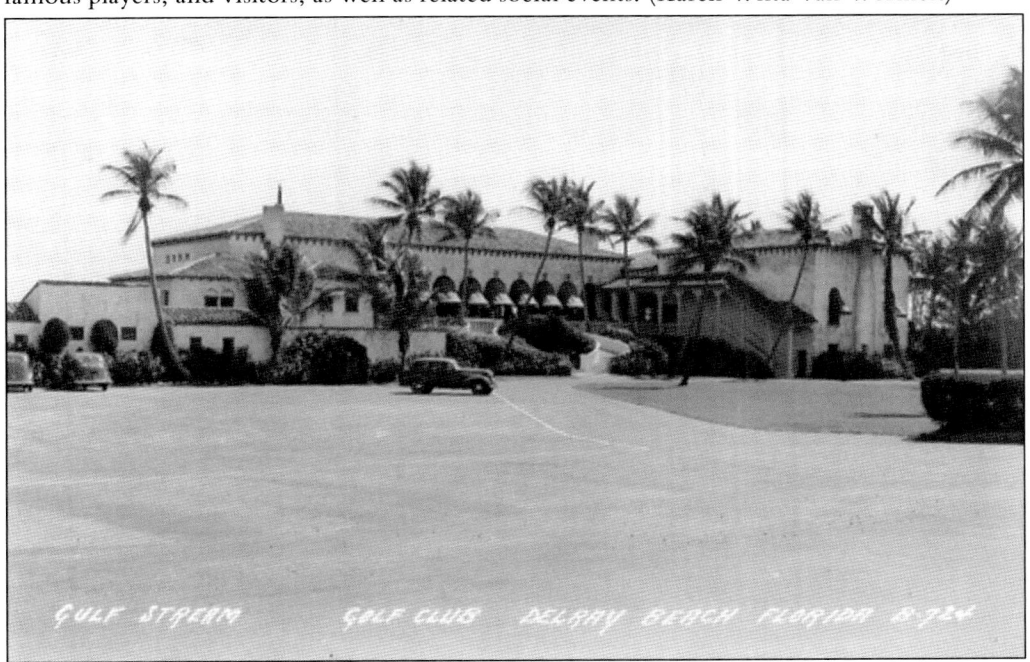

GULF STREAM CLUB. The Gulf Stream Golf Club was designed by famous South Florida architect Addison Mizner on the ridge overlooking the Atlantic Ocean. Published by the L. L. Cook Company, this postcard shows the exclusive Mediterranean Revival–style club during the 1930s.

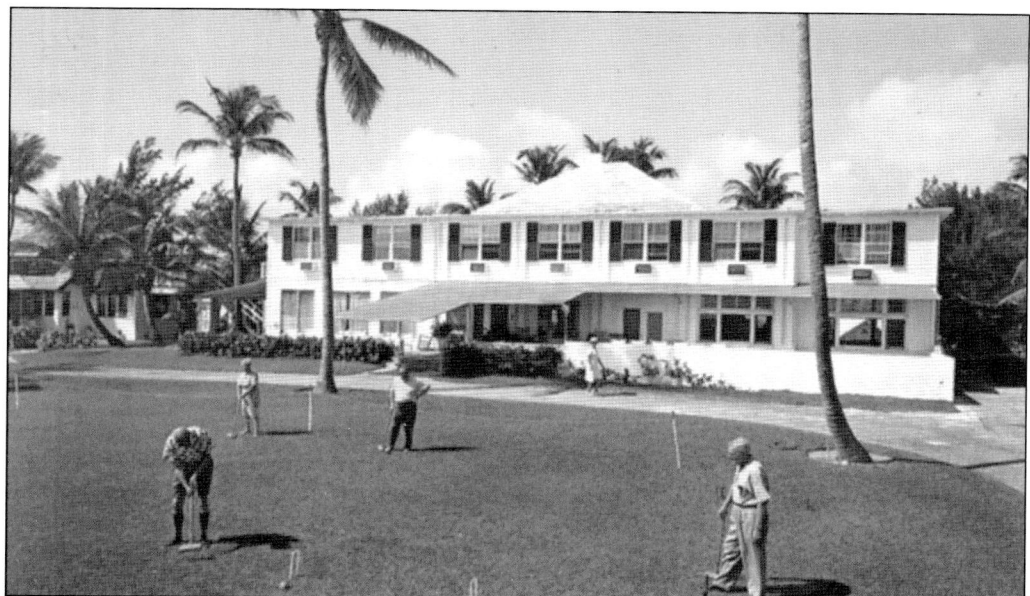

THE SANDOWAY. Established in 1934, the Sandoway offered a lodge, cottages, fine food, and a lawn for croquet (pictured) at 108 South Ocean Boulevard. Local photographer Stan Sheets published this postcard. The original owners decorated the hotel in a Caribbean-island style in what had been an old home on the beach. A nature center and a beach parking area are now named for the hotel.

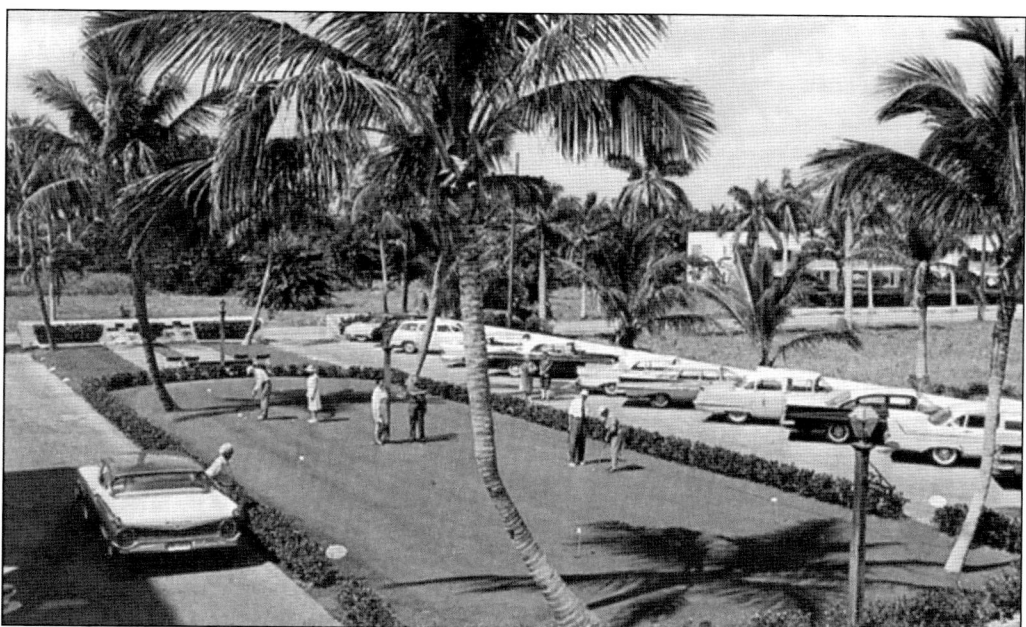

PUTTING GREEN AT THE TALBOT. Shown on a postcard from the 1960s is the practice putting green at the Talbot "on the ocean," at 125 North Ocean Boulevard. The card was published locally by Hank Cohen's Press Bureau. The scenes on these pages are evidence of the growing popularity of golf and the ongoing growth of resort facilities on the barrier island. (Henry Higgins.)

Tropical Golf Center. This versatile Tropical Golf Center advertisement opens up to show a map of the driving range on U.S. Highway 1, along with a list of three local rules. On the opposite side is a penciled-in scorecard, and on the back is a mailing area with an address area and space for a 4¢ stamp. (Henry Higgins.)

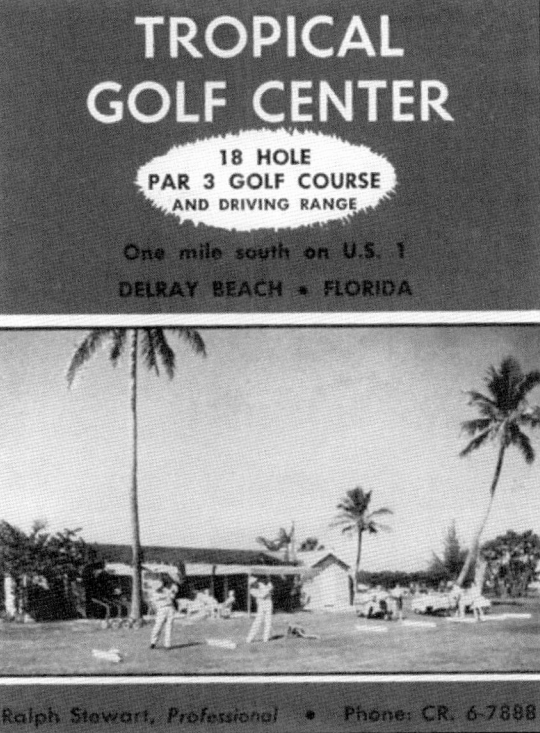

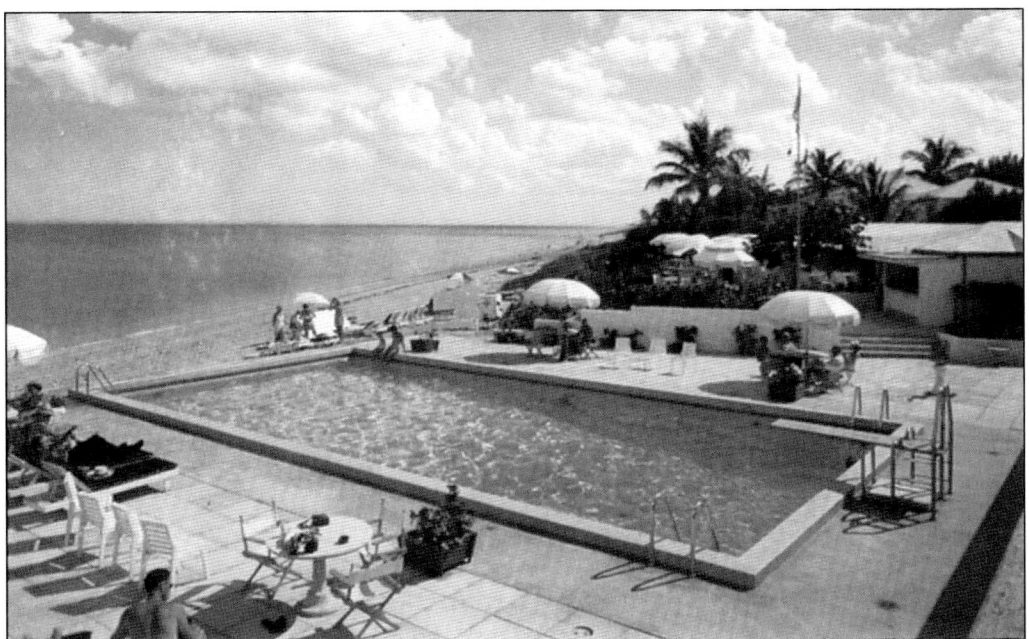

The Seagate. Promoting the Seagate and the Seagate Beach Club, this postcard shows an inviting pool with a view of a beautiful ocean and sky. The photographer/publisher is Charles Justus Wick of Delray Beach. At the time, the Seagate consisted of 38 ocean units with complete hotel service and exclusive club facilities.

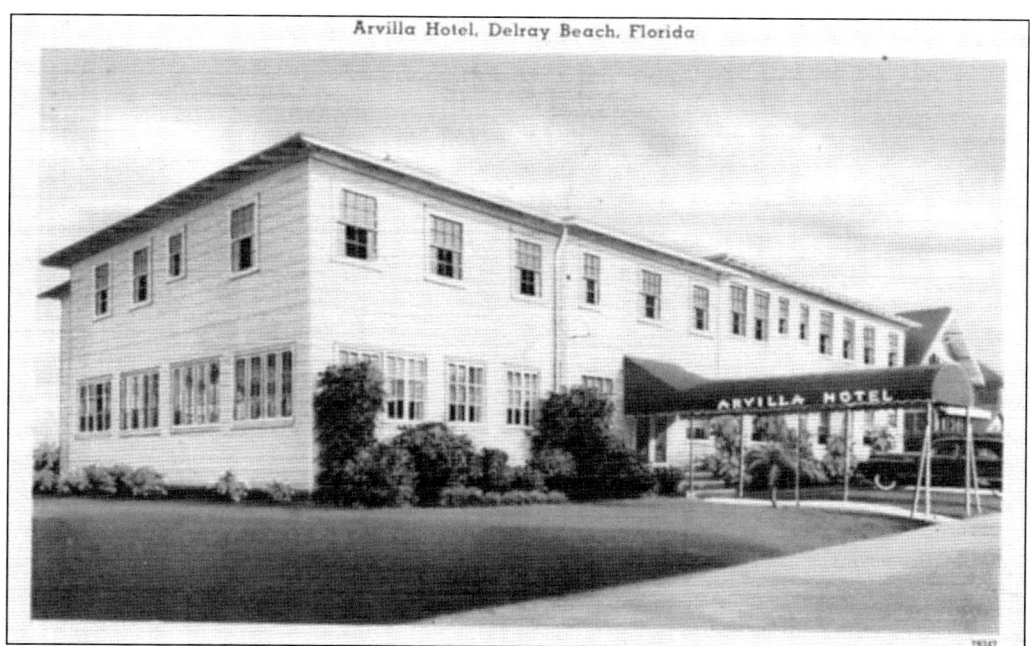

ARVILLA HOTEL IN THE 1950S. The Arvilla Hotel takes its name from the tearoom that originally inhabited the same location, at 5 Salinas Avenue, a few steps from Highway A1A. After 1950, the Arvilla is listed in local directories under hotels rather than restaurants, although there continued to be a restaurant or tearoom in the hotel.

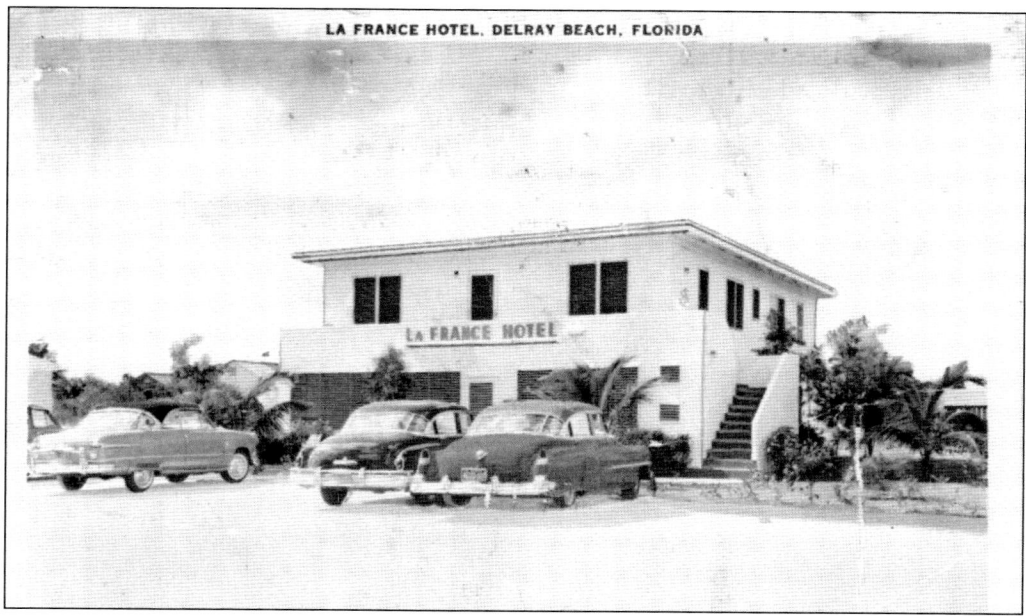

THE LA FRANCE. This hotel was the concept of Charles Patrick Jr., an African American entrepreneur in the old Sands neighborhood of Delray Beach during the days of segregation. He built the La France in 1949 because there was no hotel in the area for the African American waiters and chauffeurs working at the winter colony resort. (EPOCH.)

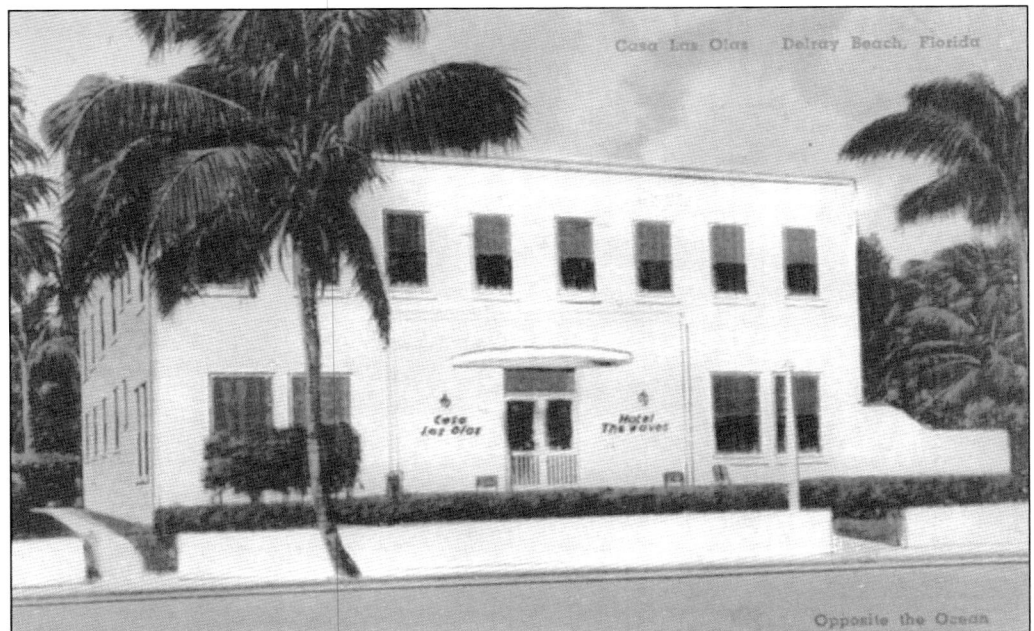

CASA LAS OLAS. This hand-colored card from the Albertype Company was sent out as a hotel advertisement in 1950. The new managers, Helen and Ed, invited locals to enjoy their home cooking. The Casa Las Olas offered a coffee shop and dining room, as well as "new, modern luxuriously appointed rooms each with bath." The building later became Boston's Restaurant.

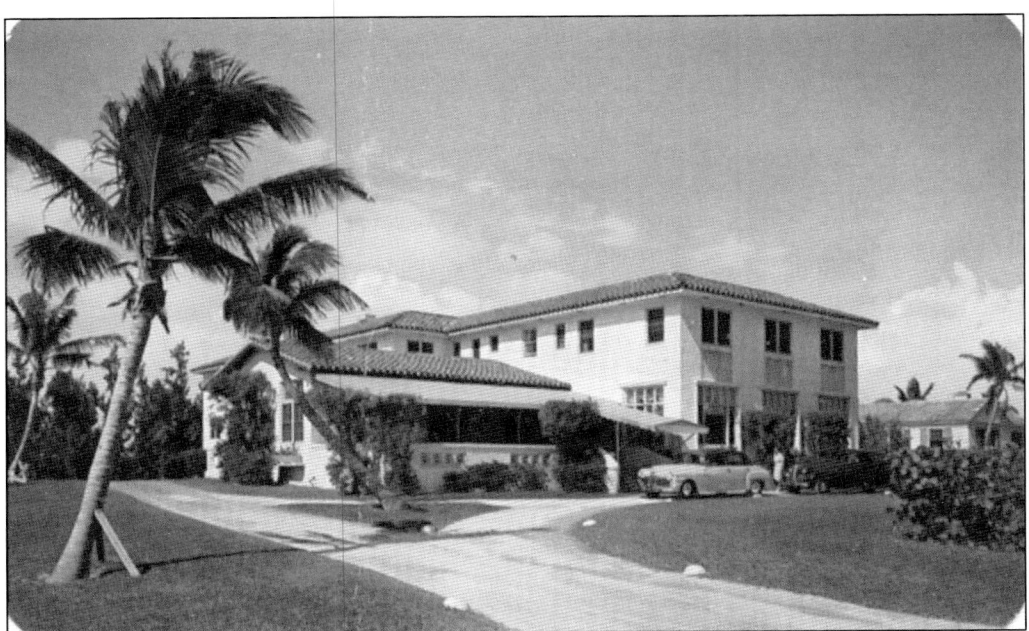

THE DELRAY BEACH HOTEL. Pictured on this L. L. Cook Company Kodachrome card is the Delray Beach Hotel, which opened in January 1940. Guests soon discovered a pastime other than sunning at the beach or playing golf: watching foreign ships at sea. World War II had begun in Europe, and British cruisers were observing German ships docked in Florida ports.

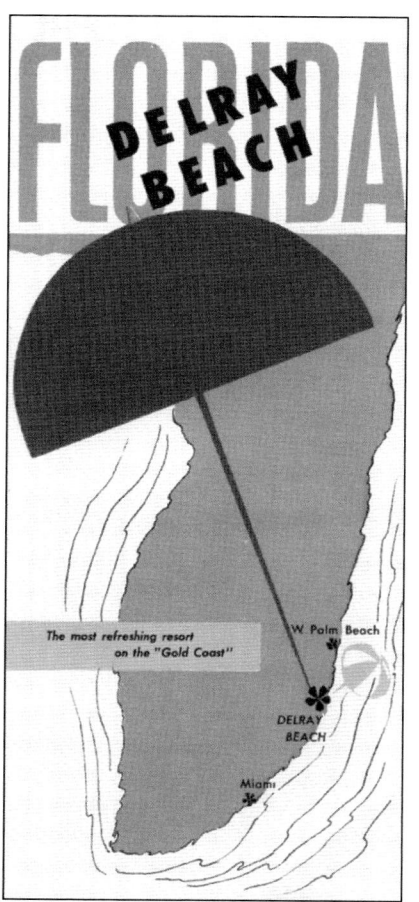

CHAMBER OF COMMERCE BROCHURE, c. 1950. This brochure of Delray Beach places the town on a Florida map with the text, "The most refreshing resort on the 'Gold Coast.'" The elaborate four-fold and fold-down brochure was published by the Delray Beach Chamber of Commerce. It includes an interesting collage of photographs in the shape of Florida and line drawings of fishing, golfing, card playing, dancing, and dining. Inside is more evidence that Delray Beach is a four-season resort, with images of polo playing, boating, exploring the Everglades, beach going, shopping on Atlantic Avenue, and more fishing. (Henry Higgins.)

PRESS PASS. The pass below is from a 1950s scrapbook assembled by Midge and Bill Archer. Midge was employed by the *Ft. Lauderdale News* and was active in the Delray Beach Chamber of Commerce. Bill worked at WPTV in Palm Beach.

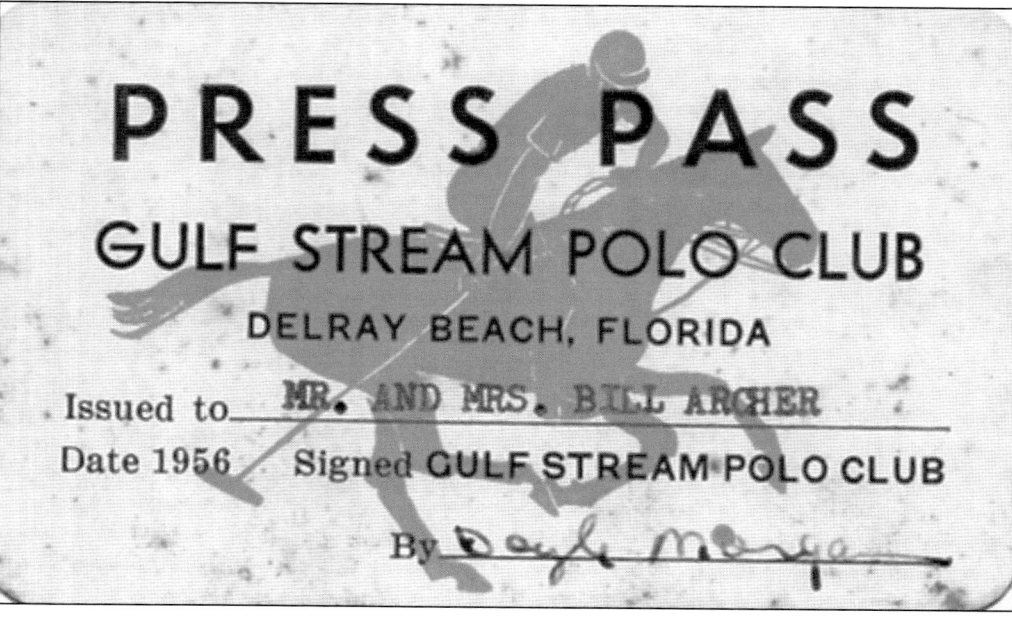

Four

ANCHORS OF SMALL-TOWN LIFE

In the archives of the Delray Beach Historical Society are multiple images of churches, schools, clubs, and sports. These anchors of small-town life engaged Delray citizens and fostered a strong, close-knit community.

The first churches were established when the town was still called Linton: Greater Mount Olive Missionary Baptist Church in 1896 and Mount Tabor, now St. Paul African Methodist Episcopal (AME) Church, in 1897. After 1902, the construction of other pioneer-period churches followed in close succession. Two public schools existed before 1898: School No. 4, Colored; and Linton School No. 17. These facilities were the centers of community life and the sponsors of many sports events. School buildings also hosted music and drama performances. Civic organizations were soon created, starting with the Free and Accepted Mason's Lodge, No. 275, in 1899; and the Ladies Improvement Association, later the Woman's Club of Delray Beach, in 1902.

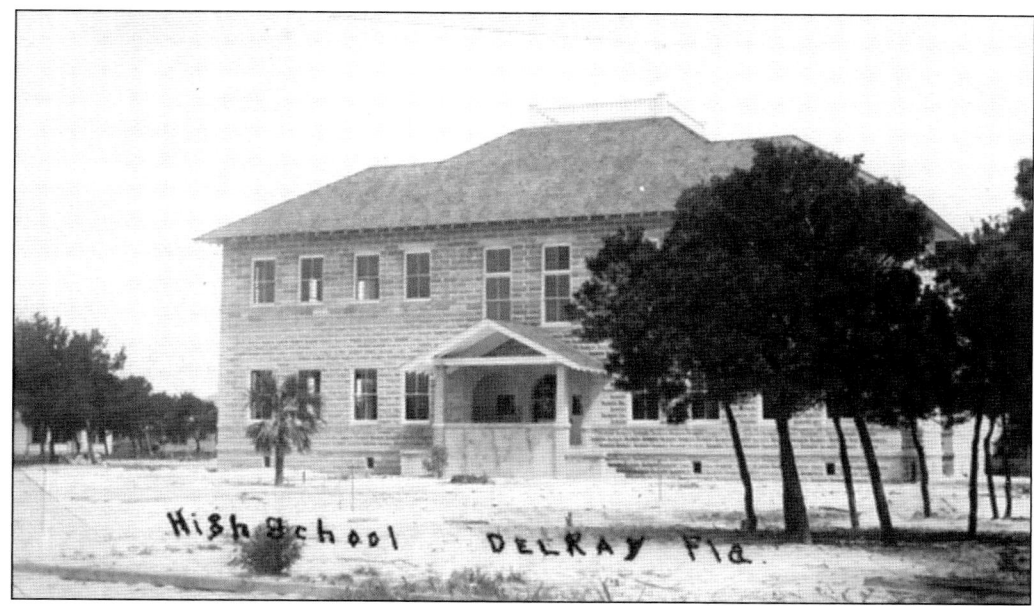

THE DELRAY SCHOOL. In 1896, School No. 17 was built on the spot indicated as the school block on the original town of Linton plat. The school board demolished the small frame Linton School, which faced Atlantic Avenue, in 1913. This substantial two-story masonry vernacular schoolhouse, consisting of four rooms upstairs and four downstairs, replaced the frame building.

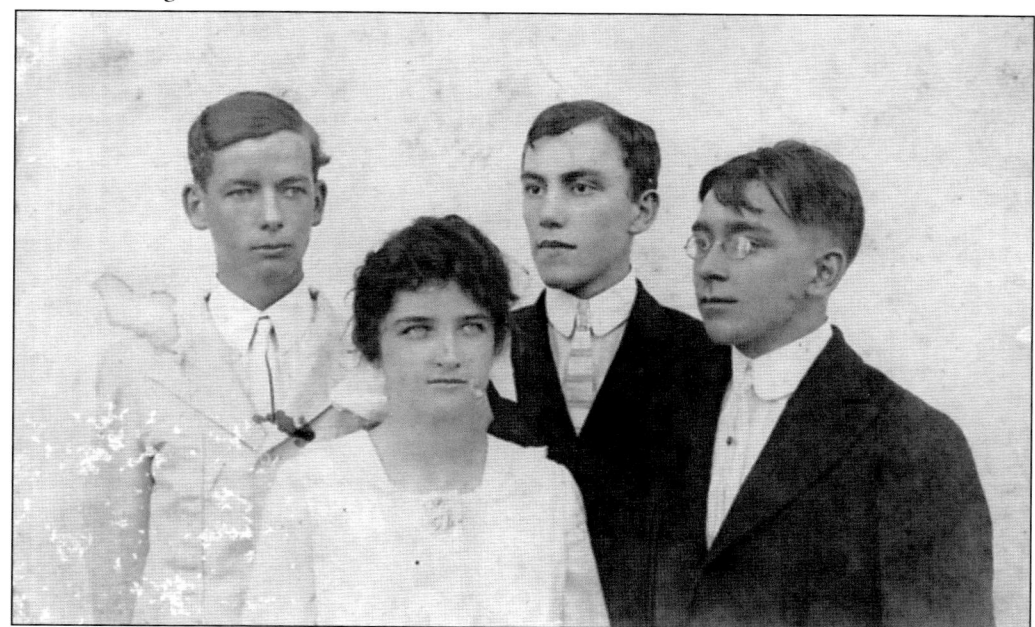

CLASS OF 1915. The first graduating class of the Delray School included, from left to right, Ben Sundy, Betty Ferguson, Lauren Hand, and Bill Sperry. Ben Sundy was the son of Mayor John S. Sundy. After graduation, Lauren Hand worked on his Ph.D. in chemistry at Berkeley but returned to Delray Beach to become editor of the *Delray Beach News*. Hand also founded the Delray Book Shop, now Hand's Office Supply.

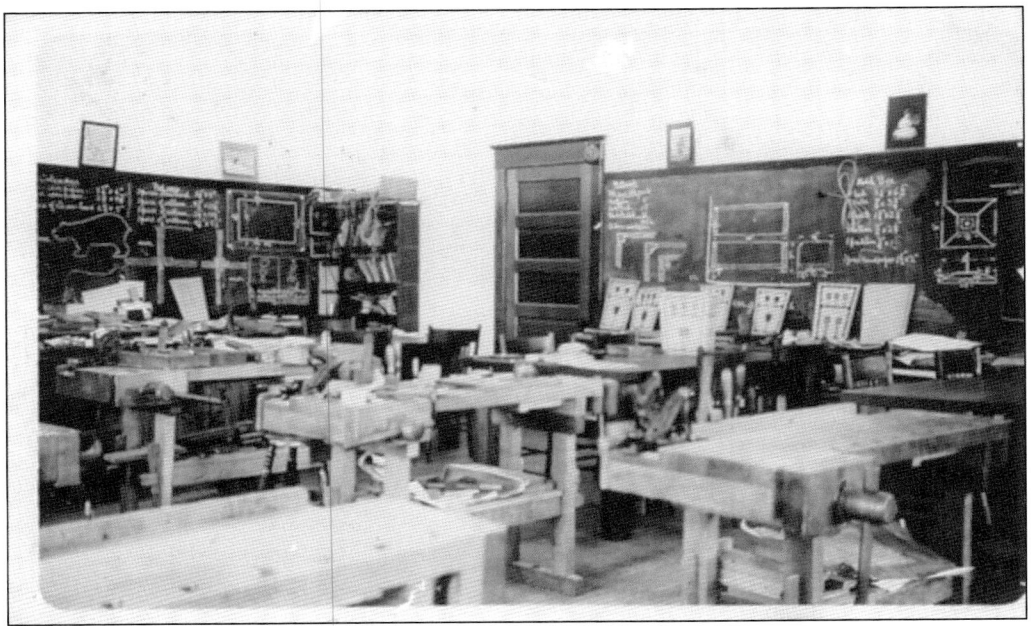

MANUAL ARTS. A 1913–1914 school photograph shows the newly furnished manual arts room on the second floor, which was reserved for high school classes. Principal C. H. Lander taught the classes and probably chose the equipment. He had studied biology and botany at the University of Michigan, Harvard, and Rutgers. Lander came to believe that students who were not academically gifted should also have a chance to excel.

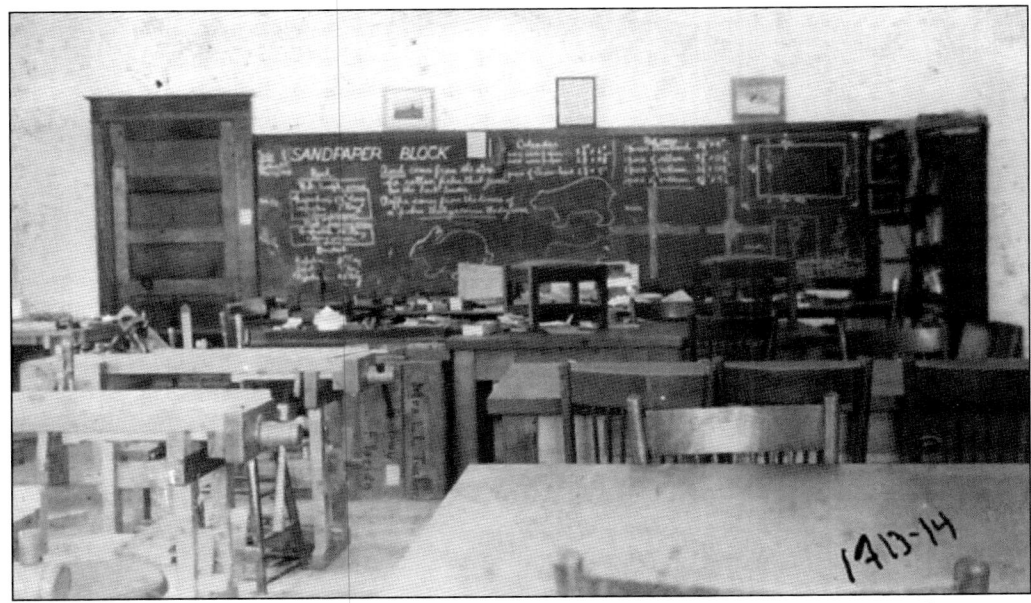

VIEW OF CLASSROOM. Principal Lander photographed a skillfully finished set of mission-style furniture built in the classroom shown above, On the photograph, now in the archives, Lander wrote, "A boy from our class did this. His father said [to me], 'At last we have found something.'"

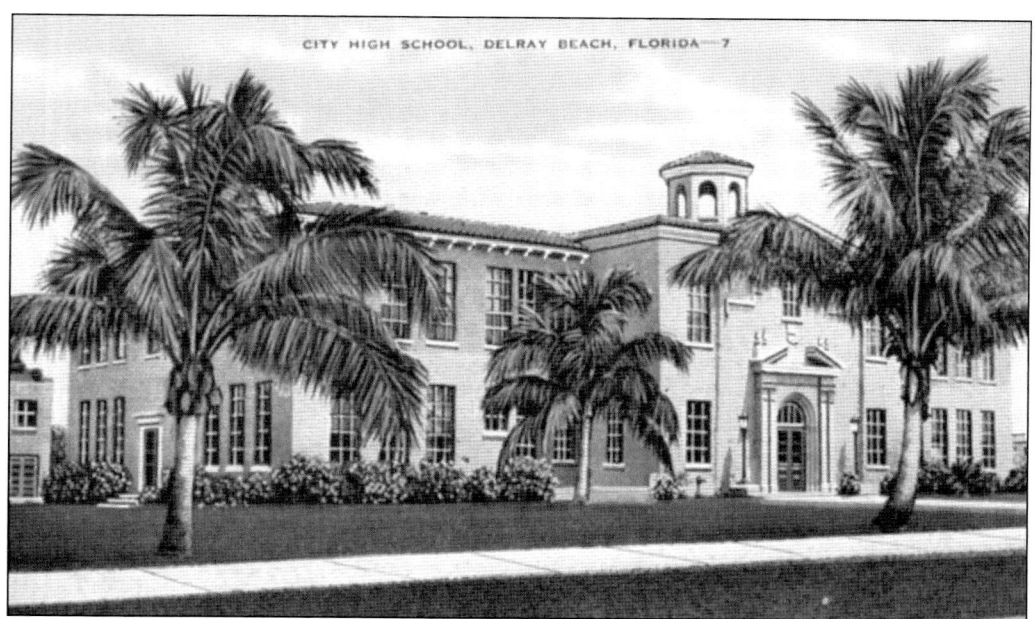

DELRAY HIGH SCHOOL. At the height of the 1920s real estate boom, townspeople saw the need for a separate high school to accommodate population growth. Delray's first registered architect, Sam Ogren Sr., designed the new school in the popular Mediterranean Revival style. By 1926, the building was ready, though the gymnasium built at the same time would soon be destroyed in the 1926 hurricane. (Karen Wiita Van Wormer.)

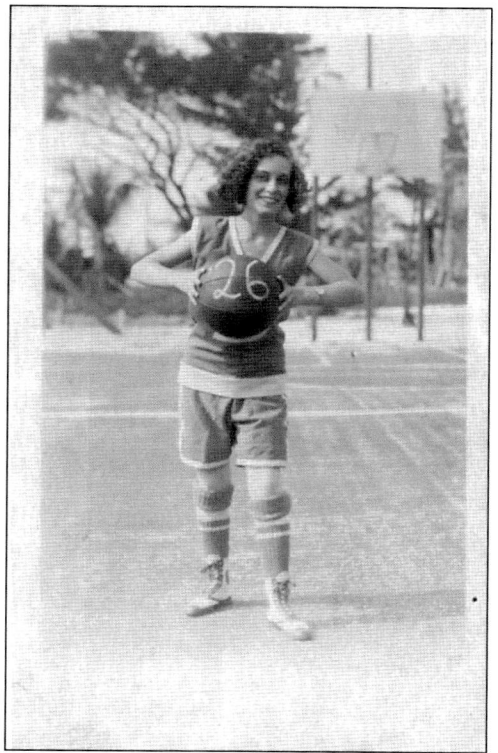

BASKETBALL TEAM. The next seven postcards show individual members of the Delray High School's 1926 basketball team. The first is Irene Moore of the girls' team. The uniforms employ a new logo with the letters D and H intertwined. Notice the class year is drawn on the basketball. Each year, the team posed holding a ball showing the year.

ROY BAKER HOLDS THE BALL. Roy Baker was one of 10 members of the Seahawk boys' basketball team. The first move he made in a February game with Coconut Grove was a two-pointer in Delray's favor. The team caught the spirit and won with a score of 24 to 14. Baker earned the highest number of points.

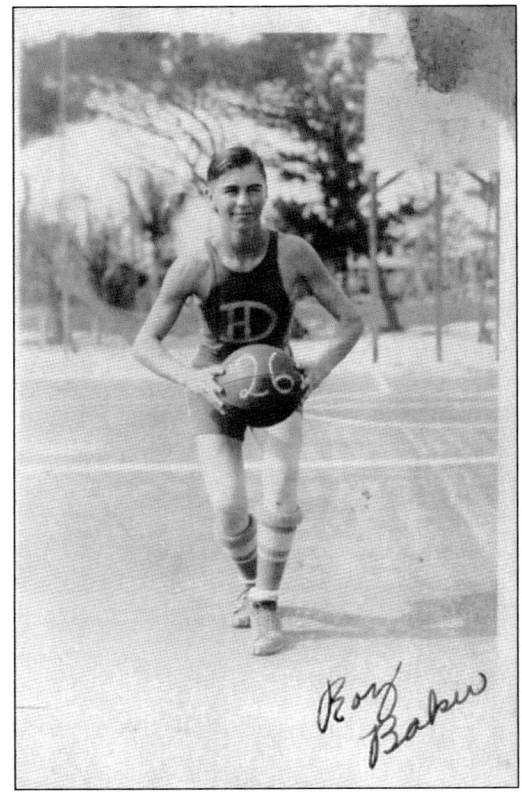

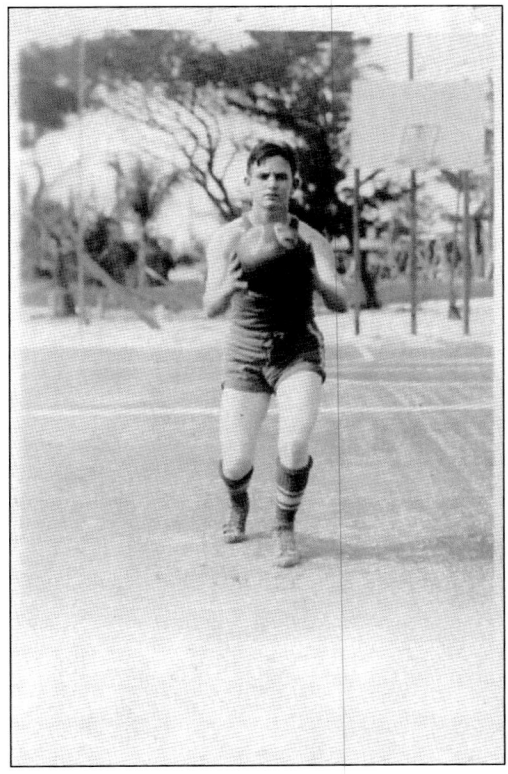

LEON BARWICK. Here Leon Barwick prepares to shoot a basket. The June 1926 school paper, *The Ocean Breeze: It's Fresh*, recorded that the boys' team had lost four and won four games for 1925–1926. Earlier that year, the team had traveled by train to Key West for a match-up. The Conchs won 25 to 11. Leon's father, L. L. Barwick, helped pay the expenses for the trip. Barwick Park and Barwick Road bear his name.

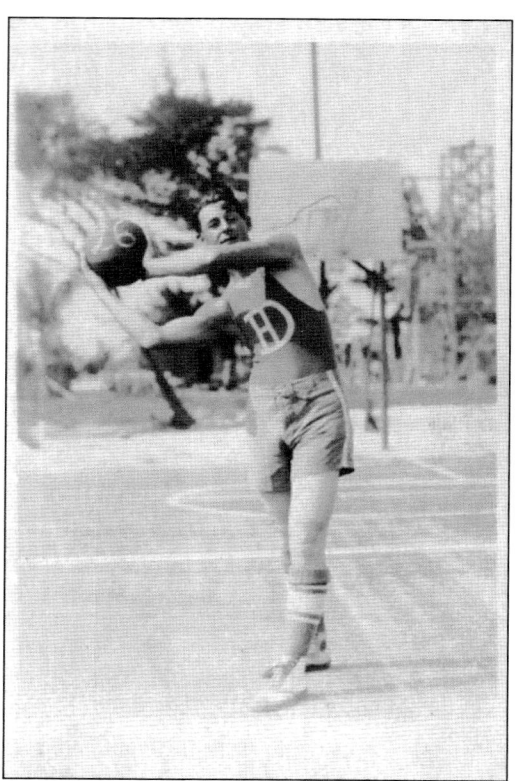

THE 1926 TEAM. Harry Carver poses in front of the goal. The same school paper stated, "Harry Carver never fails when it comes to guarding. . . . Much credit can be given to Carver for our boys' victories." In the loss to Key West, the opposing team never penetrated the Delray defense; all the Key West points were made by long shots.

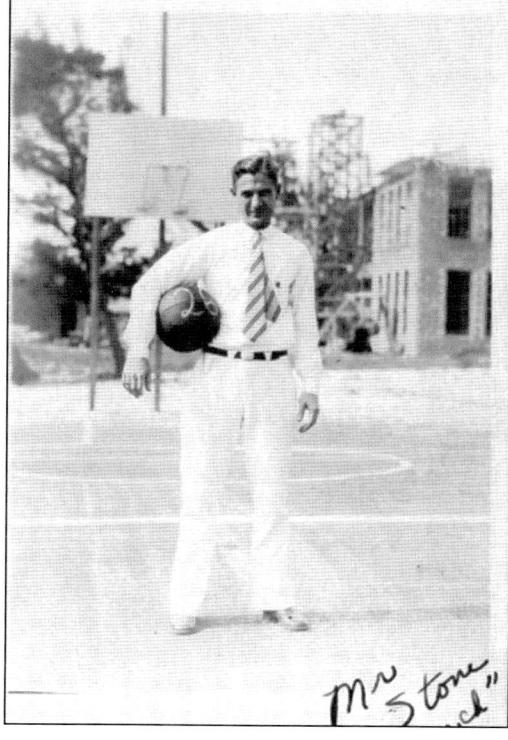

COACH STONE. Coach Stone stands on the court. Newspaper reports reveal that the new Mediterranean Revival high school was completed at a cost of $125,000 around August 1, 1926. It appears that the scaffolding was still up when this photograph was taken. On September 18, a severe hurricane demolished the adjacent gymnasium and badly damaged many other buildings in town.

"CAP." Phil "Cap" Brennan, captain of the team, also ran up the scores at games. In the official high school photograph of the 1926 team, he is in the center of the first row holding the ball.

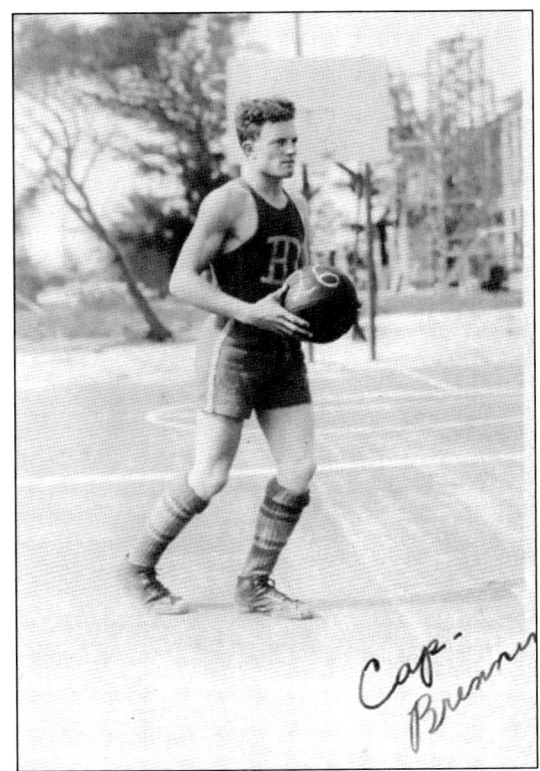

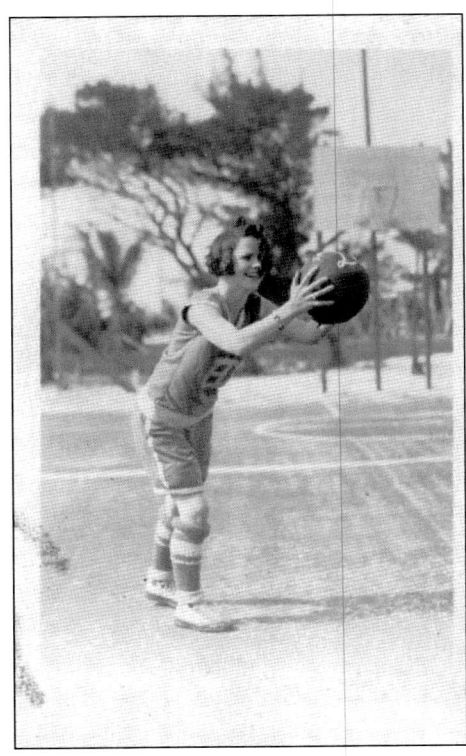

THE BARWICKS. Lorraine Barwick, Leon's sister, was a member of the girls' team. Miss Jennings served as coach, and Mr. Stone was manager. The school paper reported that Lorraine had been suffering from skinned knees and elbows. It seems that all the Barwick children had names beginning with "L" and all played basketball. Livingston ("Lib") and Leon Barwick played in 1928, when Delray won recognition as the East Coast champion.

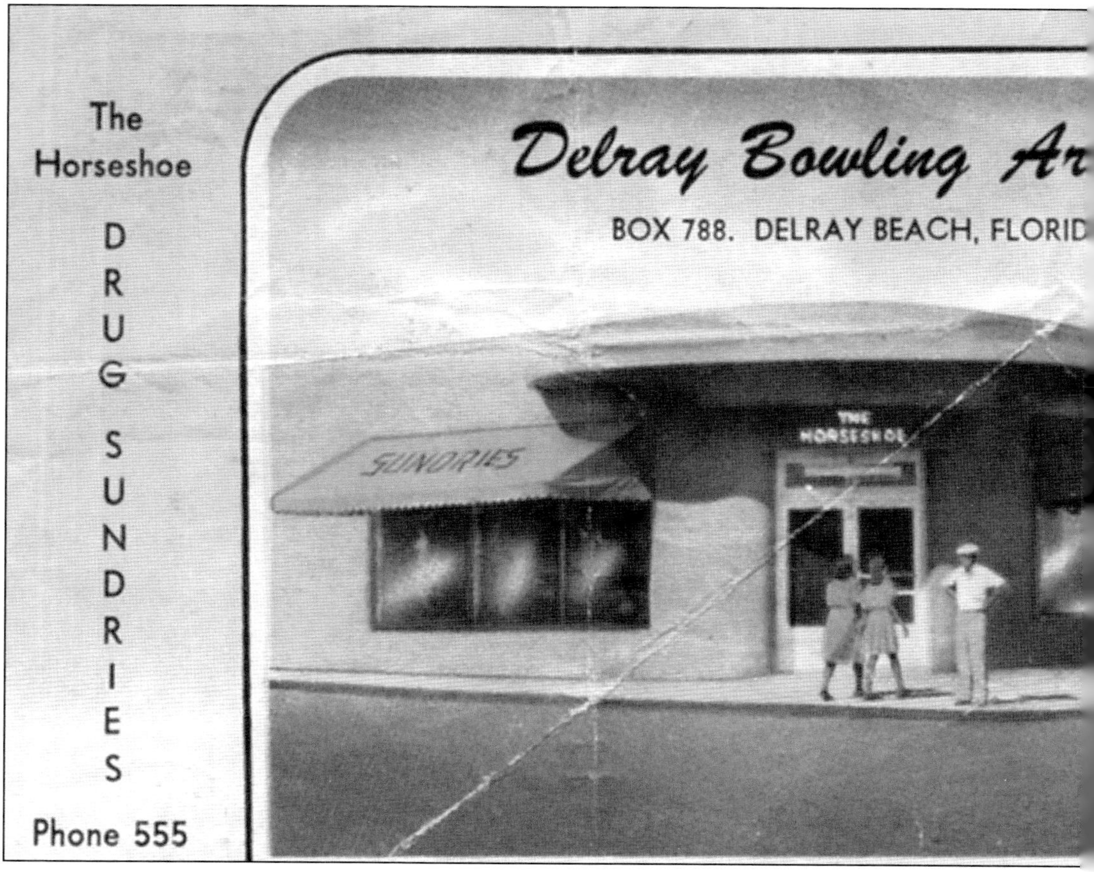

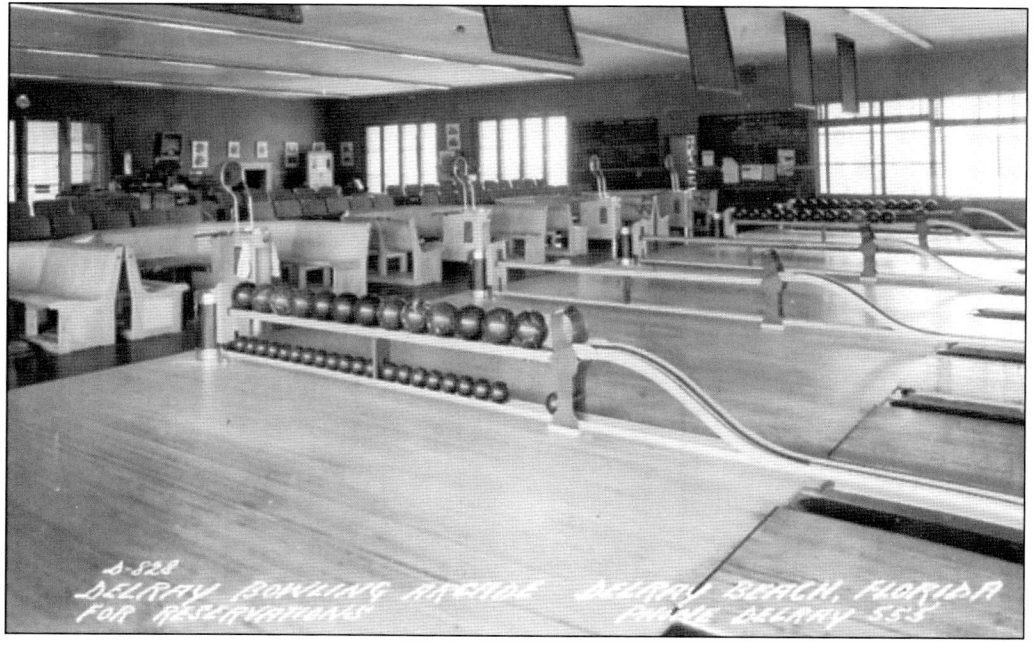

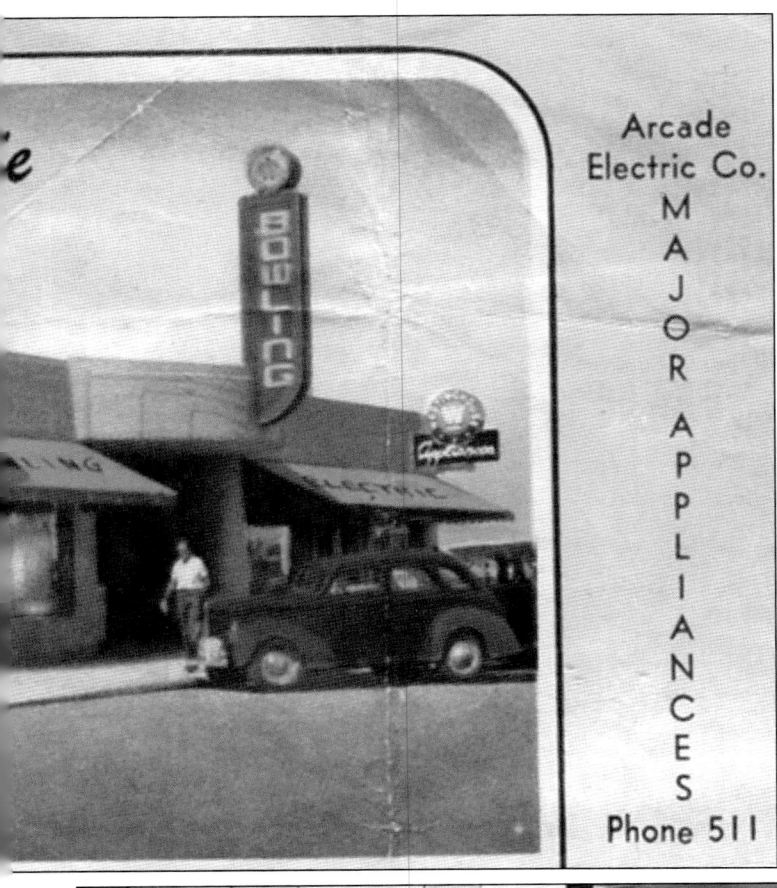

THE DELRAY BOWLING ARCADE. The Delray Bowling Arcade was built in the Streamline Moderne style in the 1940s. Note how the rounded lines of the car match the architectural style. The spare design of the exterior was reflected in the interior, as evidenced by the four views on the right. The lounge contained leather furniture, a fireplace, and a lion skin rug. W. Seward Webb established the Atlantic Avenue bowling alley as a place where military personnel were offered hospitality throughout the duration of World War II. This included procuring daily hometown newspapers for military patrons. The card on the lower right was sent to a sergeant at Fort Benning, Georgia, in December 1942.

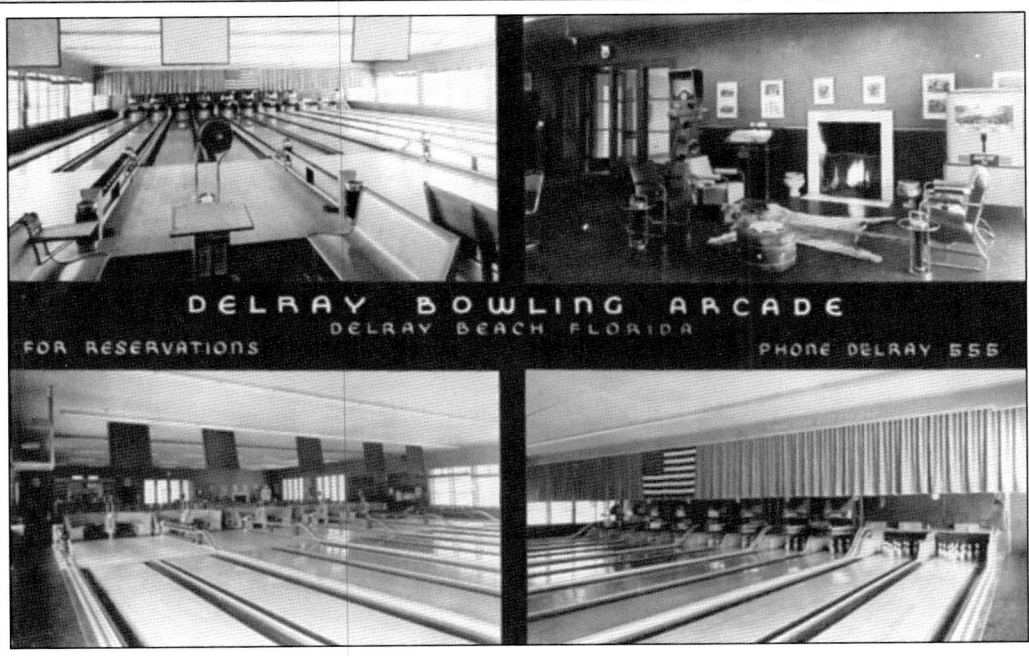

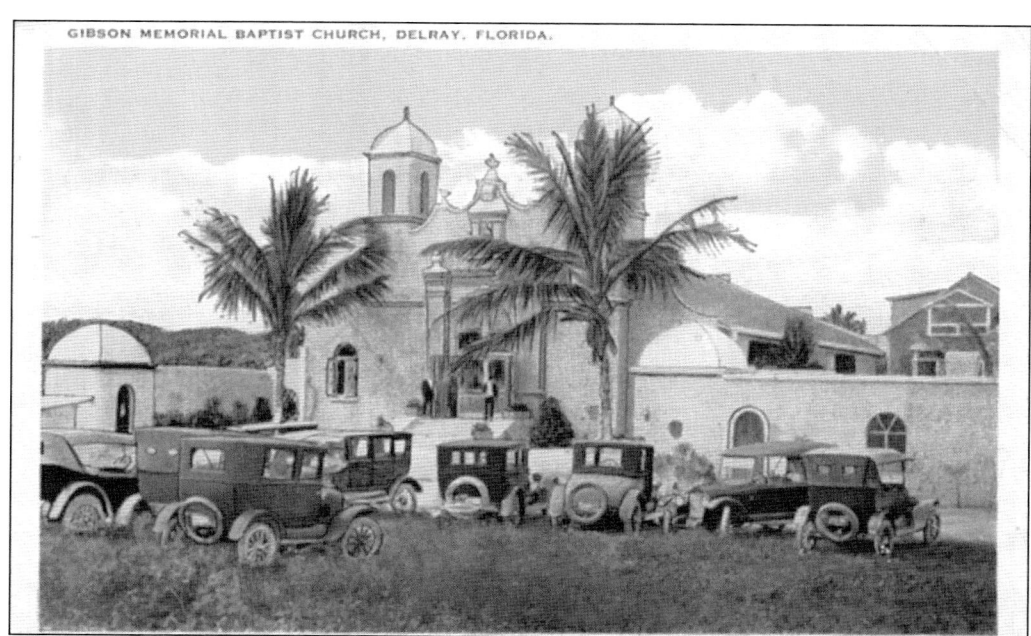

GIBSON MEMORIAL BAPTIST CHURCH. The only church on the barrier island was constructed on the site of an old orange grove. Maps from the 19th century refer to the location as the Orange Grove Haul-over. The 1924 church was completed by architect and builder F. J. Schrader, a member of the board of trustees, who used an image and floor plan of a church in Florence, Italy, for inspiration.

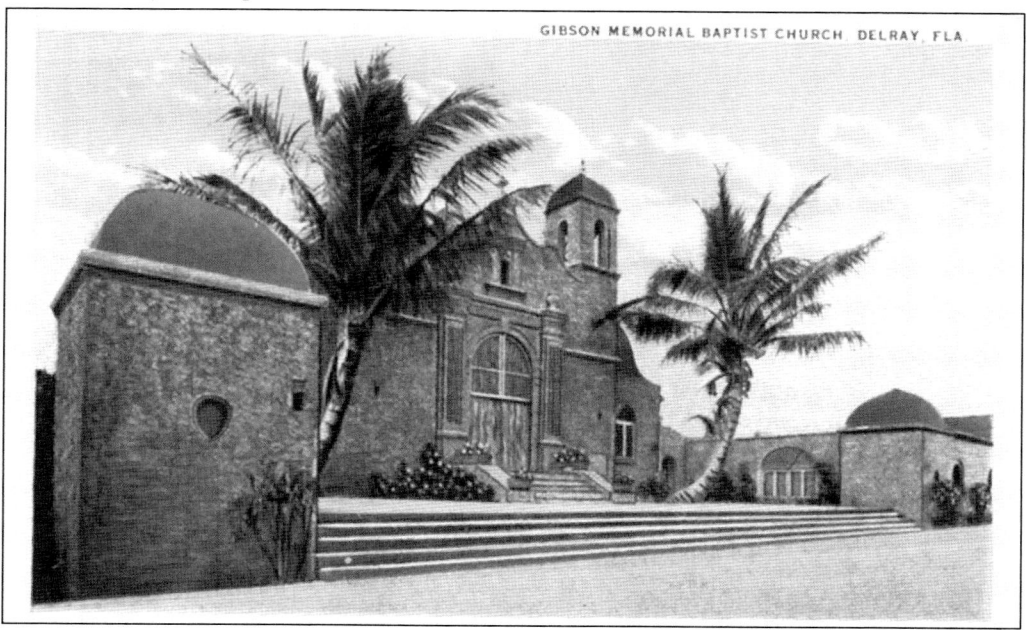

BAPTIST CHURCH, DELRAY, FLA. With its twin bell towers and surrounding wall, the church acquired the look of an old Spanish mission. It was built as a result of a split within the First Baptist Church, but by 1928, the congregation had been reunited. The building was rented and eventually purchased from F. J. Schrader by the Presbyterian Church.

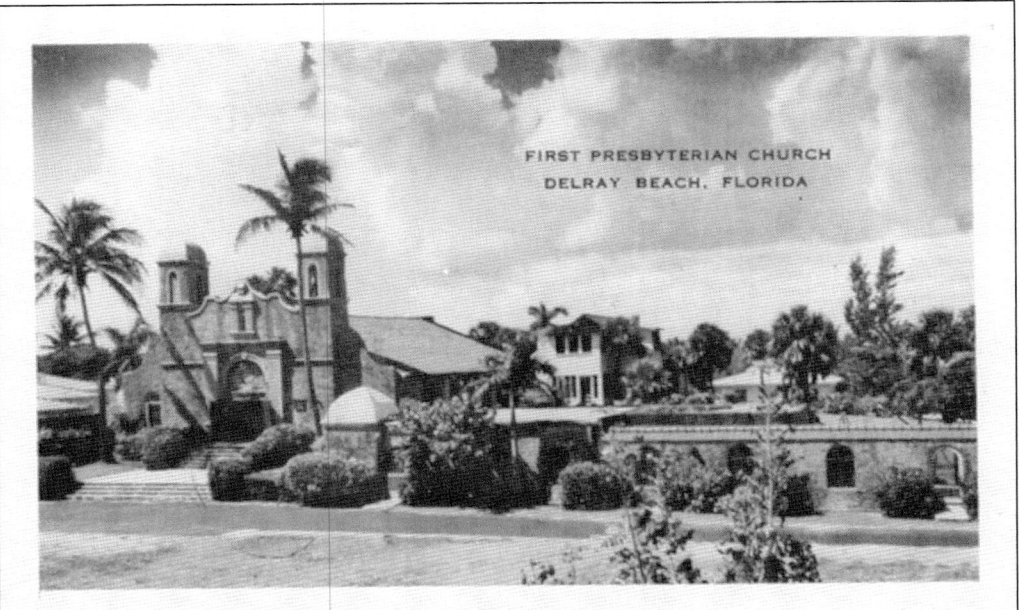

First Presbyterian Church. Several years later, the church, now Presbyterian, stands in an open setting amid lush vegetation. In 1959, on the 30th anniversary of the building, Schrader explained that he had not made this church as elaborate as that of the original in Italy. Locally, the style of the church was thought to be quite "Florida" and suitable for its subtropical location.

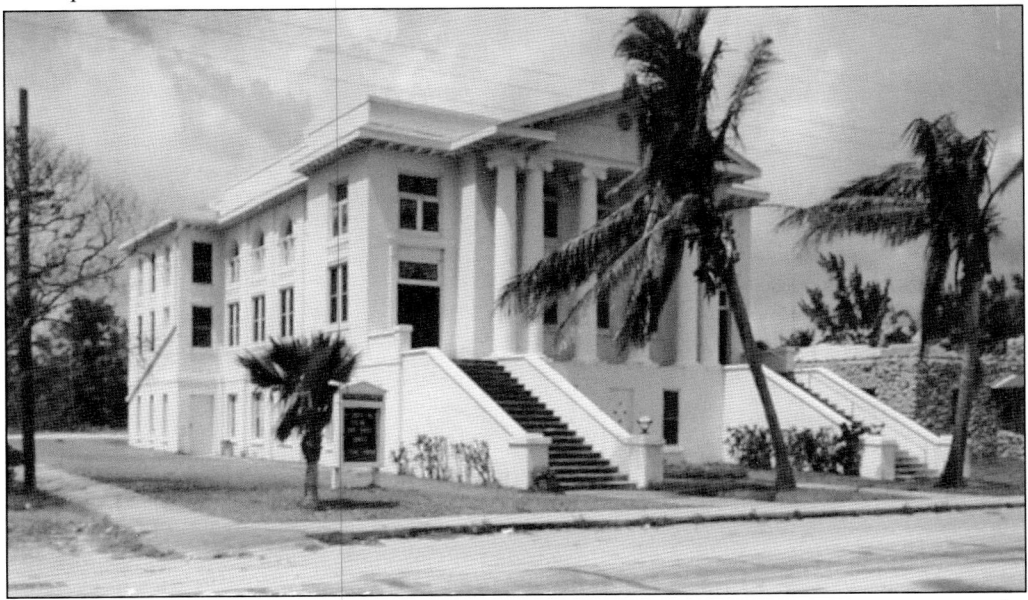

First Baptist Church. After beginning in a frame vernacular building later destroyed by the 1928 hurricane, the congregation built this impressive, Corinthian-columned church on the corner of South Federal Highway and First Street in 1926. A local newspaper article from the 1950s states, "For many years picture post cards of the sanctuary were sent all over the country by admiring winter visitors."

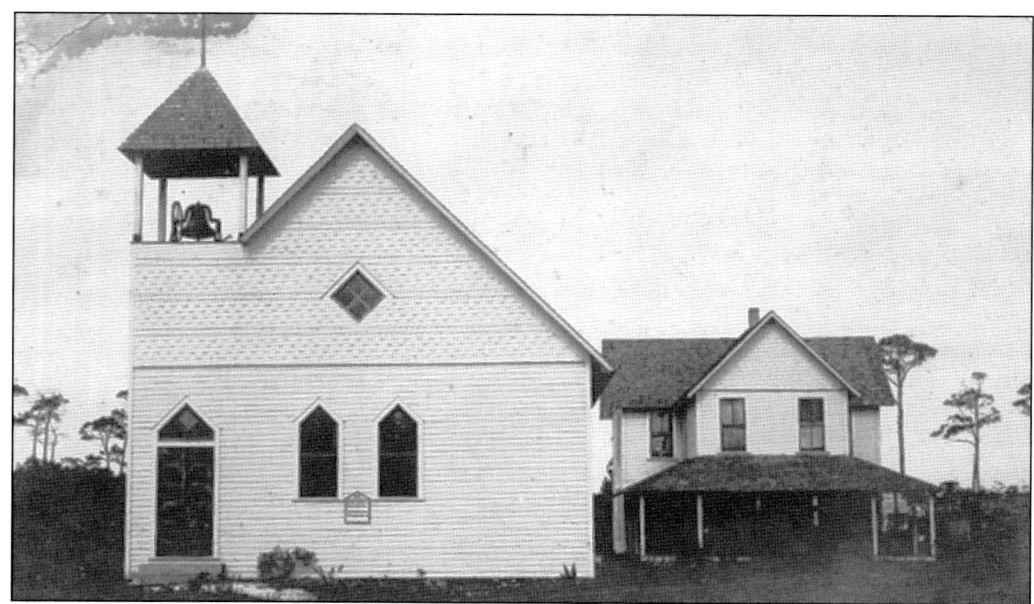

METHODIST CHURCH. The Methodist church was organized and constructed in 1903. H. J. Sterling, a founding member, and J. R. Leatherman, a United Brethren minister and carpenter by trade, completed the building work. The parsonage at right was built a few years later. Notice the repetition in the shape of the bell tower roof, the roof peak, the diamond-shaped window above, and the door, windows, and sign.

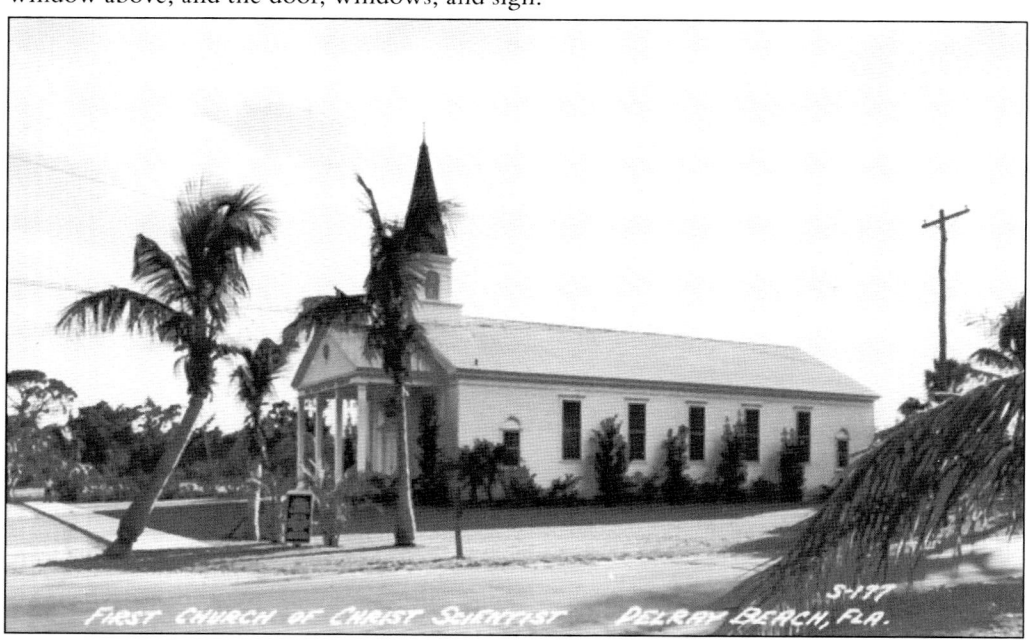

FIRST CHURCH OF CHRIST SCIENTIST. Shortly after World War II, this church, which had been a chapel at Boca Raton Air Field, was moved to Delray Beach and situated west of the Intracoastal Waterway at Southeast Seventh Avenue and Southeast Second Street. In 1949, architect Sam Ogren Sr. designed and executed a new facade and renovation for the spare military chapel. Ogren called the style Southern Colonial Revival.

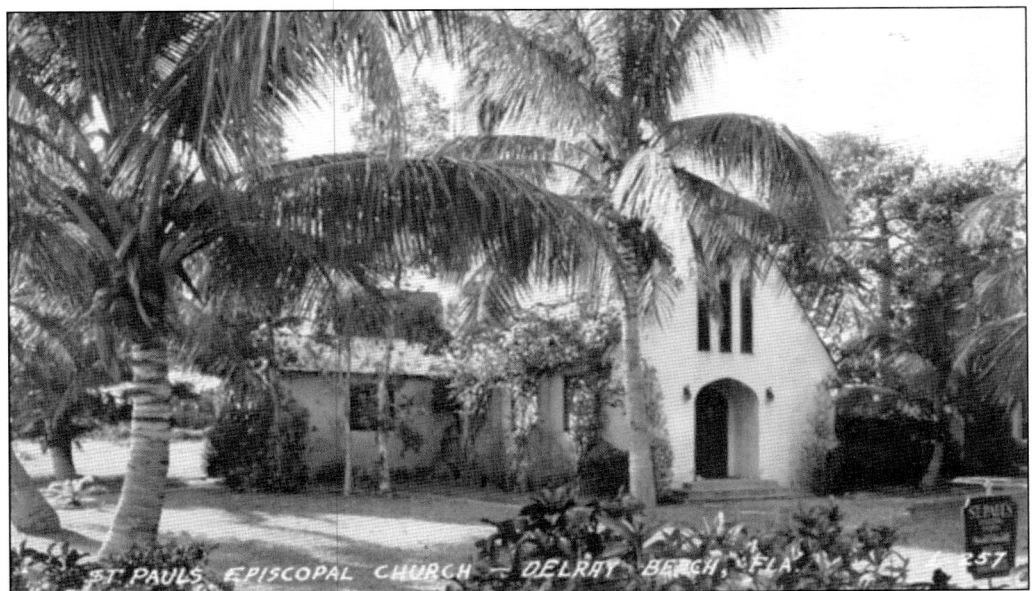

ST. PAUL'S EPISCOPAL CHURCH. First constructed in 1904, the church was later destroyed (like most of the others in town) by the 1928 hurricane. Episcopalian women from across the country donated $5,000 toward rebuilding. Harold Hair of Winter Park served as architect and John I. Thieme of Delray Beach as builder. This image shows the church that was reconstructed in 1929.

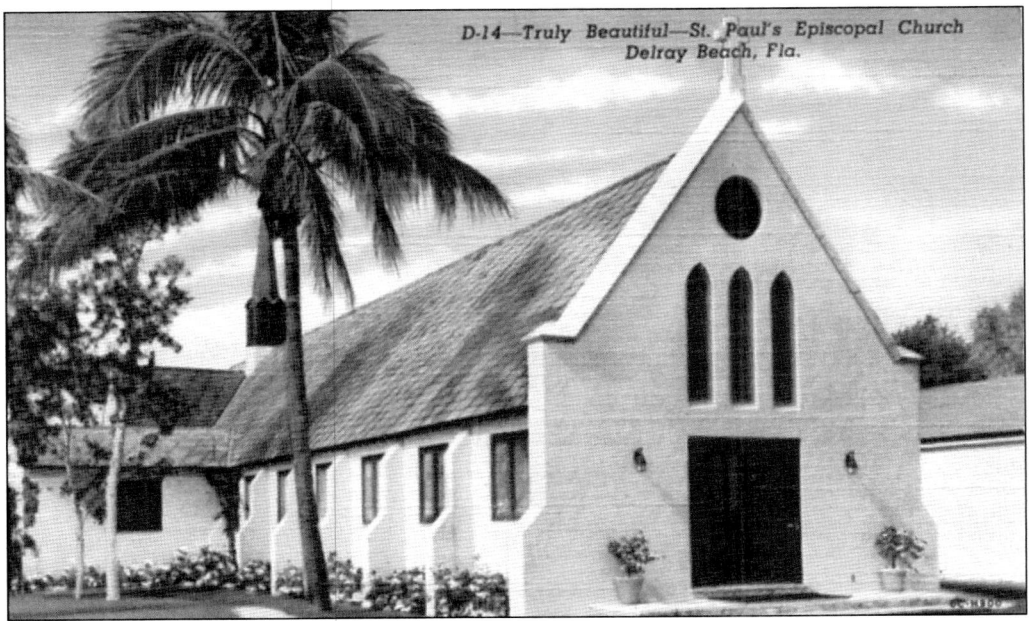

CHURCH, DELRAY BEACH, FLA. This view, published by the Florida East Coast (FEC) News Company of West Palm Beach, depicts St. Paul's Episcopal Church after it was enlarged and a new Sunday school building added in 1955. The population of Delray Beach was never static. Although a small town for many years, the city increased in residents by a significant percentage every decade. (Henry Higgins.)

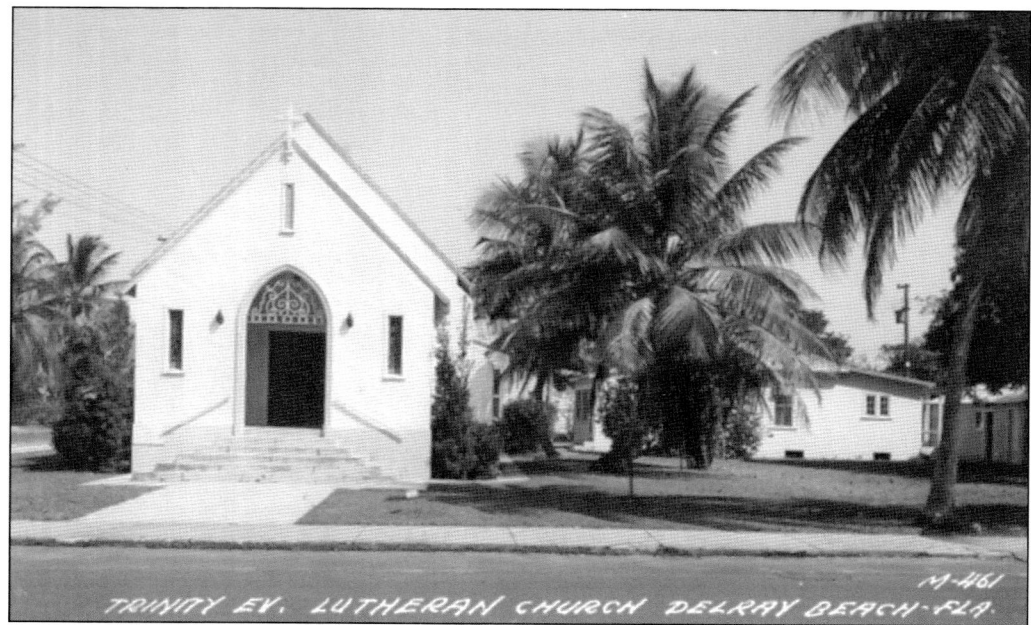

TRINITY LUTHERAN CHURCH. Trinity Lutheran Church is pictured after its 1938 renovation at its original location on Federal Highway at Northeast First Street. Three men were on the building committee in 1904: Adolf Hofman, C. F. Miller, and John Wuepper. The only survivor of Delray's original churches, it still stands at the present North Swinton Avenue site.

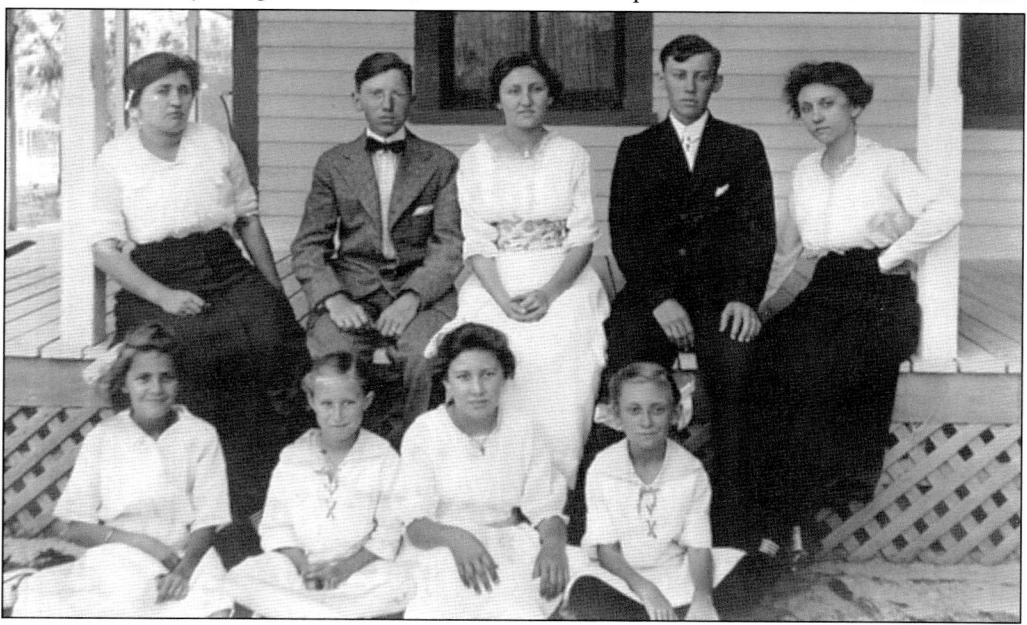

WUEPPER FAMILY. The only notation on the reverse of this postcard is "Wuepper Family." The family arrived in Delray during 1903. Three years later, John Wuepper and John Zill established the Zill and Wuepper Store on Atlantic Avenue between Fifth and Sixth Avenues. The Wueppers were faithful, active members of the Lutheran church. In fact, Margaret Wuepper (top left) reportedly refused to unpack until a church was built.

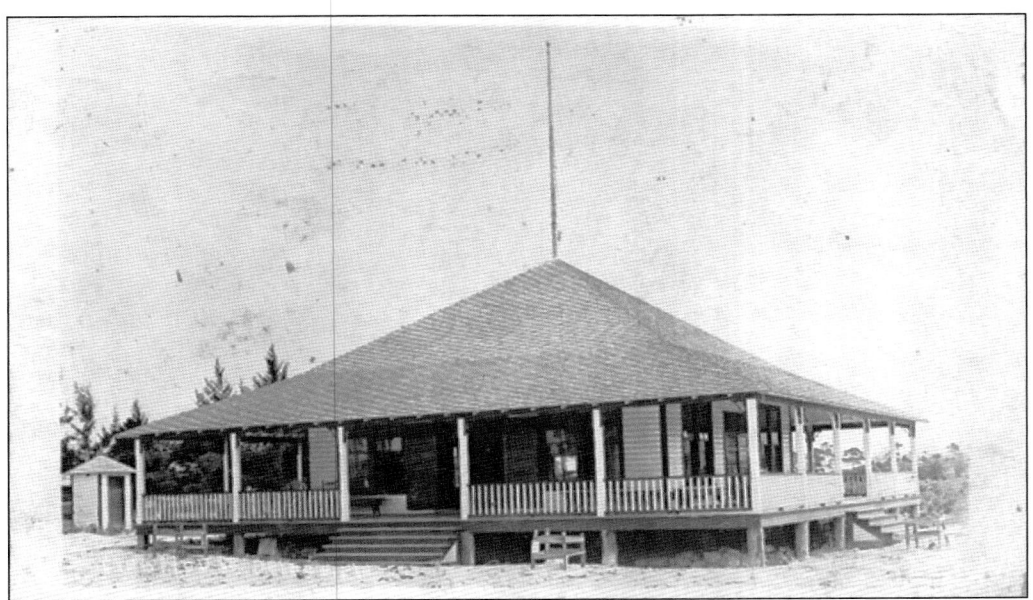

THE BOOSTERS HALL. This c. 1911 building, with its wide and inviting front porch, was located at 29 Southeast Fourth Avenue. It could be called the building of many purposes, as it served as a meeting place for the Boosters Club (forerunner of the chamber of commerce), a Fireman's Hall, the Delray Playhouse, the USO Club during World War II, and the city recreation center.

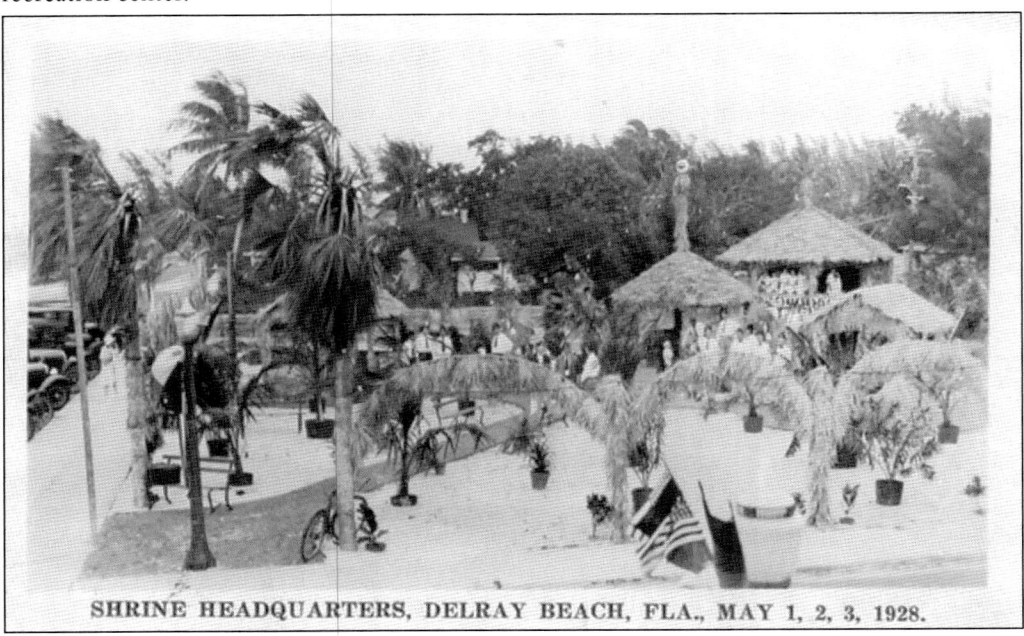

SHRINERS' CONVENTION. In 1928, the Delray Beach Chamber of Commerce mailed out this postcard. The message was as follows: "NOBLES, We want you to enjoy Delray Beach with us. 'The Ocean City of Palm Beach County' so called because it is the only city right on the ocean front. Golf, ocean bathing, polo, fishing and June weather every day in the year. Splendid hotels and apartments at reasonable rates."

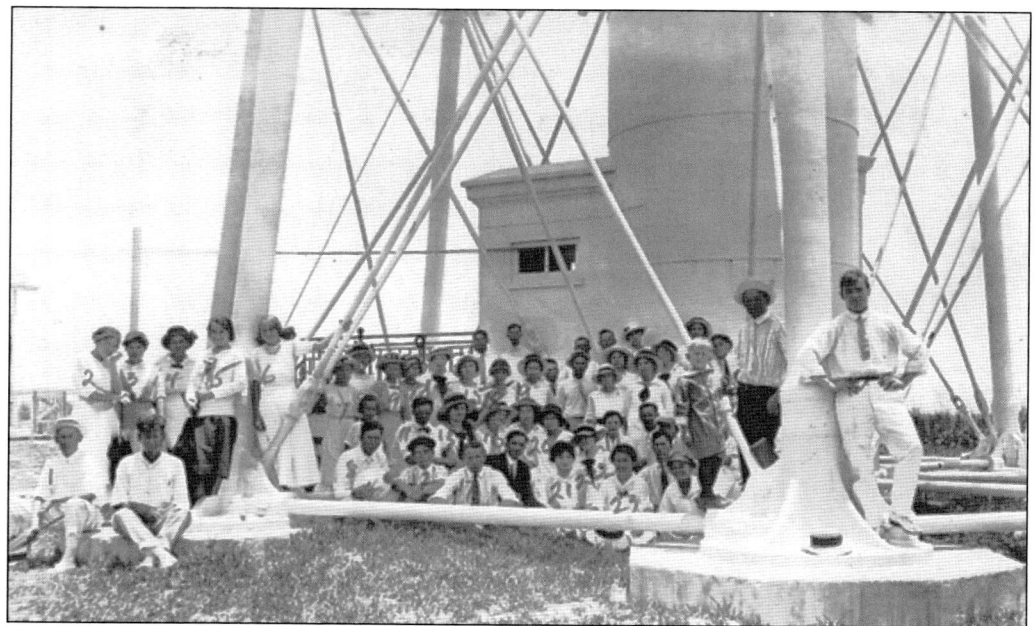

SUNDAY SCHOOL PICNIC. The Hillsboro Inlet Lighthouse was the site of this Sunday school picnic in 1914. The name of the church is not noted, but participants may have been members of youth groups from several Delray churches. The lighthouse stood at the Hillsboro Inlet, 25 miles south of Delray. The picnickers are gathered around the framework that supports the lighthouse.

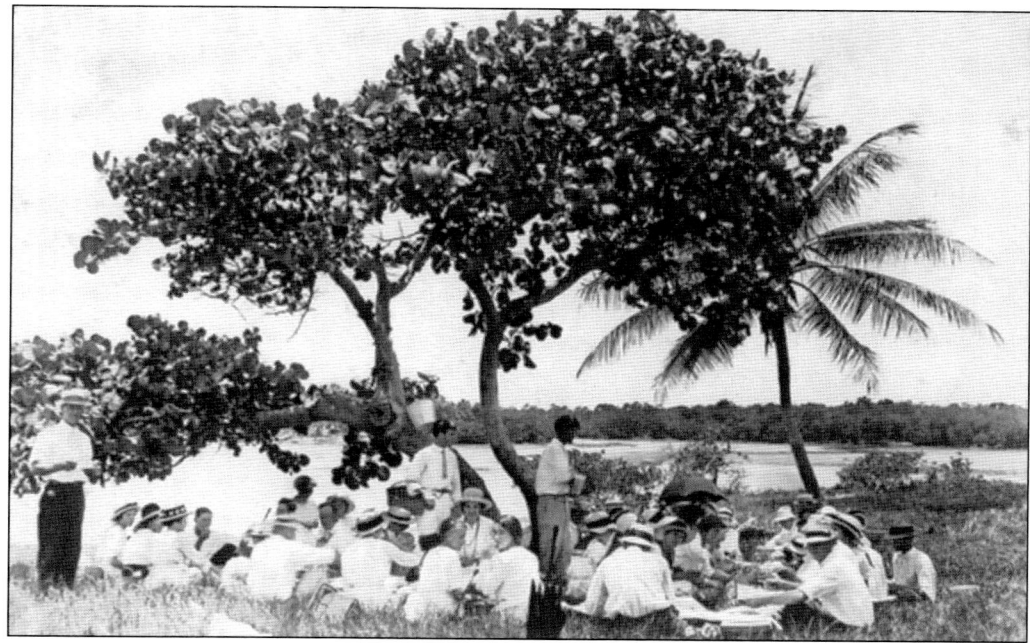

PICNIC AT POMPANO. Here the same group eats a picnic meal under the sea grape trees. Some participants appear to be wearing hats with a ribbon of stars around the crown. If this was July 4, 1914, hopefully the picnickers did not miss all the festivities back in Delray.

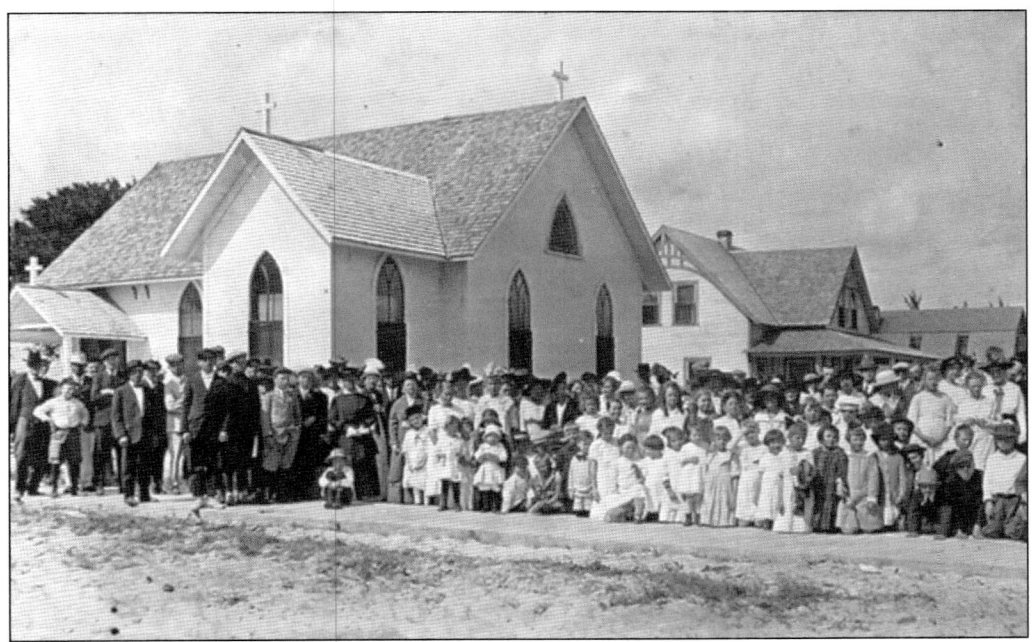

SUNDAY SCHOOL DAY. Worshipers from most Delray churches gather for a photograph in front of St. Paul's Episcopal shortly after 1904. This group portrait probably includes many of the townspeople of European descent. Behind them is a good view of the original 1904 church building. Behind the church are the Taylor and Zeder homes. The Taylor house directly behind the church was later moved to its present location on North Swinton Avenue.

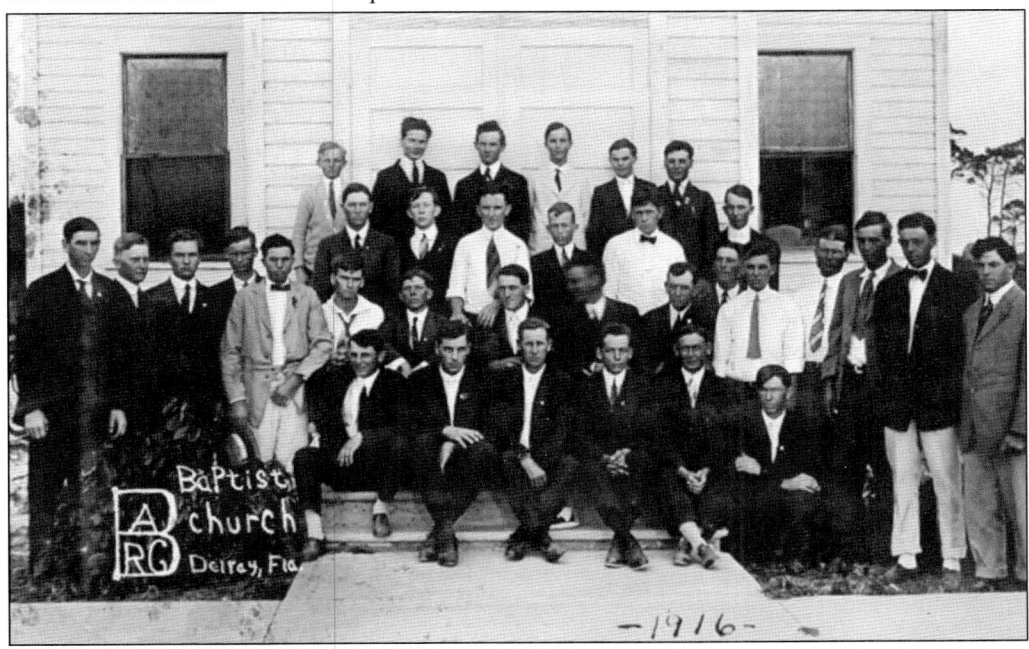

BAPTIST CHURCH GROUP. A men's group poses in front of the First Baptist Church in Delray in 1916. The location appears to be the original frame church at Southeast Fourth Avenue and Third Street, which opened its doors on Easter Sunday in 1912.

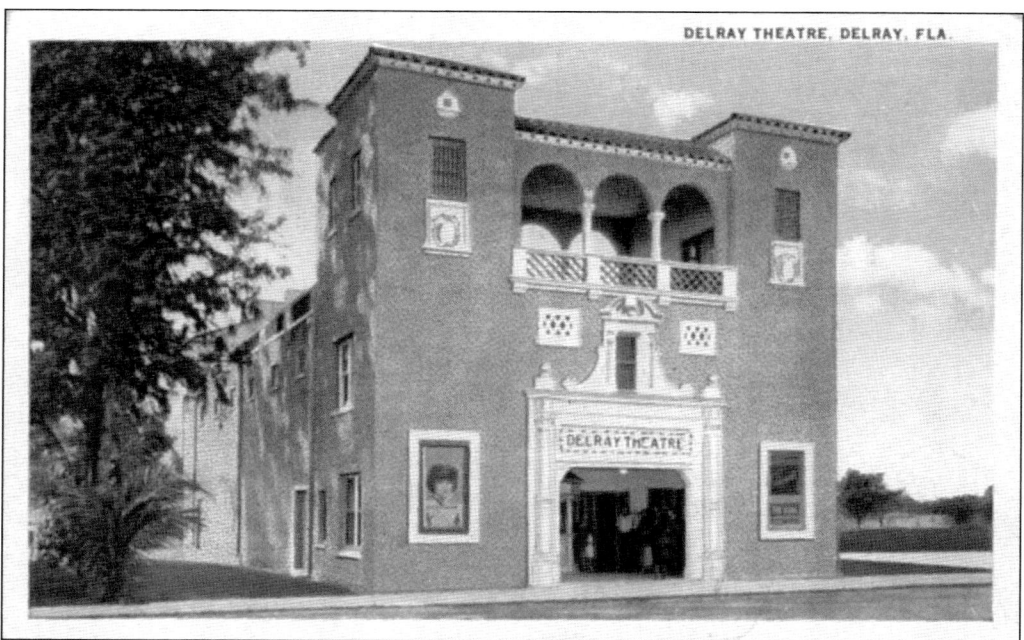

THE DELRAY THEATRE. Situated at 20 Northeast Fifth Avenue, the Delray Theatre was featured on this Beautiful Florida Series card, published by the Ashville Postcard Company. The movie theater opened on Christmas Day in 1923 and included a dance floor on the roof. At one time in the early 1930s, it was reportedly the only operating theater in Palm Beach County. The business closed in 1959, and the building was demolished.

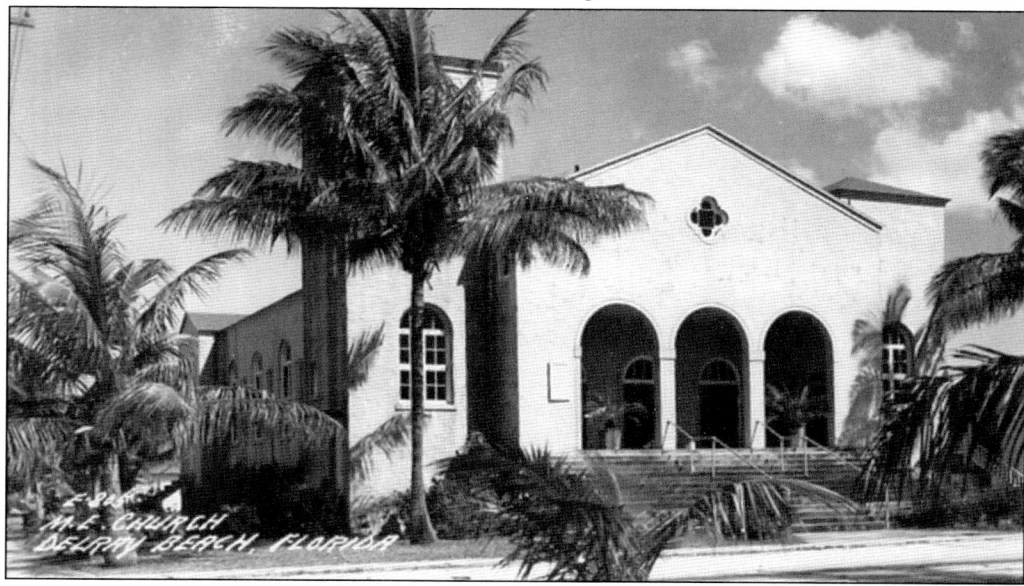

METHODIST CHURCH. Designed in the fashionable Spanish style, a new Methodist church was constructed on Federal Highway in 1926. The financial distress caused by the real estate bust and devastating hurricanes of 1926 and 1928 delayed completion. Dr. John R. Cason, a retired minister, led the drive to finish the church and pay off the debt. When a larger structure was built in the 1960s, this building was sold and subsequently demolished. (Henry Higgins.)

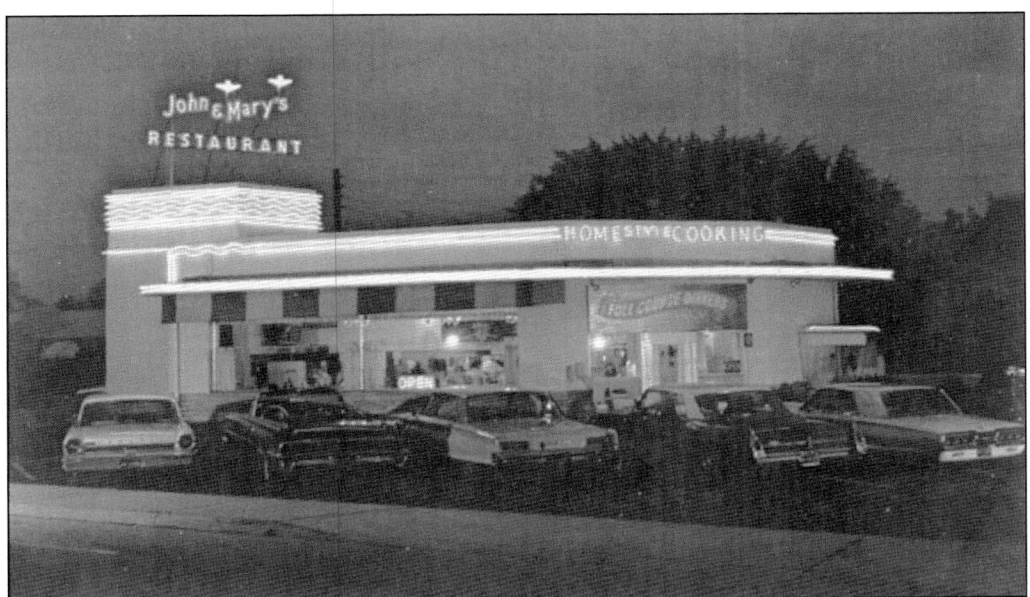

JOHN & MARY'S RESTAURANT. Located on Northeast Sixth Avenue, John and Mary's Restaurant offered home-style cooking during the mid-1960s. This night scene shows the restaurant's inviting neon lighting. Emil Mussle, who lived nearby on Northeast Second Street, originally established the business as Mussle's Drive In. Since then, the restaurant has served the community under several different names. Take-out was available at the window on the right. It is now known as Graingers.

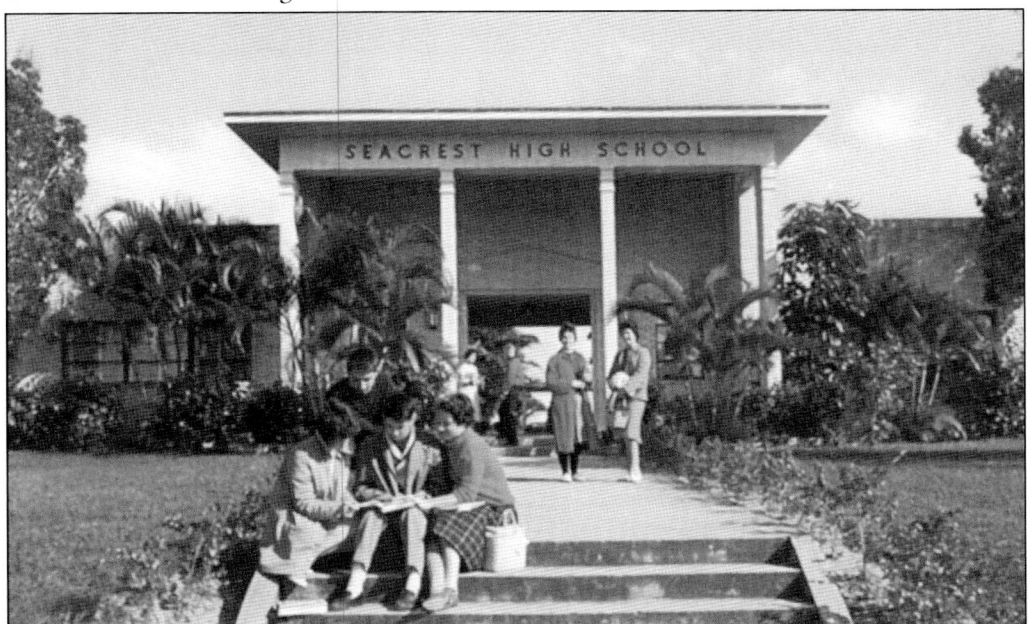

SEACREST HIGH SCHOOL. This photograph, gracing the cover of the *Nautilus*, was made into a postcard published by the yearbook staff in 1961. Delray Beach High School had closed in 1949 after this high school was constructed on Seacrest Boulevard. In 1950, the name of the yearbook was changed from the *Seahawk* to the *Nautilus*.

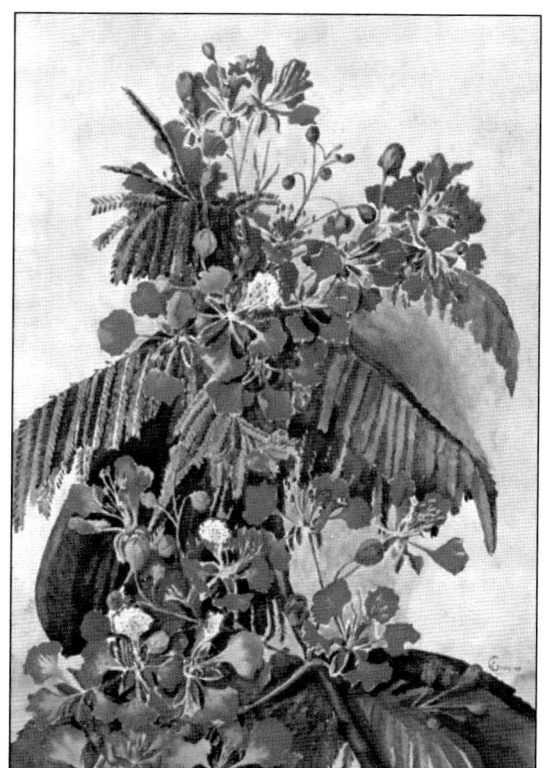

ROYAL POINCIANA. The Garden Club of Delray Beach was organized in 1939. This postcard comes from the 1947 scrapbook, now held in the historical society archives. On the reverse, information about the royal poinciana, or "flamboyant," promotes it as the most glorious "flowering tree of the subtropics noted for its wide-spreading picturesque shape." The card, part of the Hale, Cushman, and Flint Subtropical Flower Series, was created "after a painting by Wilhelmina F. Greene."

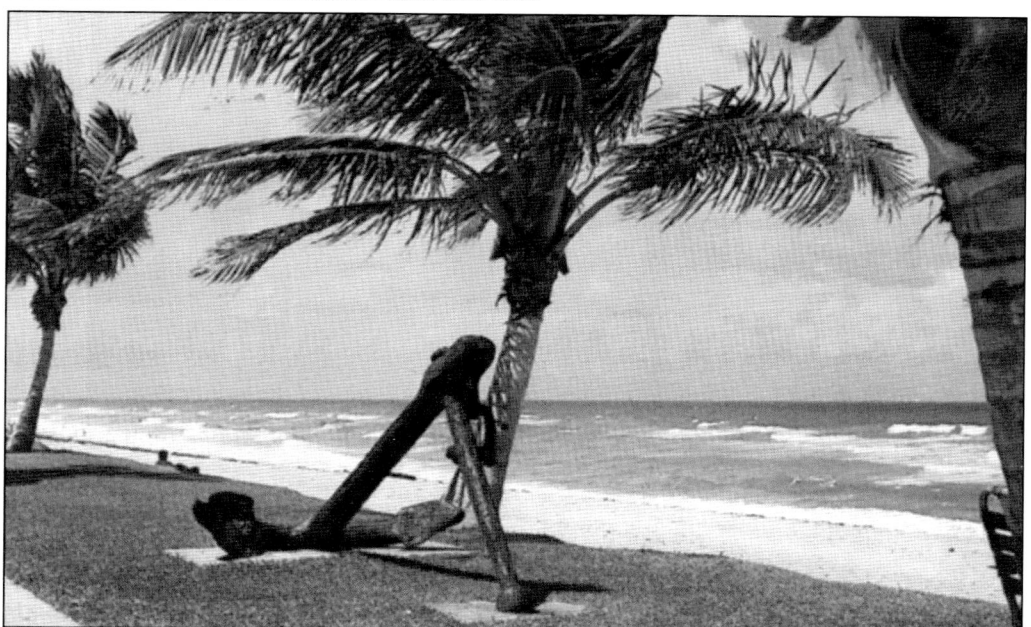

ANCHOR. Estimated to be about 200 years old, this anchor came from a sailing ship that wrecked south of Delray in about 10 feet of water. In the 1950s, local men using heavy equipment decided to drag the anchor to the southern end of Delray's municipal beach. Anchor Park is the present site. (Henry Higgins.)

Five

SHIMMERING WATERWAYS

The water-filled aspect of the state of Florida is reflected in the postcards in the Delray Beach Historical Society archives. The images in this chapter give proof to the watery environment consisting of ocean, canals, lakes, aquifers, Everglades, humid air, huge white clouds, and thunderous rainstorms.

The Intracoastal Waterway was simply called the canal by pioneers. Dredging in the 1880s worked to connect natural lagoons and create a waterway 50 feet wide and 5 feet deep at low water. The waterway has been widened and deepened through the years. In 1925, dredging began to open the South Lake Worth (known by most people as Boynton) Inlet. By 1926, the Atlantic Ocean had become more easily accessible to sports fishermen and pleasure boats from Delray Beach and the surrounding areas. Before Florida had completed so much drainage work, and before the water table had dropped due to a growing population, Seminole Indians in their flat cypress boats poled through lakes, ponds, and wetlands.

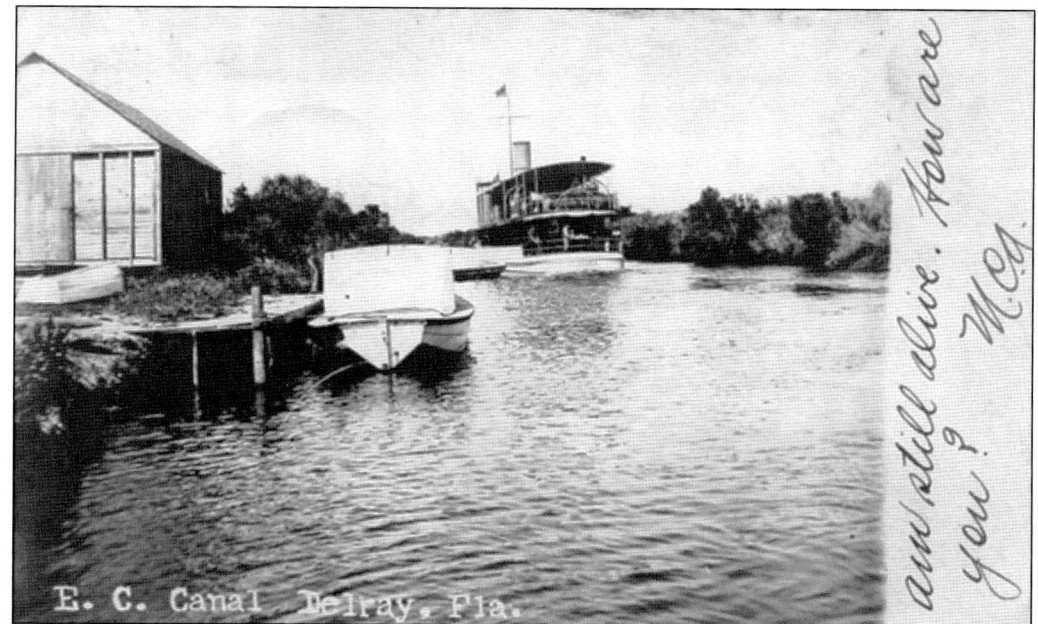

"AM STILL ALIVE." Postmarked March 1907 in Delray, this card was sent to Detroit, Michigan, where some settlers had friends and family. The scene is the Atlantic Avenue canal crossing, where there was a small dock and boathouse but not yet a bridge. The only way to cross the canal in those days was by barge or lighter. A steam-powered tourist boat is arriving from the south. (Henry Higgins.)

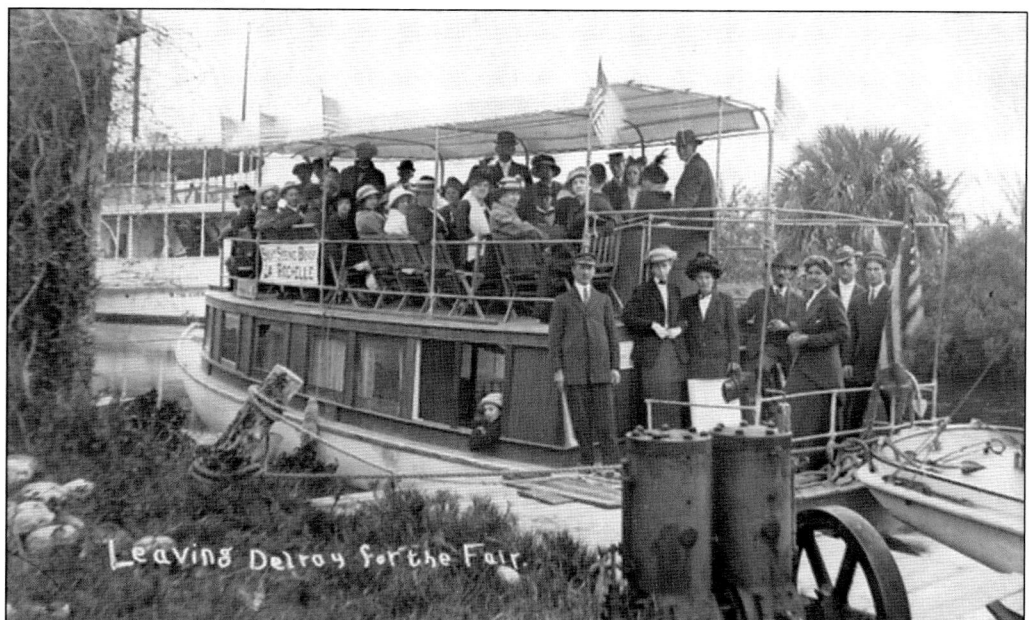

LEAVING DELRAY FOR THE FAIR. It appears that someone started to address this postcard to a Mr. and Mrs. Alswede. The sign on the boat reads, "Sight Seeing Boat, La Rochelle." The man in the center wears a uniform, and the woman in front with the dark hat carries an alligator handbag. Townspeople evidently used the sightseeing boat for trips to West Palm Beach.

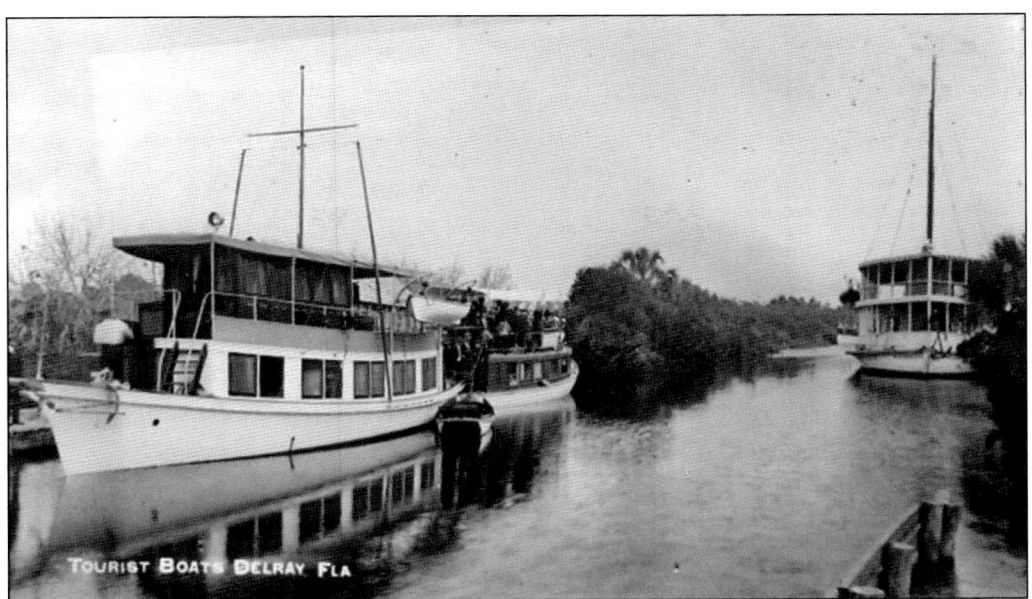

TOURIST BOAT. The note on the reverse states, "East Coast Canal near the bridge in 1913–14 when we first saw it." The photograph could possibly have been taken the same day as that on the previous page, as it appears to be showing the *Rochelle* in the rear, filled with people. Excursions such as this were popular with visitors and residents who craved to see more than just small-town Delray.

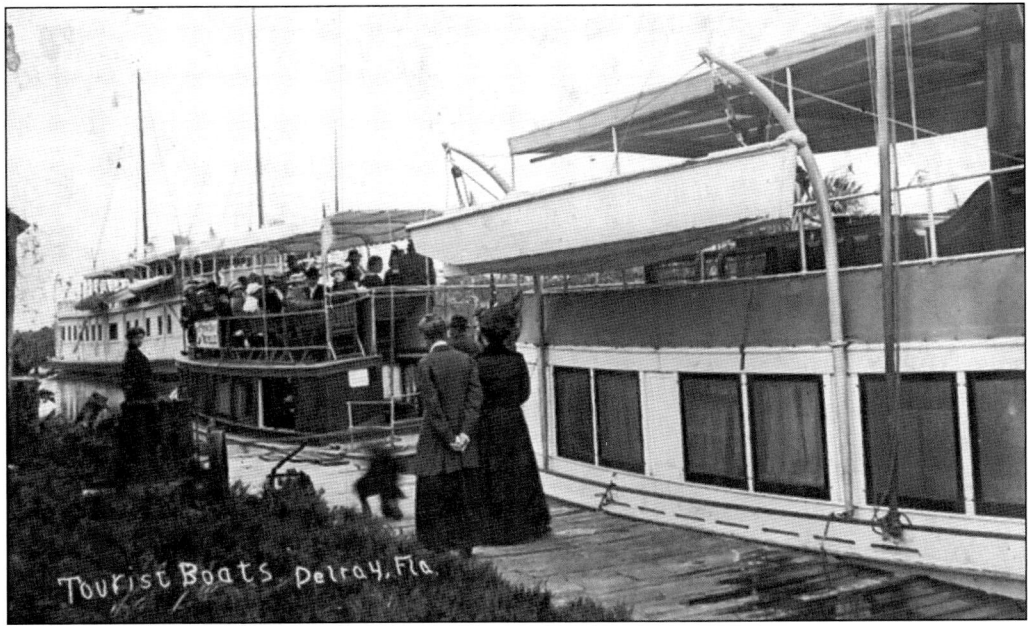

TOURIST BOATS, DELRAY, FLA. This scene appears to be another angle of the same boats, with the *Rochelle* in the middle this time. Notice the clothing the people are wearing. Locals mostly wore white, reflective clothing, so the visitors from the North are probably the sightseers wearing dark colors. On the reverse is the name Mrs. E. V. K. Hopkins, Delray, Florida. (Henry Higgins.)

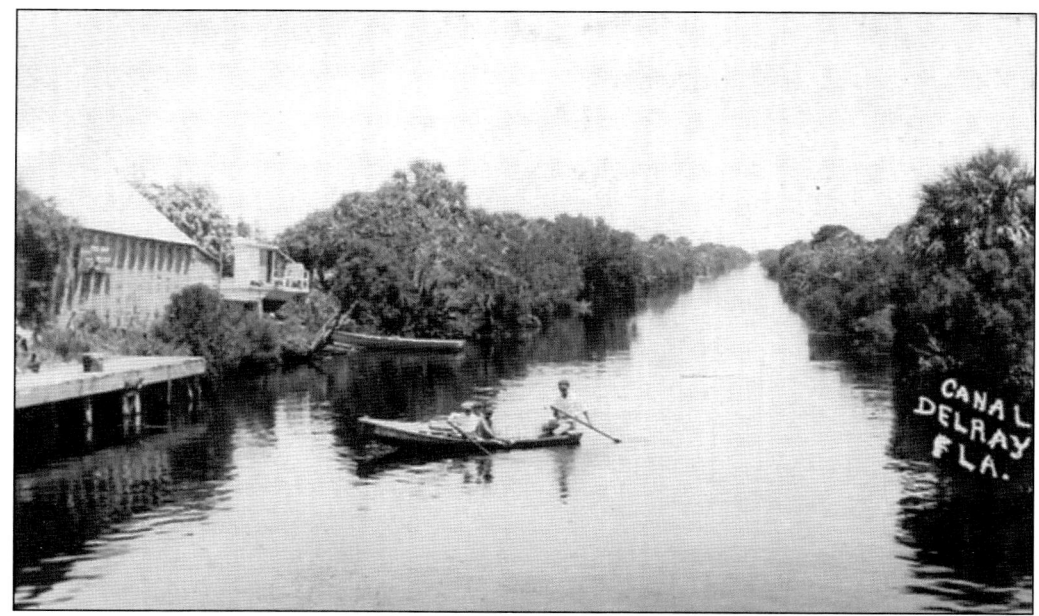

CANAL, DELRAY, FLA. No large tourist boats are docked in this scene—just four boys paddling north up the canal. The oceans and canals not only provided fun for the children; in the days of fewer roads, traversing by water was an alternate form of transportation. The photograph was taken at the Atlantic Avenue crossing.

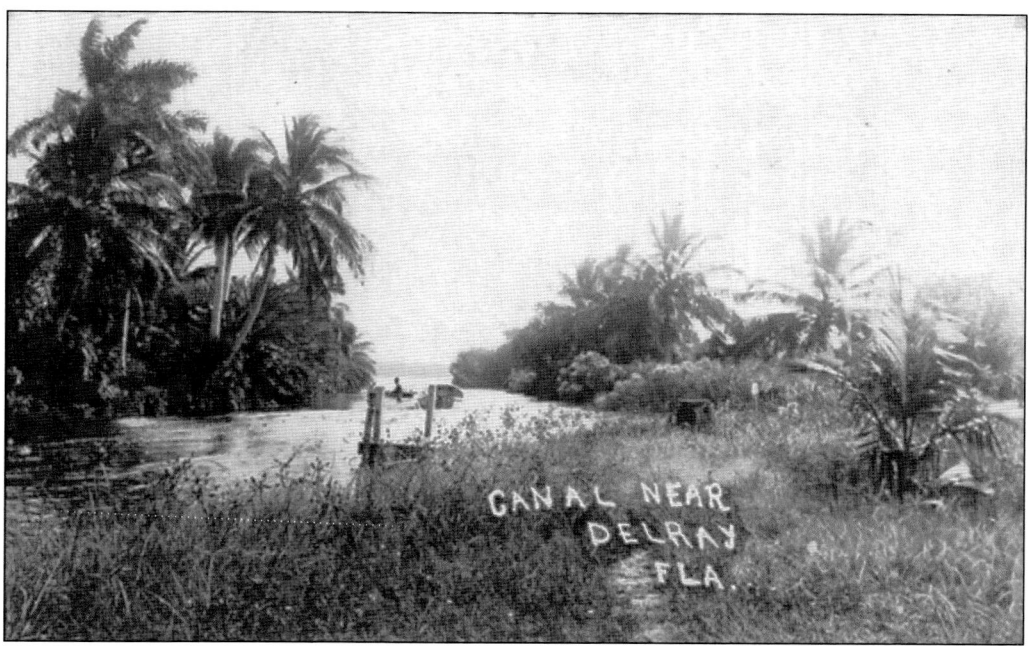

CANAL NEAR DELRAY. Two boats are visible here, south of Delray at Boca Raton. Boca Raton's first settler, Capt. Thomas Moore Rickards, owned acreage on Lake Boca Raton, and these boats may be his. A civil engineer, Rickards served as a land surveyor for the early railroads.

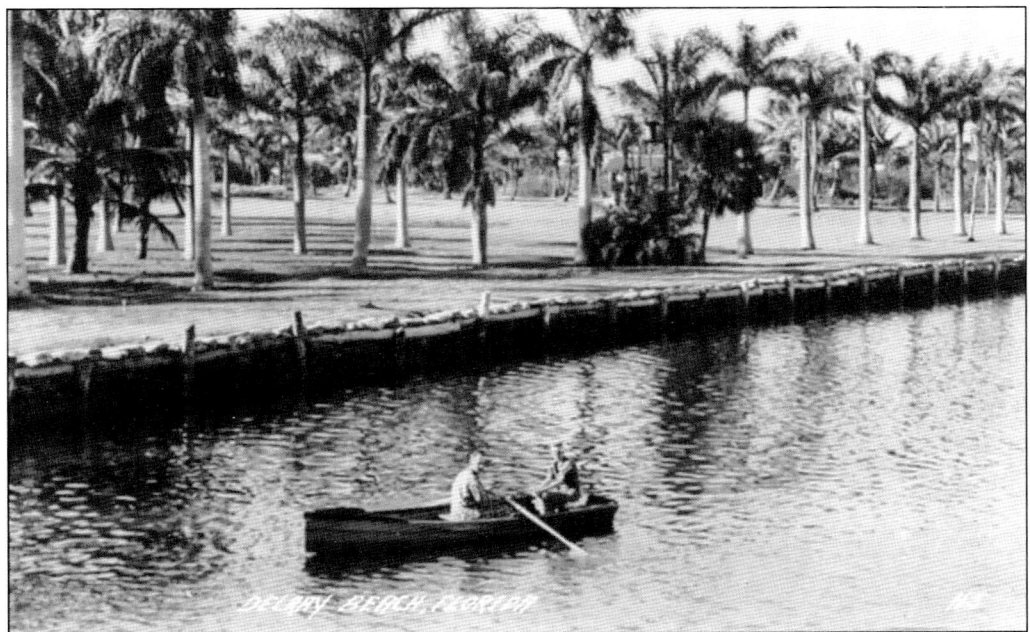

BOATING ON CANAL. This photograph was taken at a later date than the two on the previous page, as the city was called Delray Beach rather than Delray after 1927. Here boats paddle past the city park. The waterway had been dredged and the sides reinforced with a makeshift seawall.

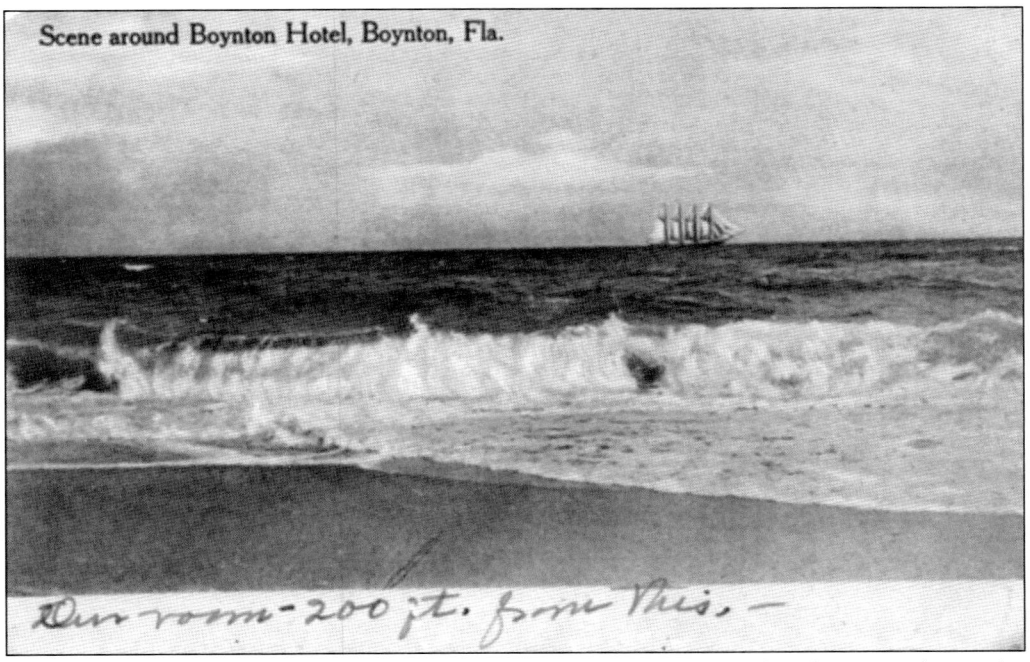

SCENE AROUND BOYNTON HOTEL. At the bottom of this lovely beach scene, the sender wrote, "Our room—200 ft. from this." On the reverse, she commented, "We are right by the ocean. Slept by its roar." The note ended with a St. Patrick's Day greeting from this mother to her daughter at Shafer Hall, Wellesley, Massachusetts, on March 17, 1912.

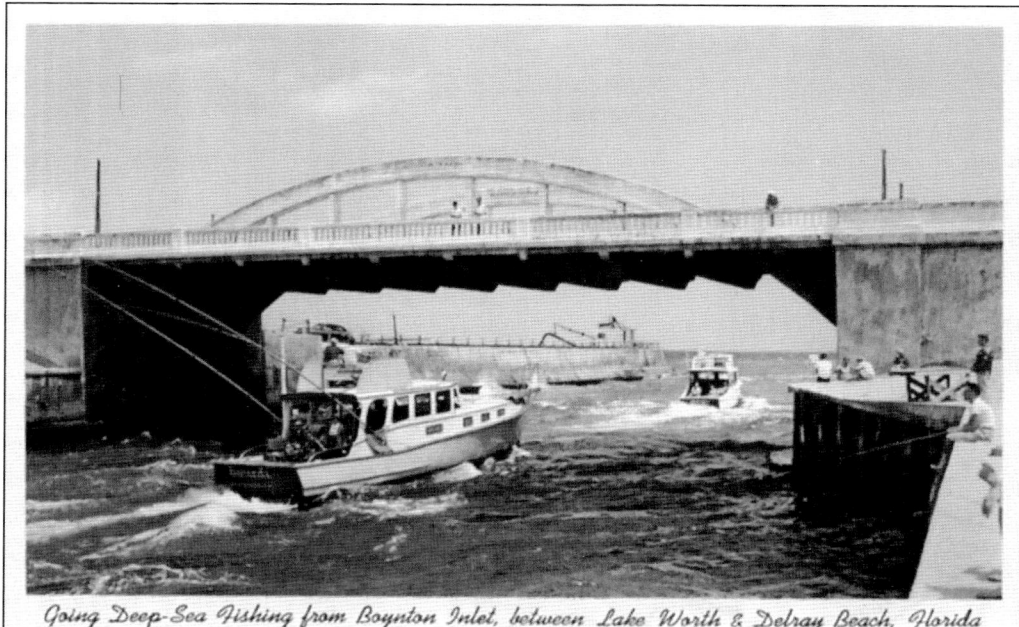

Going Deep-Sea Fishing from Boynton Inlet, between Lake Worth & Delray Beach, Florida

GOING DEEP-SEA FISHING. Since there is no ocean inlet at Delray Beach, deep-sea fishermen from Delray, like those on the *Bacardi* fishing boat, usually left from the Boynton Inlet. The arched span of bridge was replaced in 1974. This card was published by the D&M Post Card and Records Company of West Palm Beach. (Karen Wiita Van Wormer.)

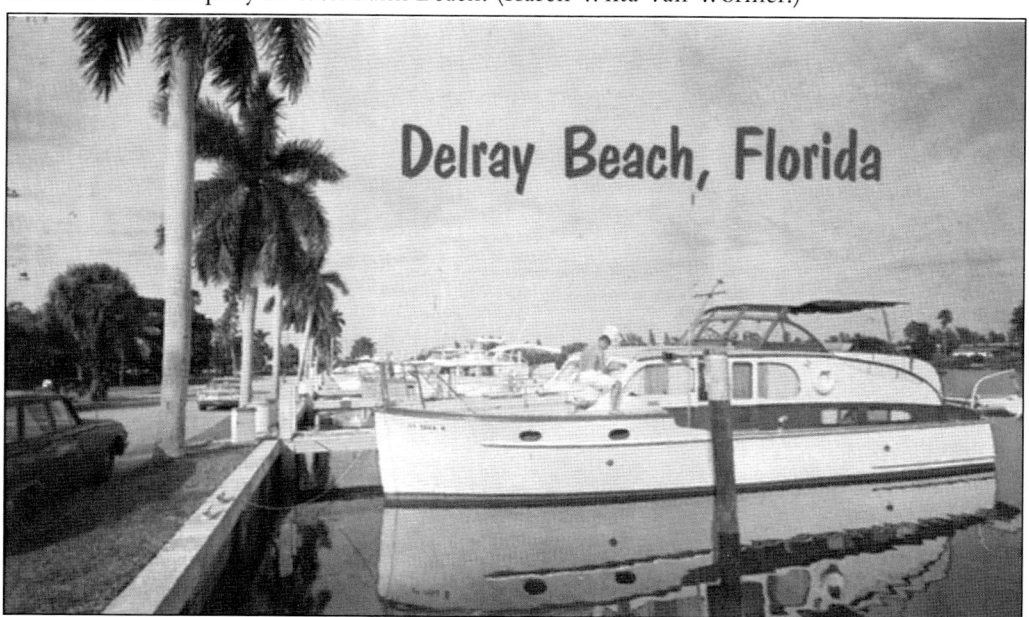

DELRAY BEACH, FLORIDA. On the reverse is the following description: "One of the many fine boats at the docks along the Intracoastal Waterway at beautiful Delray Beach, Florida on the famous Gold coast." The name *Gold Coast* is derived from the many Spanish treasure ships that ran aground or sank along the coast in centuries past. Dukane Scenics of Hollywood, Florida, published the card.

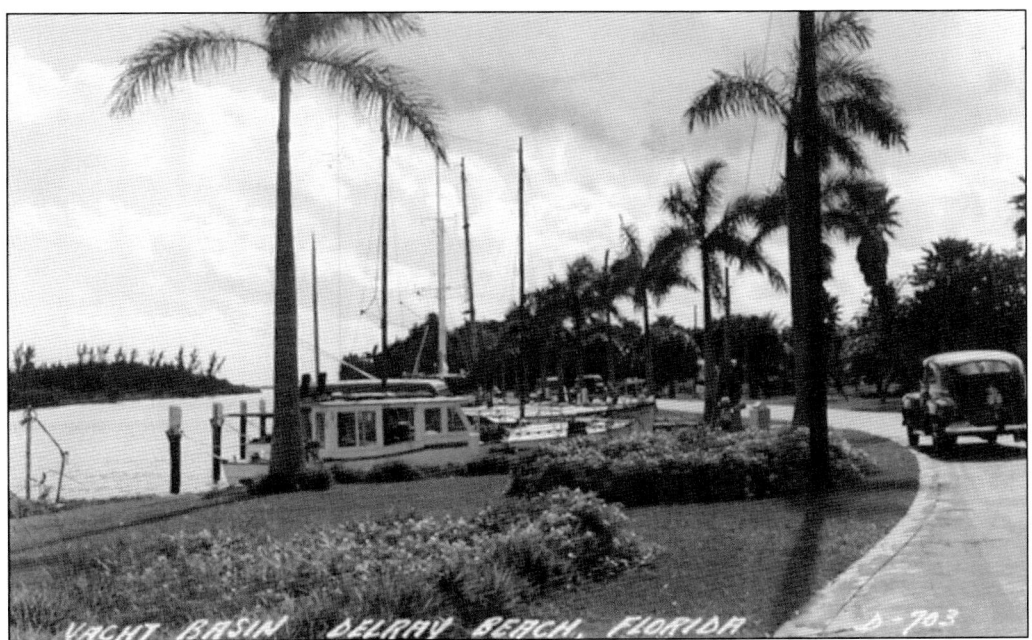

YACHT BASIN. This photograph of the city yacht basin was published by the L. L. Cook Company in the late 1940s. Note that the opposite shore of the Intracoastal Waterway is still undeveloped.

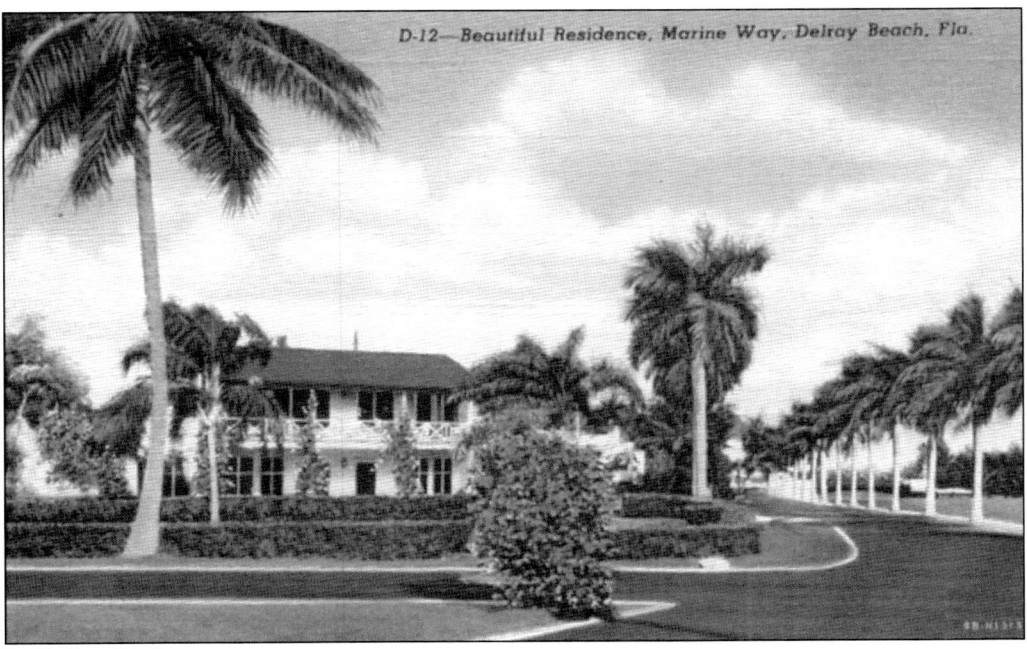

BEAUTIFUL RESIDENCE, MARINE WAY. The Anchorage was designed by two esteemed South Florida architects: Sam Ogren Sr. and Gustave Maas. It is set amid the lush tropical foliage of the waterway, close to the city yacht basin. This area, now the Marina Historic District, is one of Delray Beach's five historic districts. (Henry Higgins.)

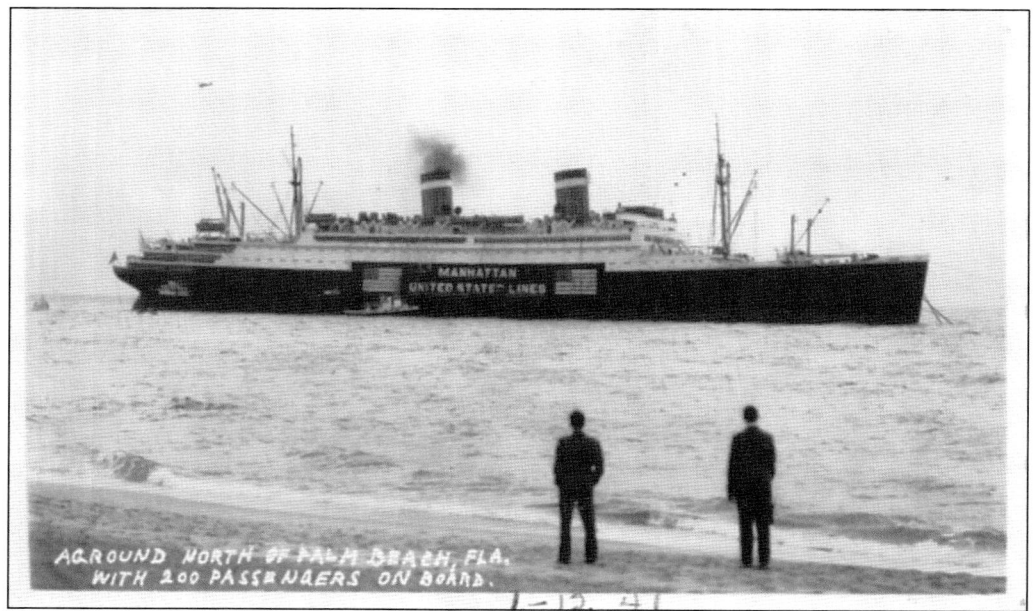

SHIP AGROUND. The 24,189-ton luxury liner *Manhattan* of the United States Line ran aground nine miles north of Palm Beach on January 1, 1941. She was finally re-floated after 22 days. In June 1941, the ship was commissioned the USS *Wakefield* by the U.S. Navy and went on to serve as the largest vessel ever operated by the coast guard until a 1942 fire gutted her hull.

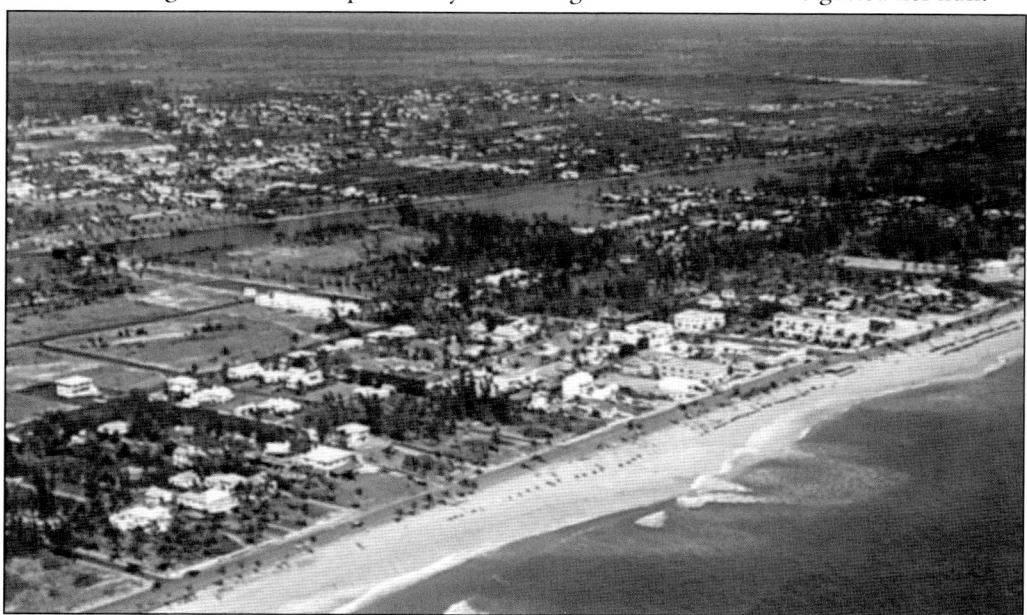

AIRVIEW, DELRAY BEACH. This photograph, taken by H. W. Hannau, shows a 1950s aerial view before several high-rise condominiums were built along the Intracoastal Waterway. Descriptive text on the reverse reads, "Delray Beach, Florida. Above photo of the beautiful beach. Behind, the Inland waterway and fast growing town." The view highlights the sparkling water of the Atlantic Ocean, Intracoastal Waterway, and the lakes and wetlands to the northwest.

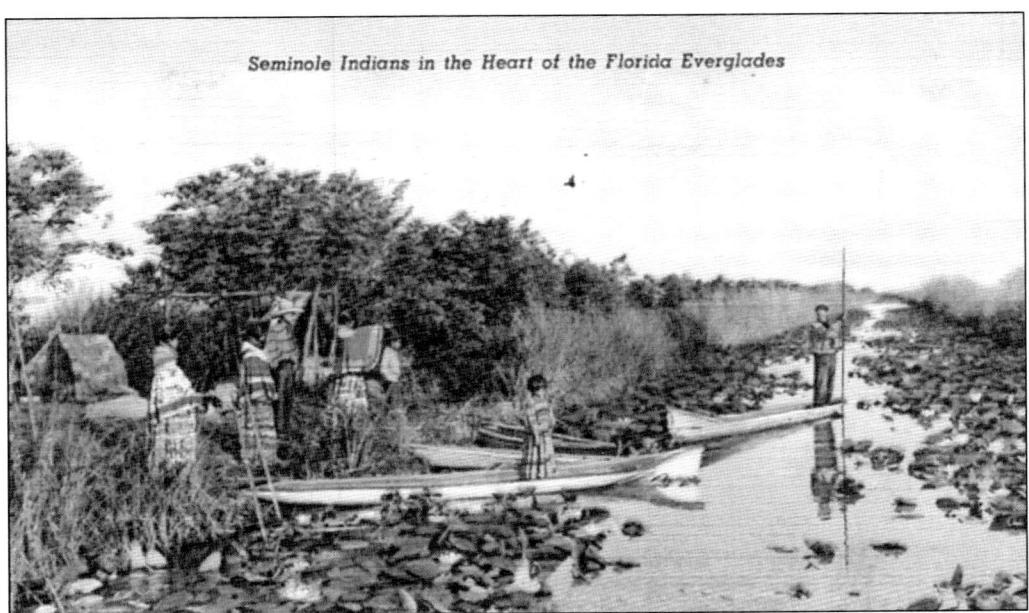

SEMINOLE INDIANS. Seminole Indians pose at a waterway described as being "in the Heart of the Florida Everglades." They are wearing traditional clothing, which began to be stitched after sewing machines became available toward the end of the 19th century. The flat dugouts carved from cypress logs are poled through the shallow water. This Tropical Florida Series card, postmarked February 1946, was created with a Charles C. Ebbets photograph.

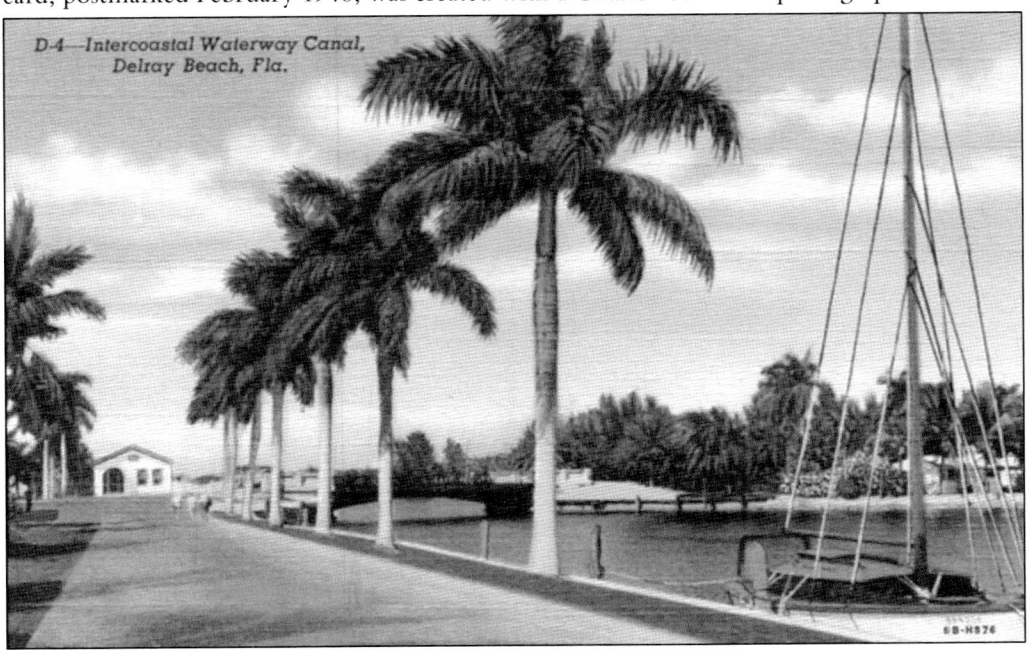

MARINA SCENE. This serene view looks north from the city marina toward the Atlantic Avenue bridge. At the time, some charter sport-fishing boats and other tourist boats for hire were docked here. The hand-tinted linen card was published by the FEC News Company of West Palm Beach. (Henry Higgins.)

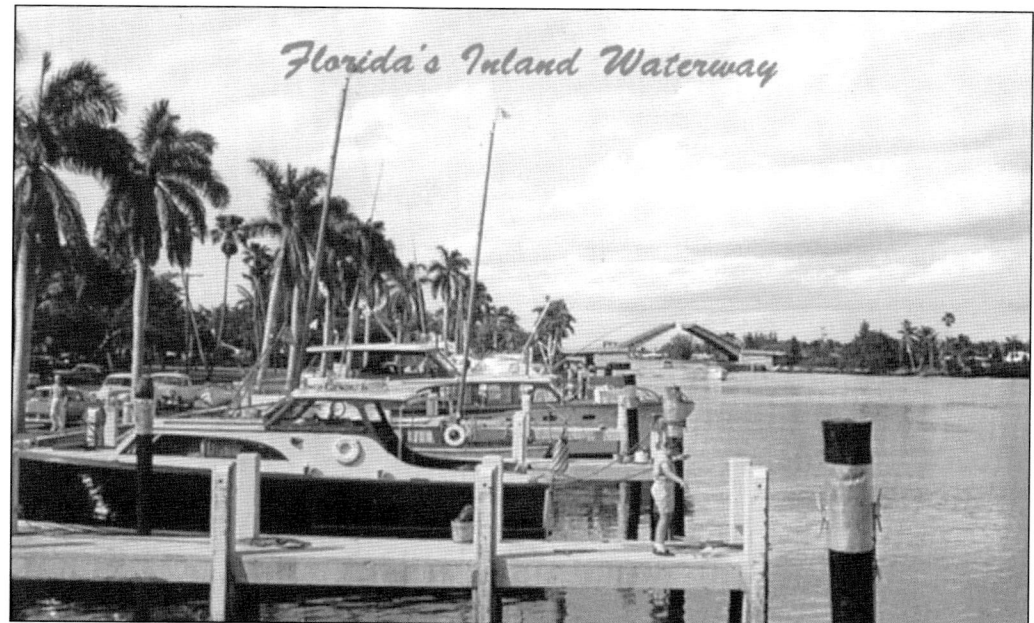

INLAND DOCKS. Children revel in the sunshine at the end of a dock on Florida's Inland Waterway. The location is the Delray Beach Yacht Basin and Marina. Some of the wooden sport-fishing and pleasure boats were moored here year-round, while other craft traveled south to Delray to enjoy the busy, balmy winter season.

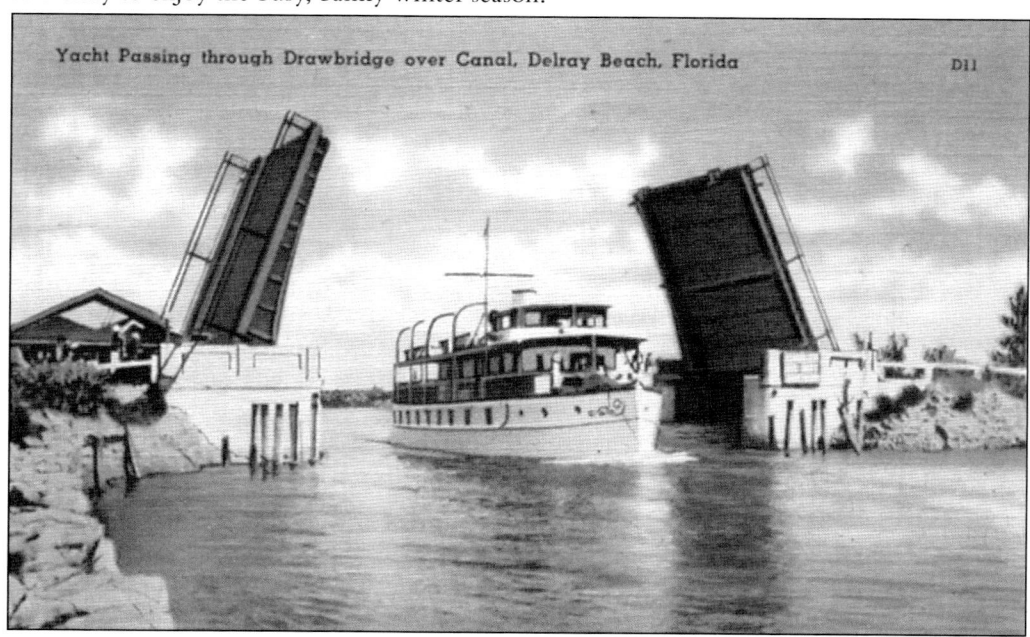

OPEN BRIDGE SPAN. While the Atlantic Avenue bridge is open, a large yacht passes. Motorists, walkers, and those on bicycles had to wait to cross over the Intracoastal Waterway at such times. In January 1946, a girl named Ruth mailed this postcard to her parents in Indiana. Part of her message says, "Be prepared to see a healthy girl." The fine weather apparently agreed with Ruth.

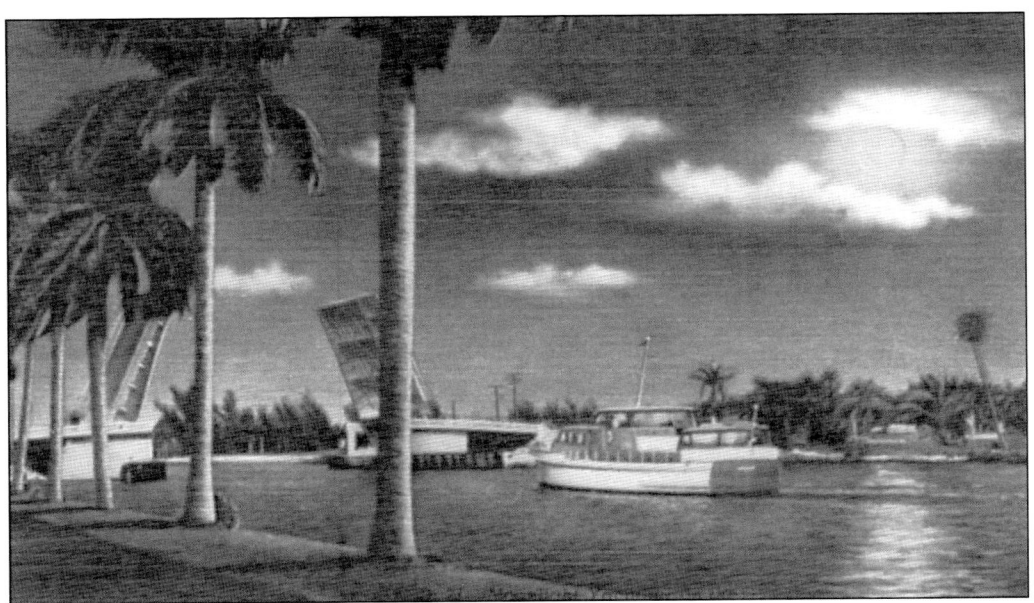

SAILING NORTH. The Atlantic Avenue bridge has again opened to allow boats to pass. This 1926 wood-and-concrete double-lift span was replaced during 1951–1952 by a Chicago-style, double-leaf Bascule bridge. The tender opened the mechanical bridge upon demand from the boaters, who tooted their whistles or blew air horns to get his attention.

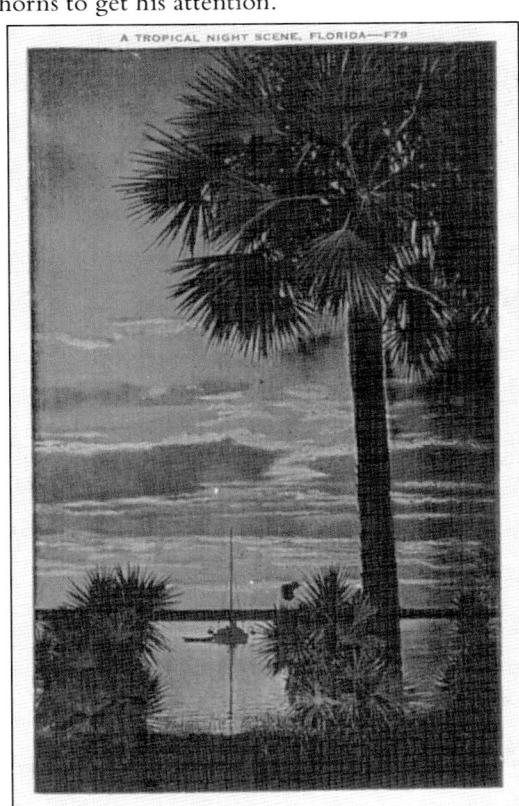

TROPICAL NIGHT SCENE. This tranquil scene is illuminated by moonlight, creating a shimmering Intracoastal Waterway. The palm tree at right is a cabbage palmetto, also known as the sabal palmetto. In 1953, the Florida legislature designated it as the state tree. These trees have tall, straight trunks and can grow to 80 feet tall. (Karen Wiita Van Wormer.)

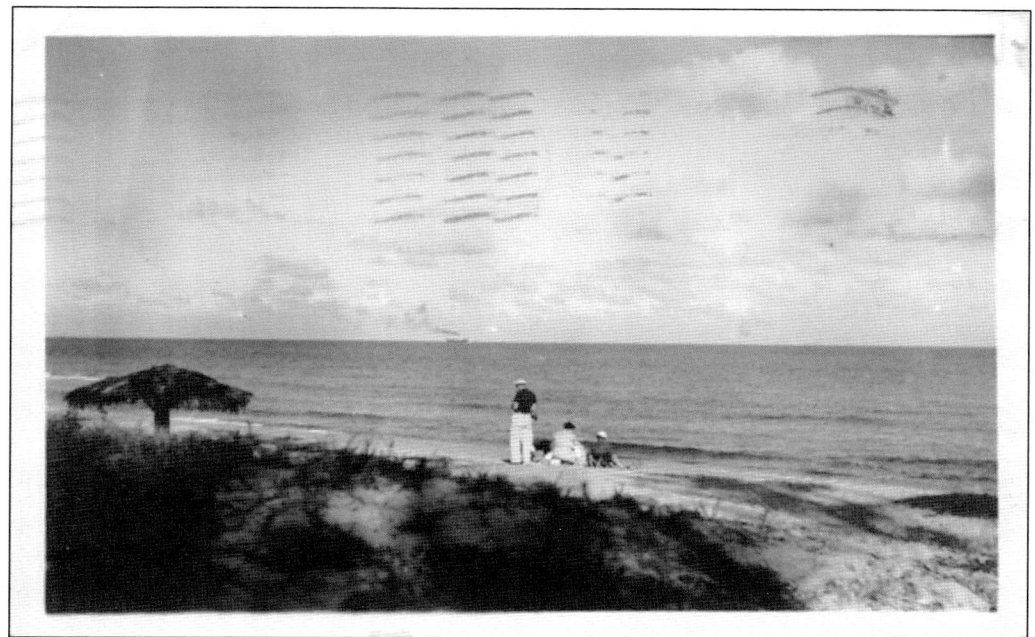

THE BEACH IN 1941. Three people in this beach scene are looking out to sea. A palmetto frond "beach umbrella," typically used in the 1940s, is visible. The postmark date on the reverse is February 24, 1941. On the horizon is the faint image of a ship. One wonders if the people are thinking about the war in Europe. In 1940, lifeguards reported that ship watching was a favorite pastime of sunbathers.

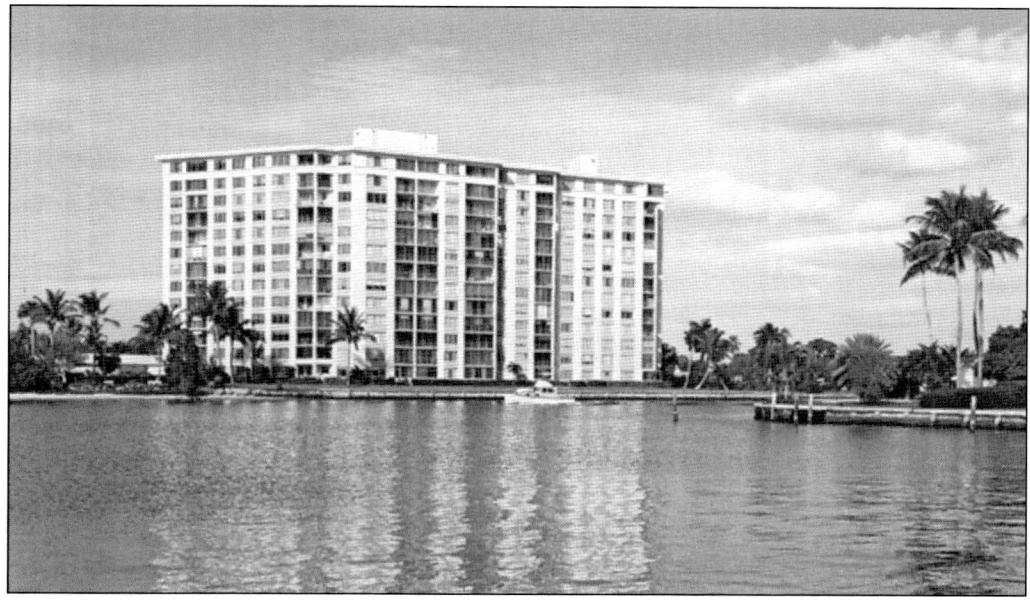

THE BARRTON. This chapter ends with completion of the Barrton in 1971. A tree-topping ceremony held in July for the 12-story Barrton was attended by Mayor Jack Saunders, Charles Barr, building company executives, and the architect. The Barr Company also built Barr Terrace, Bar Harbor, Delray Summit, and Mira Mar Garden, all situated in the Intracoastal Waterway.

Six

Always Atlantic Avenue

When E. Burslem Thomson, the civil engineer in William Linton's 1895 party, drew the first plat of the town from October to December in 1895, the main street was named Atlantic Avenue. The main street then and now, was laid out—at the suggestion of Refuge keeper Captain Andrews—with the House of Refuge on the north side and the old orange grove on the south side. It has remained the commercial heart of Delray Beach. The movie theaters, many of the restaurants, retail shops, hotels, and the first post offices were located on or near the avenue. Through the years, Atlantic Avenue has been the barometer by which the economic health of the town has been measured.

About 1915, a line of royal palms was planted from the Atlantic Avenue bridge east to the end of the road. The trees grew into a beloved colonnade of towering palms leading to the beach pavilion. Where the Intracoastal Waterway crosses the avenue, the city established a park. Residents and visitors enjoyed shuffleboard games and performances held in the park's band shell. The names of the nine Delray Beach men who did not return from World War II were chiseled on a monument erected by the Veterans of Foreign Wars, and the park became known as Veterans Park.

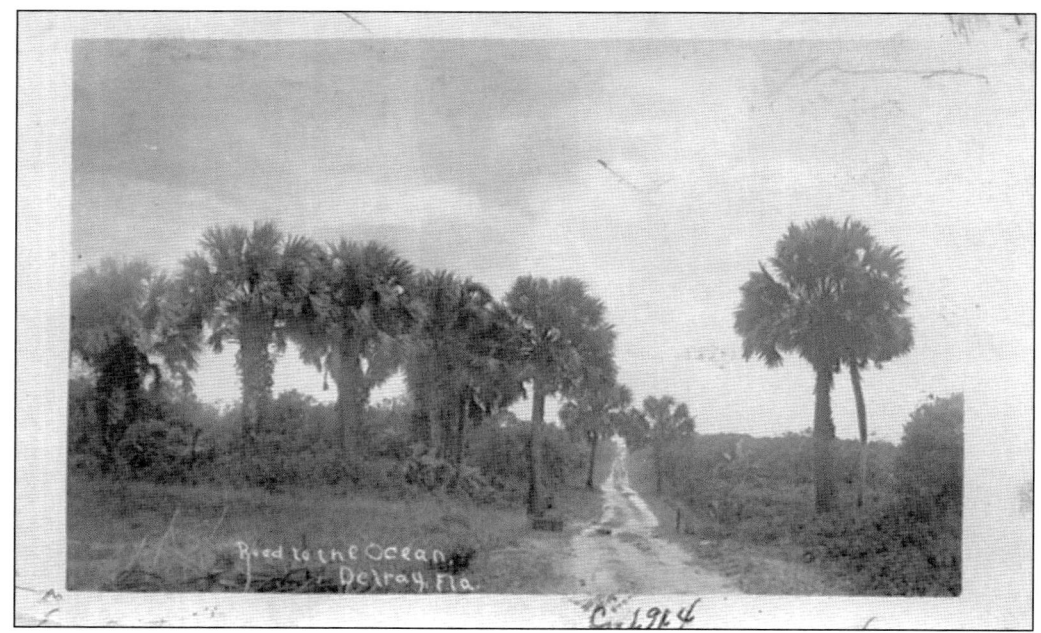

ROAD TO THE OCEAN. East Atlantic Avenue, pictured here, could truly be called the "lonesome road" in the early part of the 20th century. Notice how the road rises up over the coastal ridge, which is covered with saw palmetto. Behind the ridge are a few native sabal palms. The beach begins on the other side of the rise.

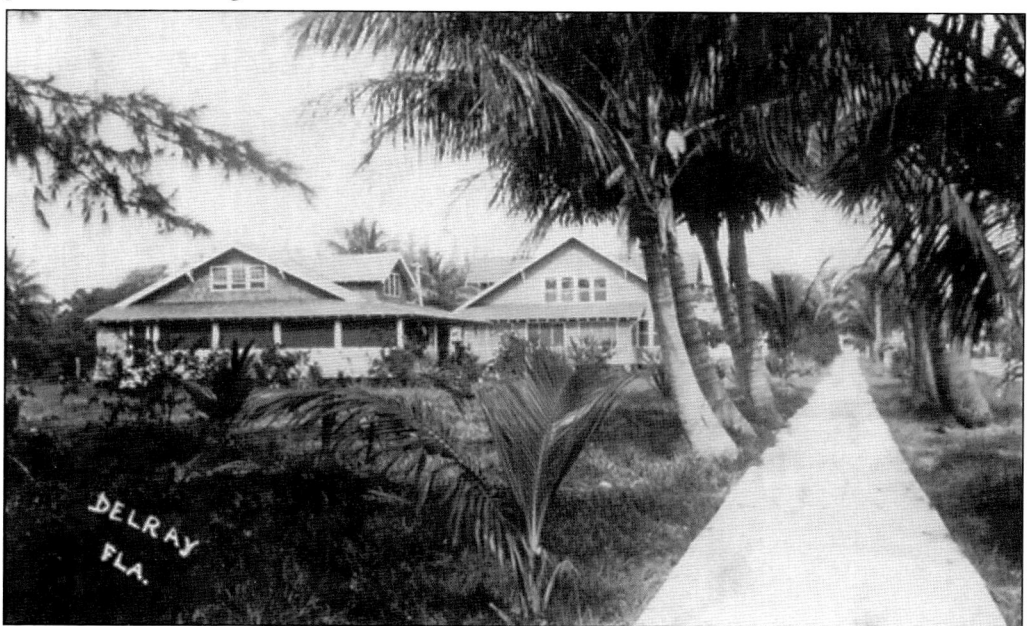

ALONG ATLANTIC AVENUE. In this photograph, taken some years later, improvements are visible, such as a better road and a sidewalk west of the beach area. Written on the reverse by the donor is this: "Stevens's house on right." Most of the housing in Delray then—and for many years—consisted of bungalows, such as the ones seen here. Atlantic Avenue can be glimpsed through the palms on the right.

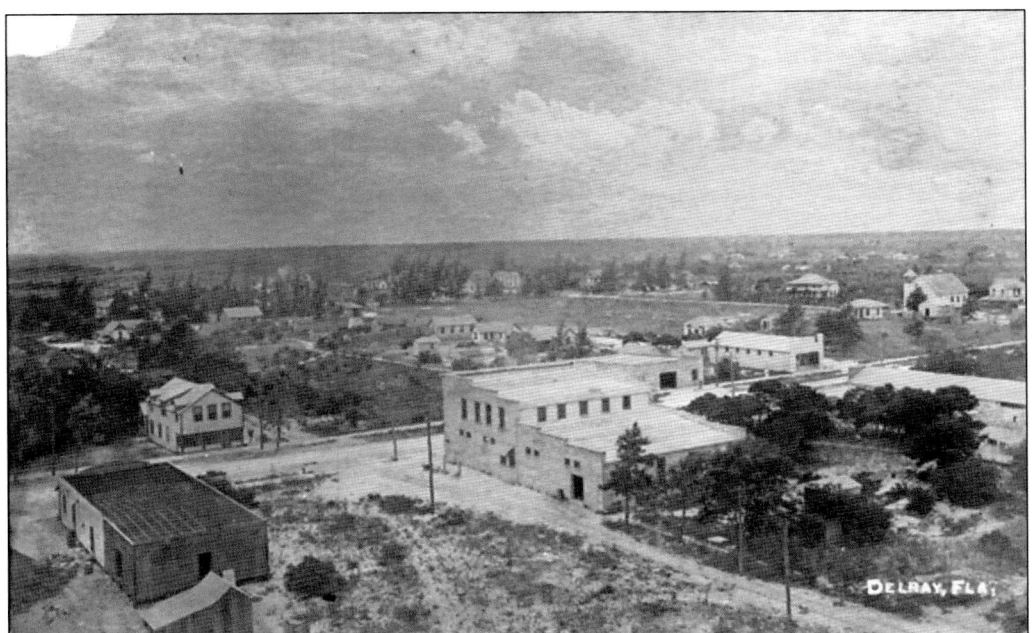

ATLANTIC AVENUE, C. 1915. This early view of East Atlantic Avenue shows the intersection at what is now Northeast Second Avenue next to the Cathcart Building, which is still there. On the reverse, the donor has listed most of the visible buildings as follows: (left to right) Ford place, Rista Hotel, Cathcart Building, Tenbrook Building, Methodist church, Cathcart Home, and Sundy Home.

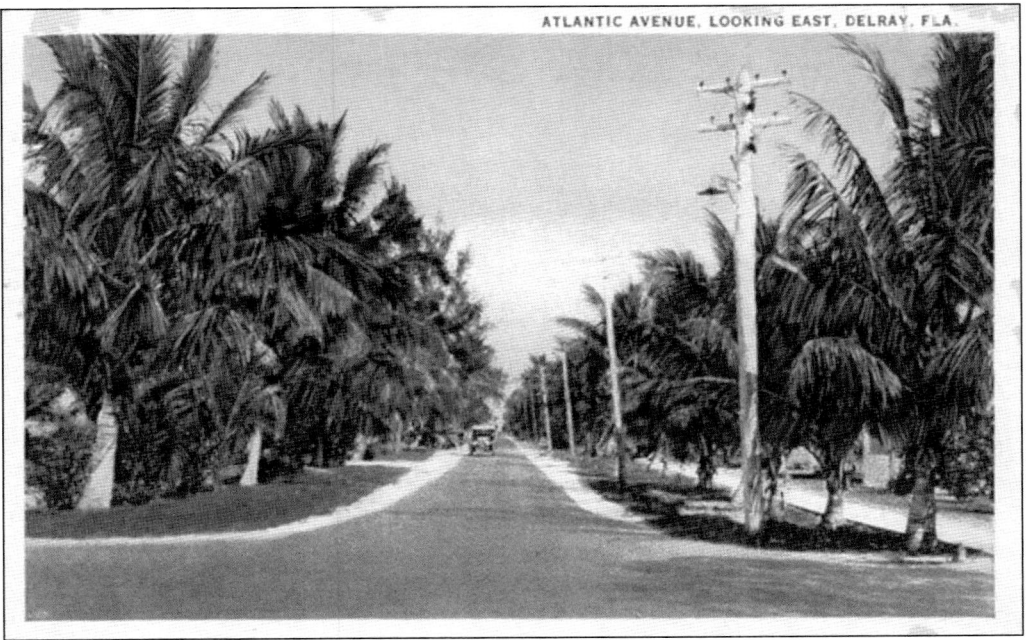

ATLANTIC AVENUE, LOOKING EAST. Another beautiful Florida Series postcard shows the main street, Atlantic Avenue, sometime in the 1920s. The avenue is looking more sophisticated, and in later images, the palms are even taller.

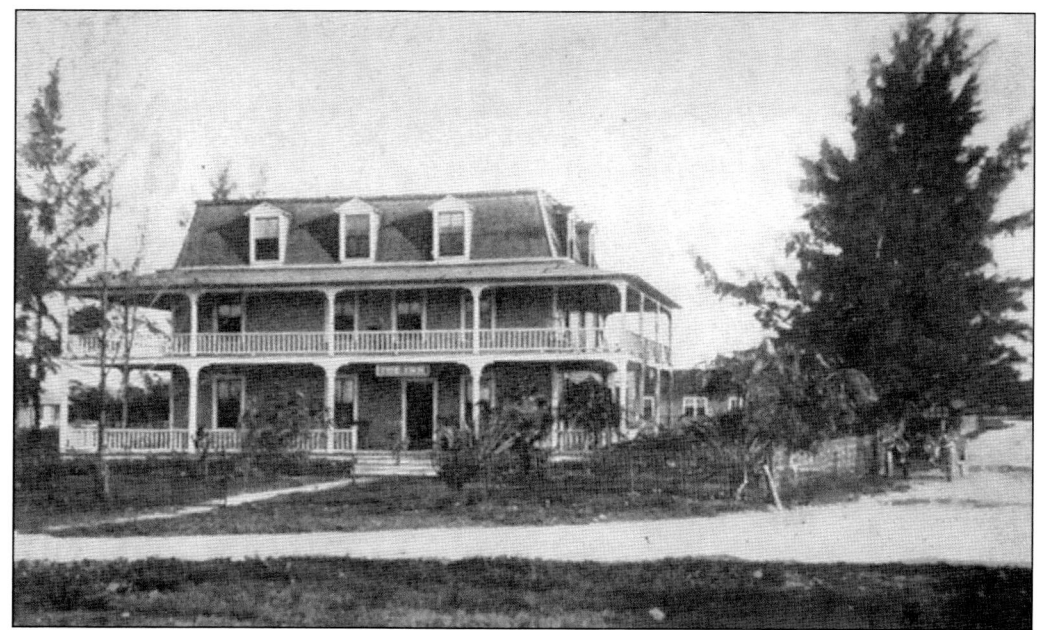

THE CHAPMAN INN. Built in 1902 in the Bahamian style by Mr. and Mrs. Frank Chapman, the Chapman Inn was the first building in town constructed for hotel use. The initial hotel register is housed in the archives of the historical society. Frank Chapman, a former railroad agent, arrived with the William S. Linton party in 1895 and served as the town's original postmaster. (Henry Higgins.)

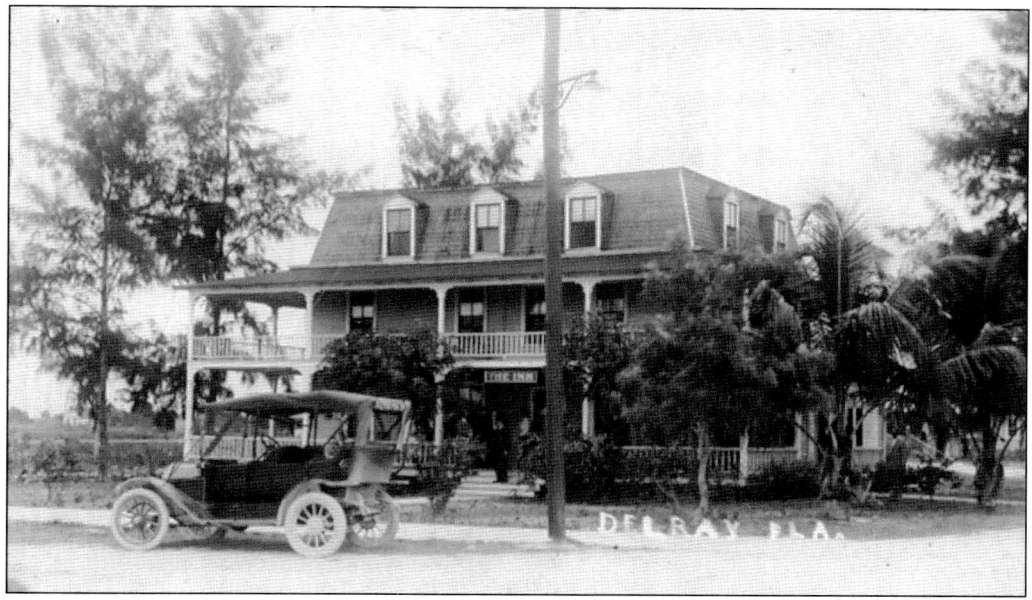

THE INN. This view captures a later time, as the trees have grown larger. A car waits, perhaps for the people standing on the porch. Survivors of the 1903 wreck of the British freighter SS *Inchulva* took refuge here. Also known as the Chapman House and the Grand Hotel, the building burned in 1927.

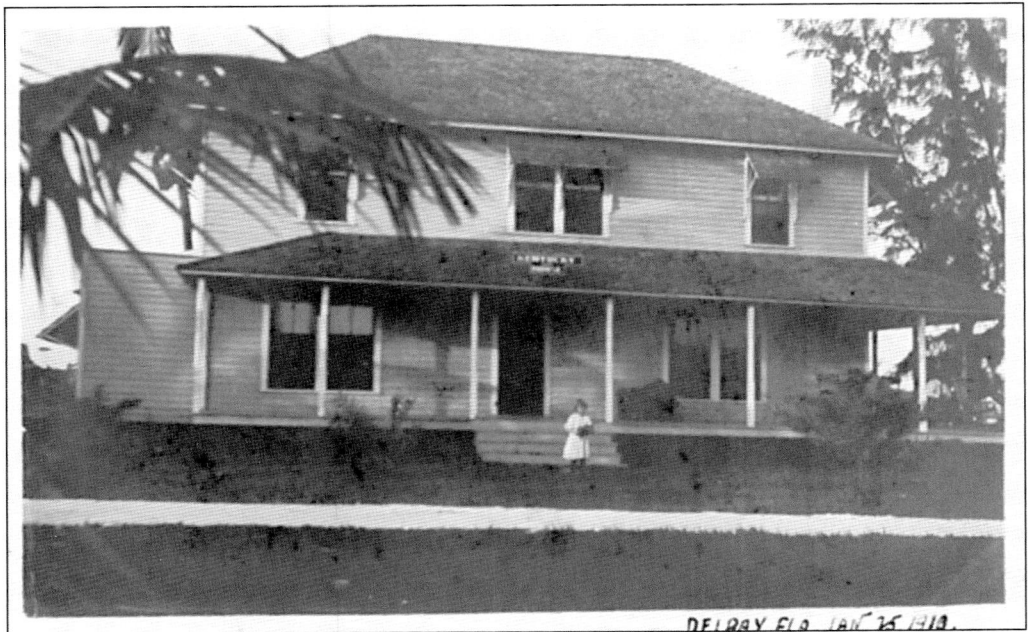

ORIGINAL KENTUCKY HOUSE. Established in 1911, the first Kentucky House is the subject of the photograph seen here. L. H. Bradshaw and his family moved to Delray from Kentucky. They had purchased a two-story frame house and two cottages on East Atlantic Avenue near the Intracoastal Waterway. Other arrivals from Kentucky asked to rent rooms, and the Kentucky House was established. The Bradshaws immediately became known for serving excellent meals. The date, January 25, 1913, is written clearly on the card.

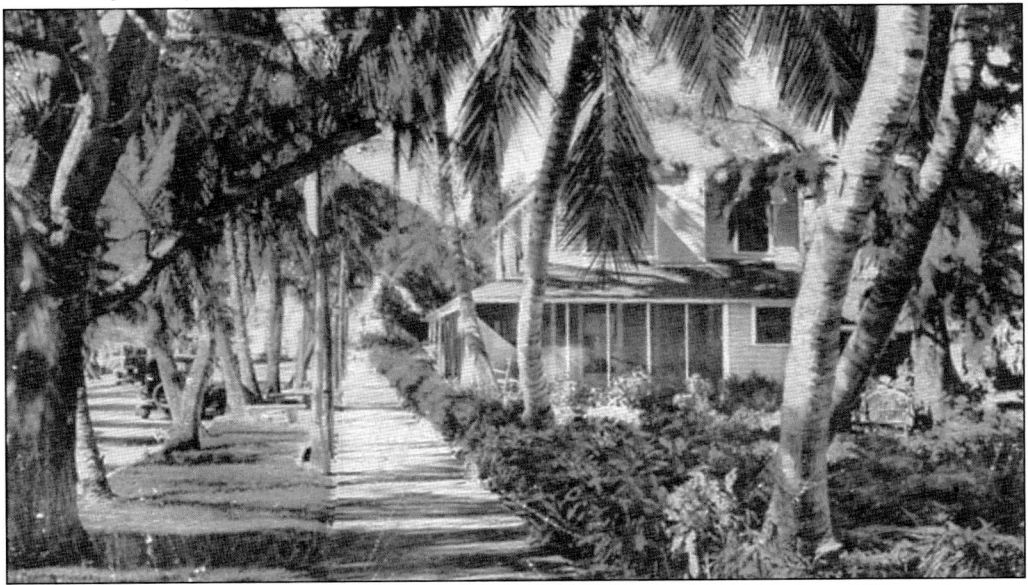

KENTUCKY HOUSE ANNEX. This hand-colored Albertype Company postcard shows the same building from a different angle after 1920, when it was renamed the Kentucky House Annex. At that time, the Bradshaws had built a large hotel adjacent to the "Annex." The porch has been screened in, and more shrubbery has been planted. (Henry Higgins.)

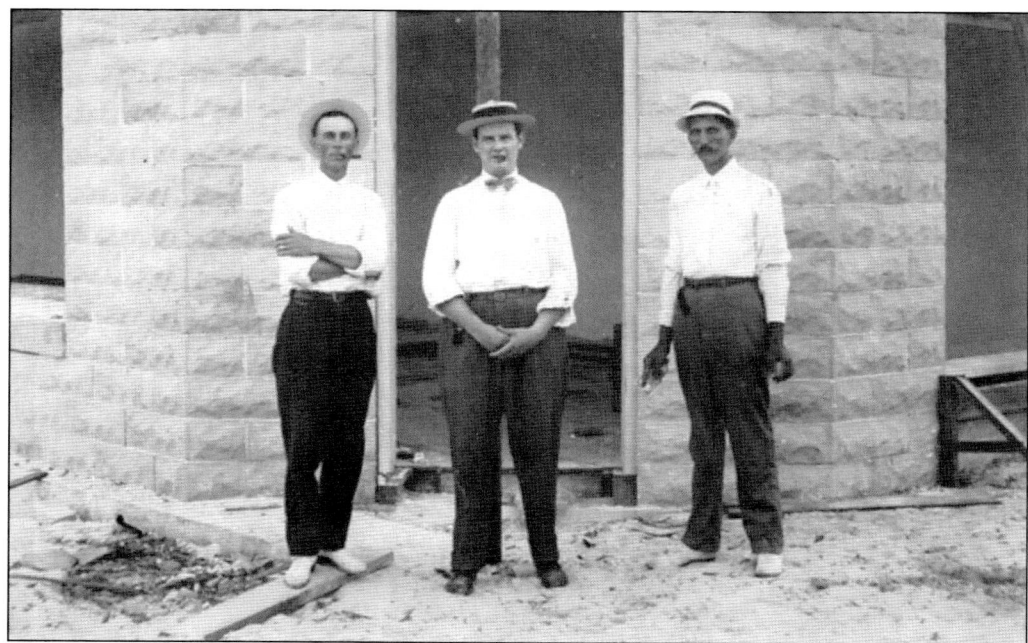

BUILDING THE BANK. J. M. Cromer (right) was a prominent local businessman and the original owner of the Cromer Block, the 500 block of Atlantic Avenue, which was one of the first masonry vernacular buildings. The first financial institution in town, the Bank of Delray was established at the east end of the building.

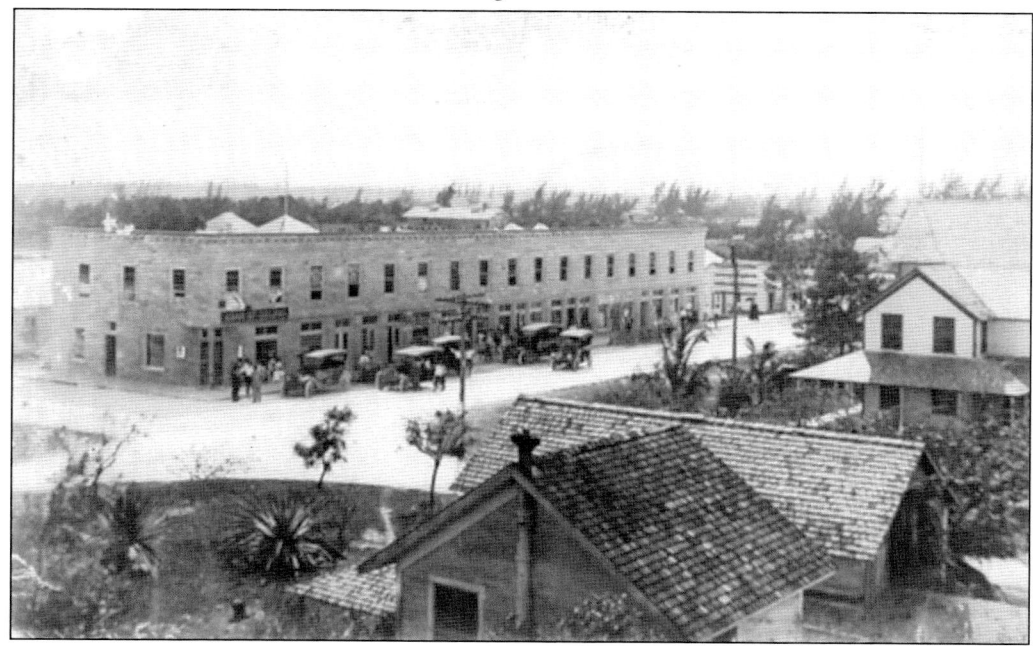

CROMER BLOCK. This view of the Cromer Block, taken from a roof or water tower, bears a captivating message from Henry in Delray to Hazel in Key West: "I just got back off of a two weeks hunt and just got your card. Don't think I am mad at you because I never answered sooner. I am going to come down to Key West this winter."

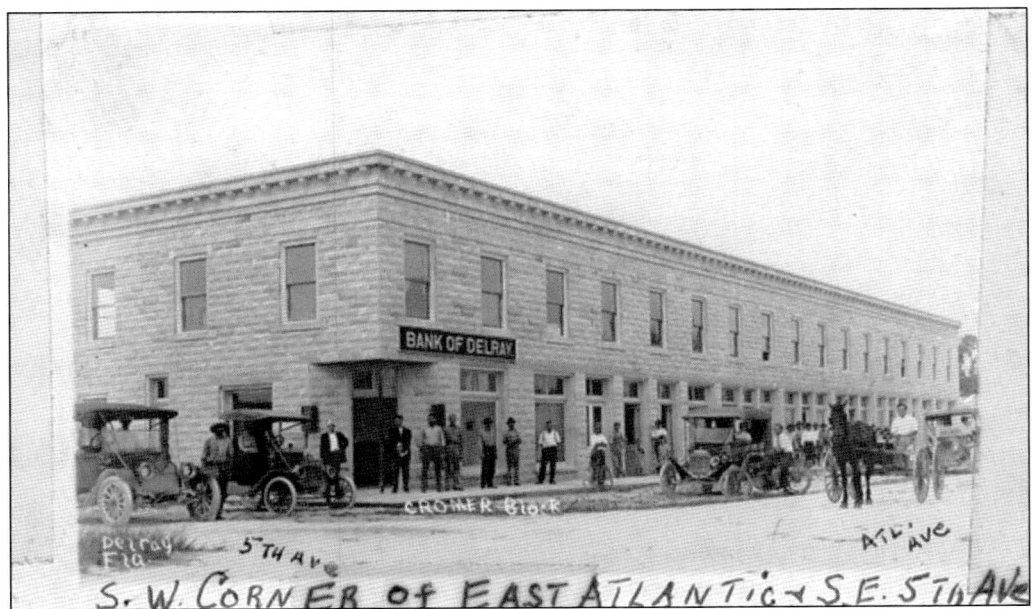

CROMER BUILDING. A closer view of the completed Cromer Block building shows the cars lined up at the new, busy commercial hub on Atlantic Avenue. Several modes of transportation are seen here: cars, a motorcycle, and a horse and wagon.

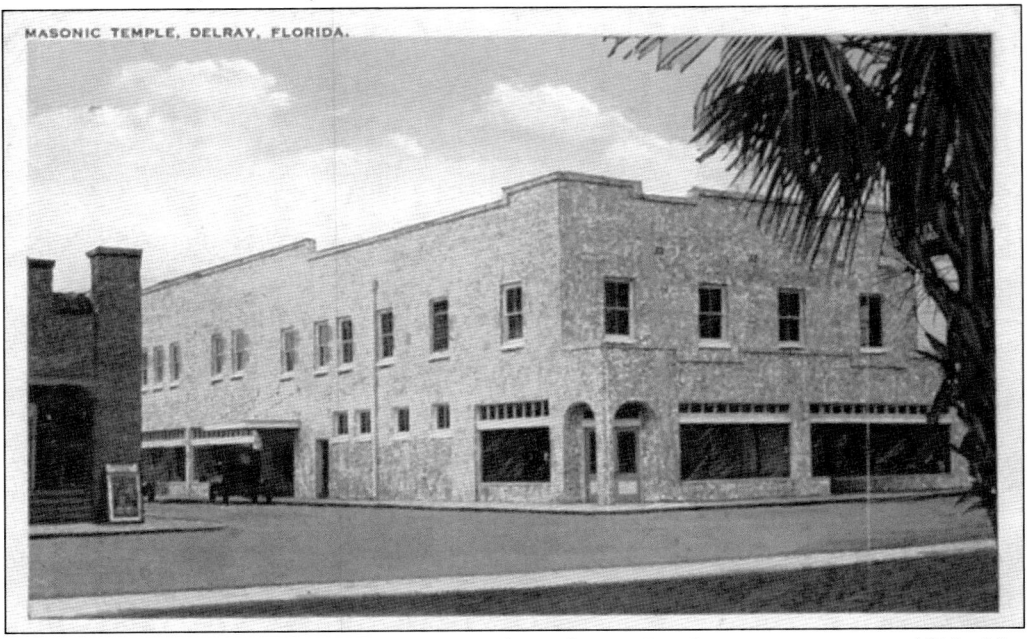

MASONIC TEMPLE. This Atlantic Avenue and Southeast First Avenue scene was published by the Red Cross Pharmacy of Delray. In the 1920s, the post office was established at the site of the car on the side street. Next door to the Masonic Building, the corner of a theater can be seen. Originally constructed in 1914 as the Bijou Theater to show silent movies accompanied by a piano, it later was stuccoed, renamed the Roxy, and continued to show movies into the 1940s.

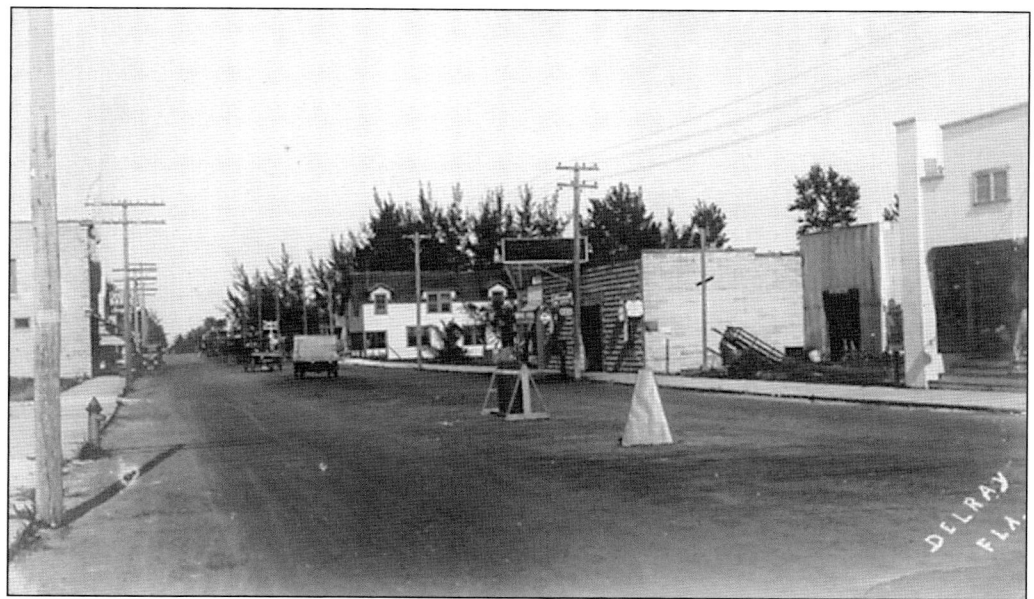

STREET SCENE. This view looks east toward the first block west of the Florida East Coast Railway tracks. In the background, the white building on the right side of the road is the Rista Hotel. The 1924 telephone book, in which Delray consists of merely a half-page, lists the Rista phone number as 48. The hotel was established in the enlarged 1896 Sterling-Russell Commissary. The first building in the right foreground is the Bijou Theater.

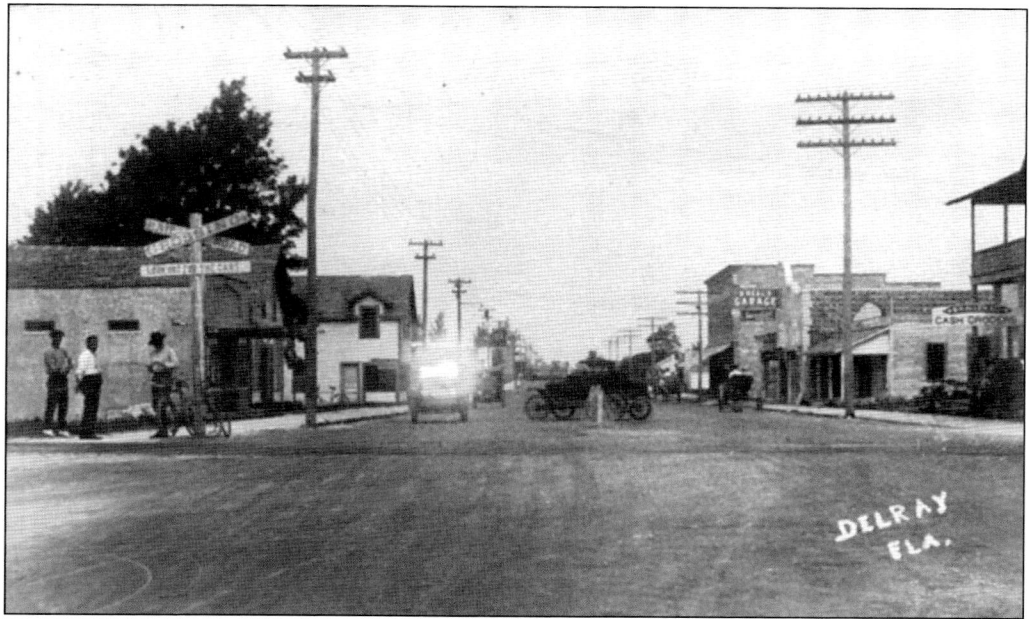

REVERSED STREET SCENE. The same block as above has been reversed, as the view looks west from the railway tracks. The Rista now appears on the left, and under magnification, the name "Sterling" can be read on a sign there. Across the street are O'Neals Garage and S. H. Allen Cash Groceries, both listed in the 1924 telephone book. Modes of transportation span from horses and wagons to automobiles and bicycles.

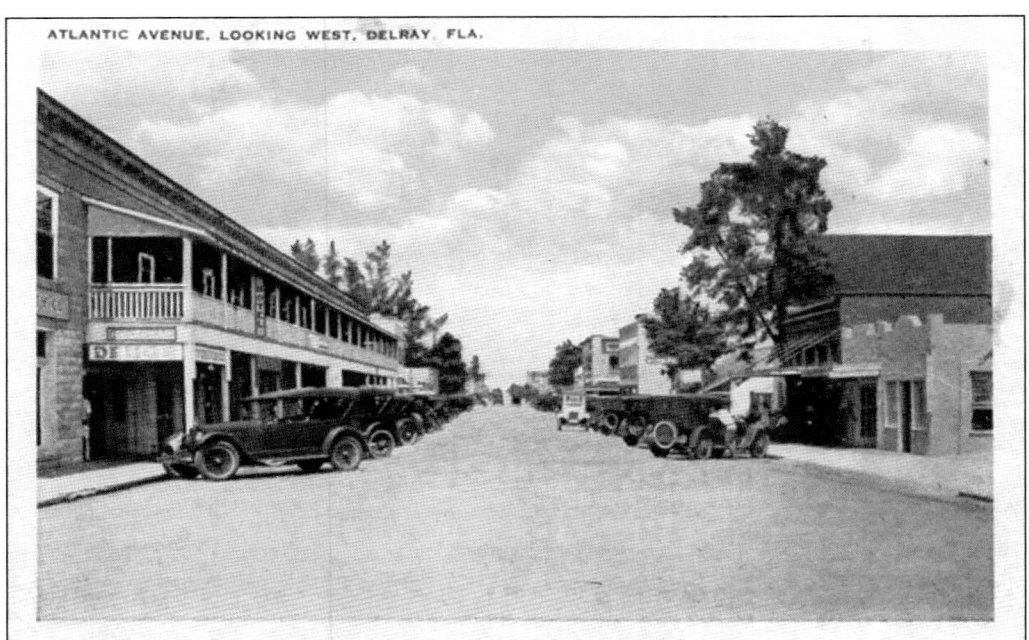

CROMER BUILDING BALCONY. This 1920s street scene of Atlantic Avenue was photographed looking west from near the intersection of the Dixie Highway. A balcony was built onto the front of the Cromer Building, shading the hotel rooms upstairs and the sidewalk and stores below. The first business below in the left foreground is a drugstore.

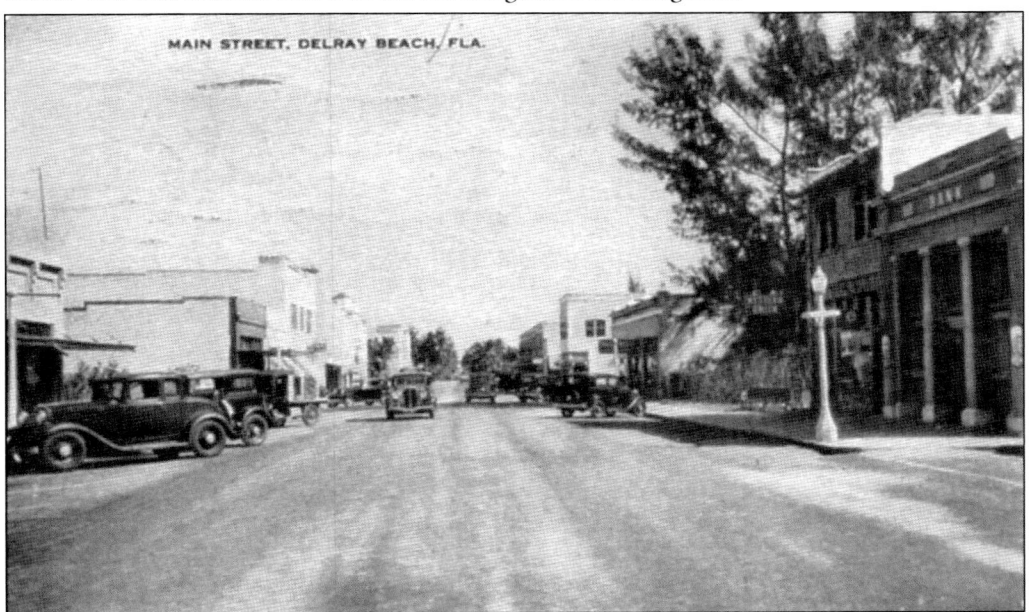

MAIN STREET, DELRAY BEACH. In the right foreground of this view is the Florida State Bank at 302 East Atlantic Avenue. Looking east on the left, one can see the Spanish-style bell towers of the Red Cross Pharmacy and the Arcade Building beyond. The Artvue postcard's message reads, "Greetings from me and Delray." It was sent to a Mr. Jackaberry in DeSmit, South Dakota, in 1935.

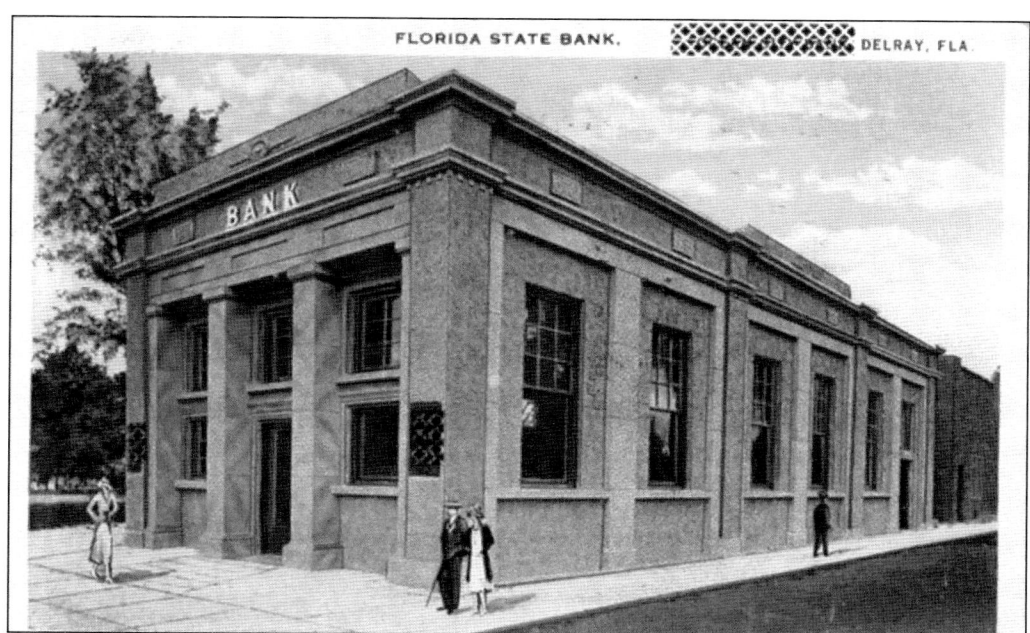

BANK. This enhanced Florida State Bank view is part of the Beautiful Florida Series. Sent from Delray Beach on May 10, 1934, the card was received in Atlanta on May 12, 1934. The note states, "Mr. J. B. Moon. Dear Sir, Your letter regarding baseball game. In reply will say, we have not formed any team here yet. And unless we get a closed park we will not have a team." (Henry Higgins.)

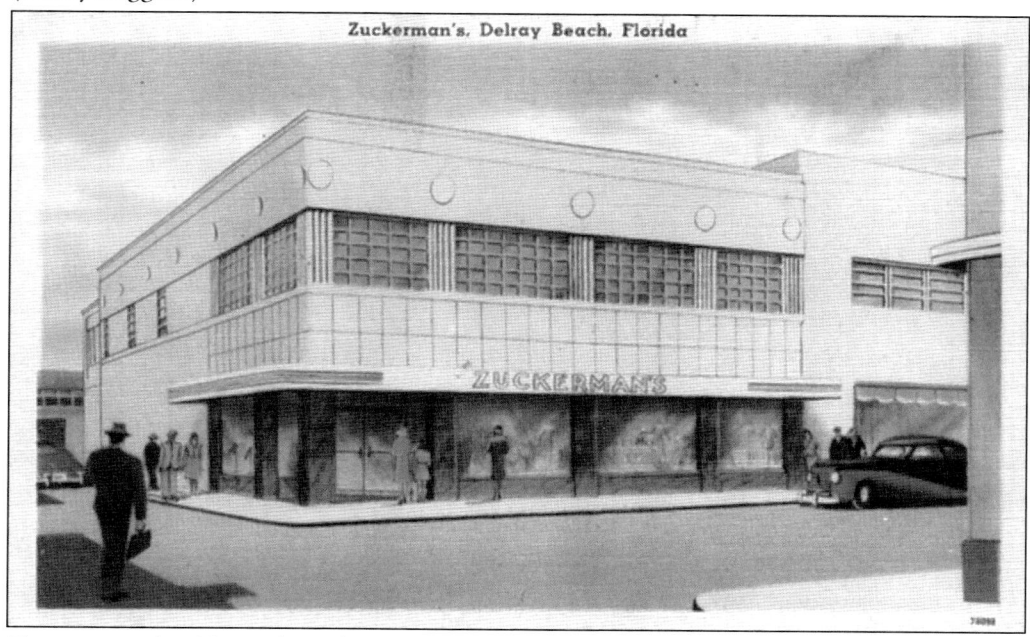

ZUCKERMAN'S. Pictured in the 1940s, Zuckerman's department store was located at 401–403 East Atlantic Avenue. A hometown department store, it used the motto of "style without extravagance." Mercer Wenzel remains in business at the same site. This Tichnor Quality View linen card was published by the Zone Sales Company of Delray Beach.

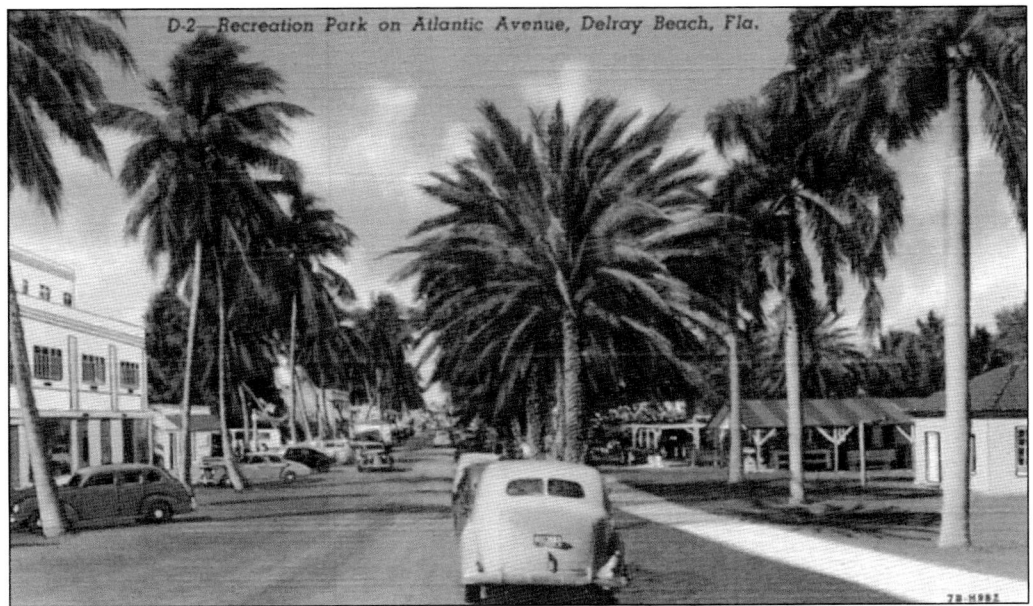

RECREATION PARK. In the left foreground, the Boyd Building stands at 824 East Atlantic Avenue. The building, constructed in 1937, was designed in the Art Moderne style by Gustav Maas. On the right are the shuffleboard courts at the city park next to the Intracoastal Waterway. This hand-tinted card was published by the FEC News Company.

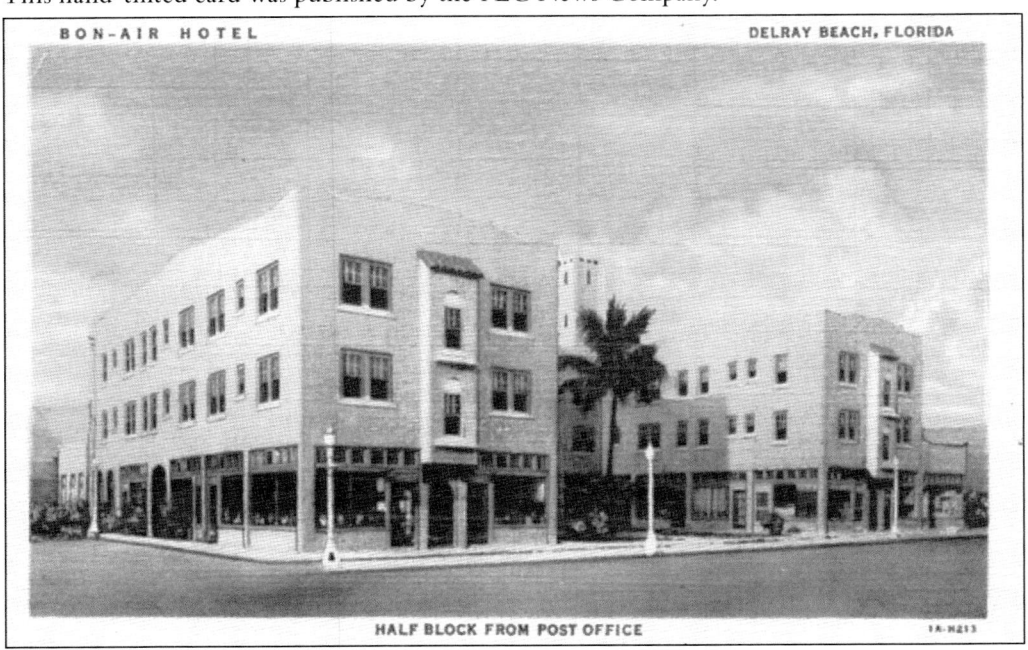

BON-AIR. The Bon-Air was situated at 126 East Atlantic Avenue. Management advertised its location as being "in the heart of the city" and a "half block from the post office." Irwin J. Sinks was the original building contractor. After the real estate crash and a period of bank management, the name was changed from Casa Del Rey to the Bon-Air. It was demolished in 1968.

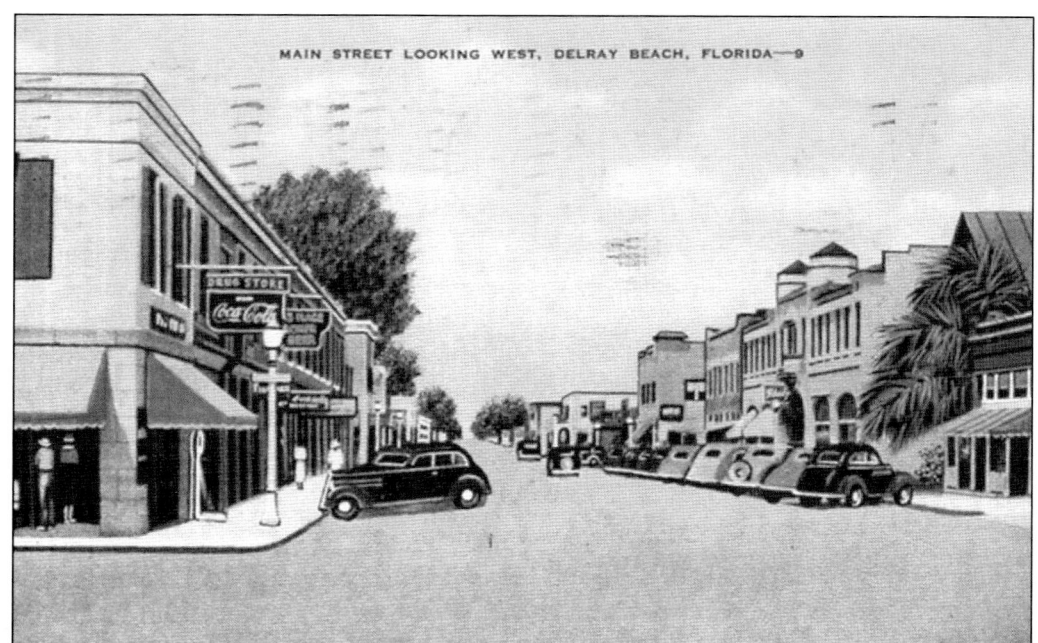

MAIN STREET, LOOKING WEST. This Atlantic Avenue scene, postmarked March 24, 1937, focuses on the 400 block with the 300 block in the distance. On the right are the Woman's Club of Delray Beach, the Arcade Building, Zuckerman's, and the Love Building with Love's Rexall Pharmacy. On the left is the Atha Building, which replaced the Cromer Block. (Henry Higgins.)

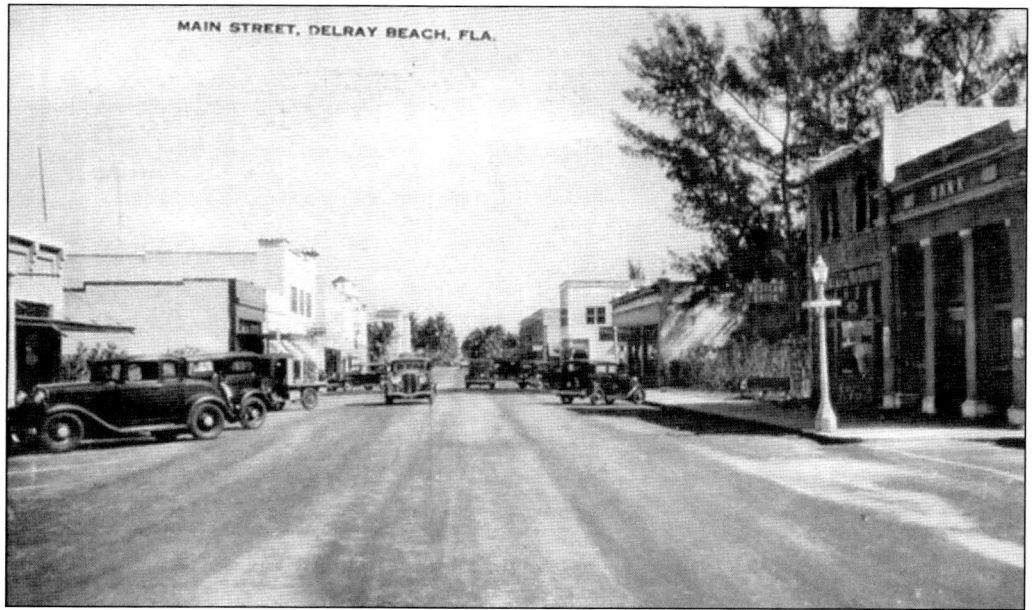

300 BLOCK, LOOKING EAST. On this Artvue postcard, the Love Building stands on the left, while the Arcade Building is pictured beyond. On the corner at right is the Florida State Bank, featured in the card on page 90. Next door to the bank is Western Union, and beyond the trees is a Piggly Wiggly. (Henry Higgins.)

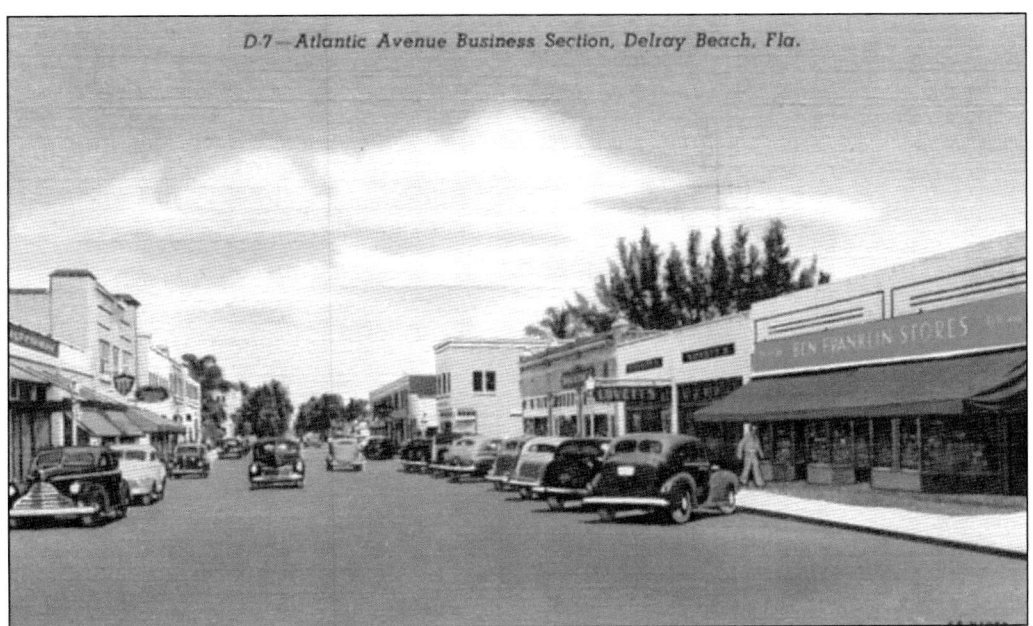

BUSINESS SECTION. This hand-tinted postcard, published by the FEC News Company of West Palm Beach, shows the 300 block a few years later. The Ben Franklin Store is listed as a department store located at 312 East Atlantic Avenue. Across the street, the Love Building can be recognized by its two small red-tile tower roofs.

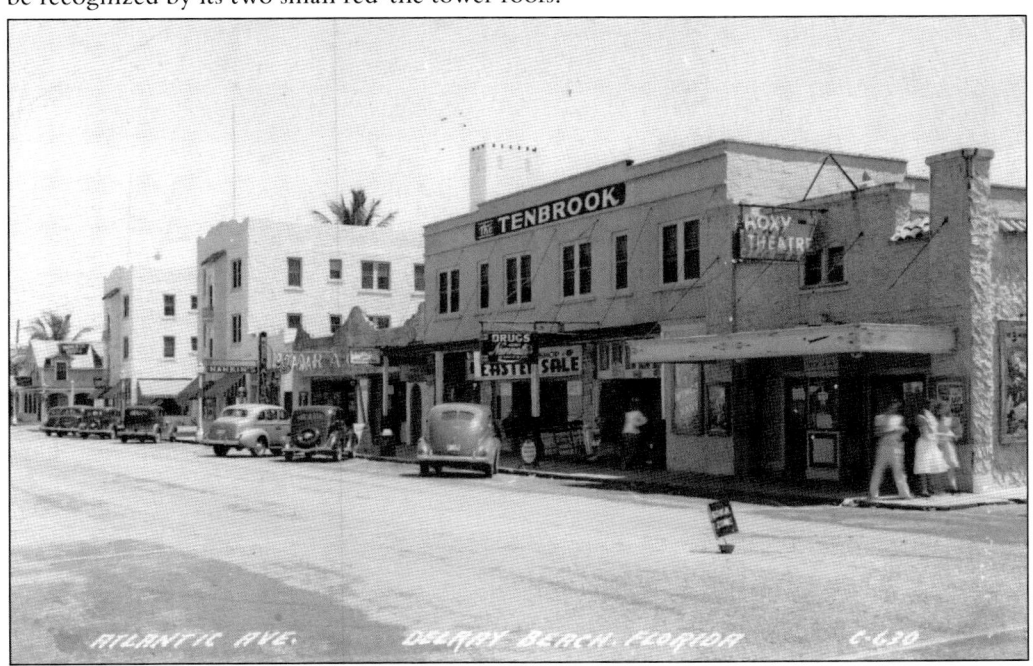

TENBROOK BUILDING. The Roxy Theater (right) was the first movie theater in town. However, in 1914, it showed silent films under the Bijou Theater name. Frank and Elizabeth Tenbrook owned and operated the Bijou. The couple also owned the adjacent Tenbrook Building. East of that building was the Bon-Air Hotel. This card is postmarked April 28, 1944.

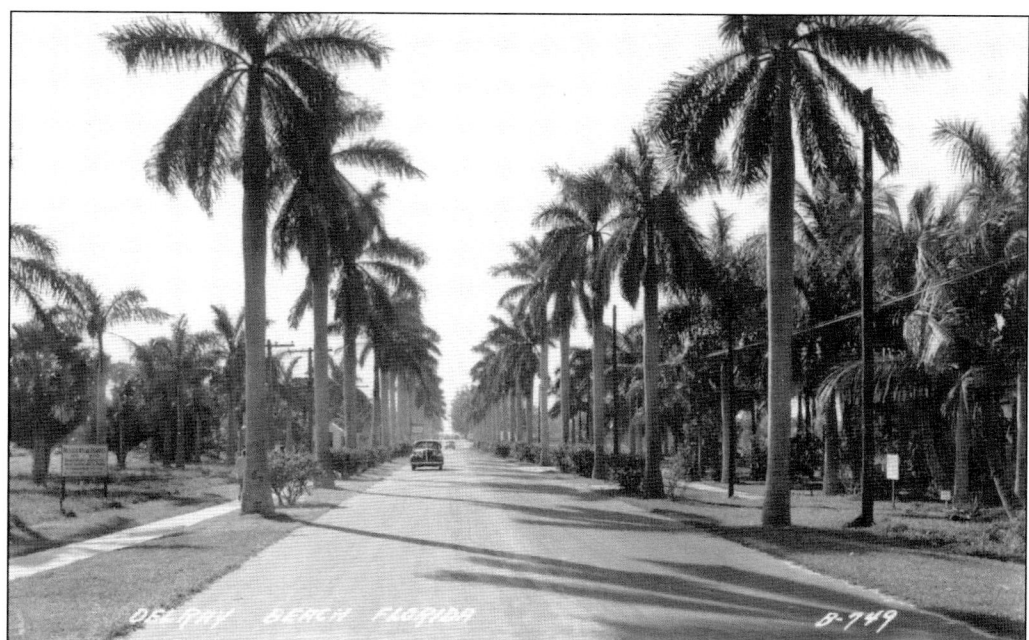

TALL ROYAL PALMS. Cars drive west on Atlantic Avenue from the beach about 1940. Notice how undeveloped the east end of Atlantic Avenue was at the time. The sign on the left reads, "Residential Estates, 100 X 200, Beautifully Planted."

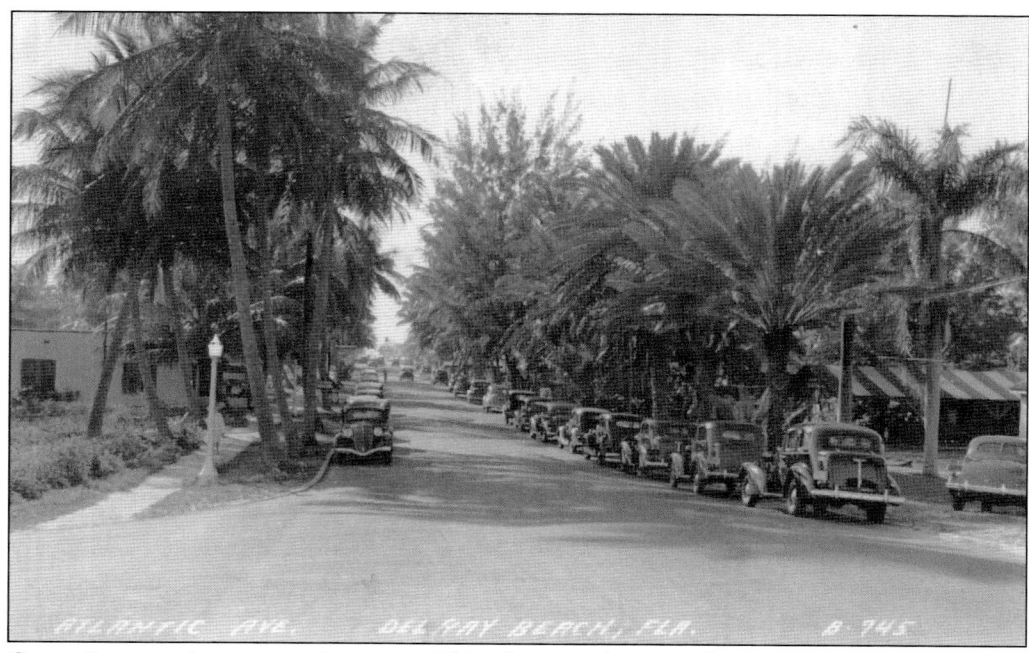

CARS LINING ATLANTIC AVENUE. This photograph was taken in the 1930s before the Boyd Building's 1937 construction. The city park on the Intracoastal Waterway appears on the right. On the left is a small building with a sign out front for "H. D. Gates, Realtor." (Henry Higgins.)

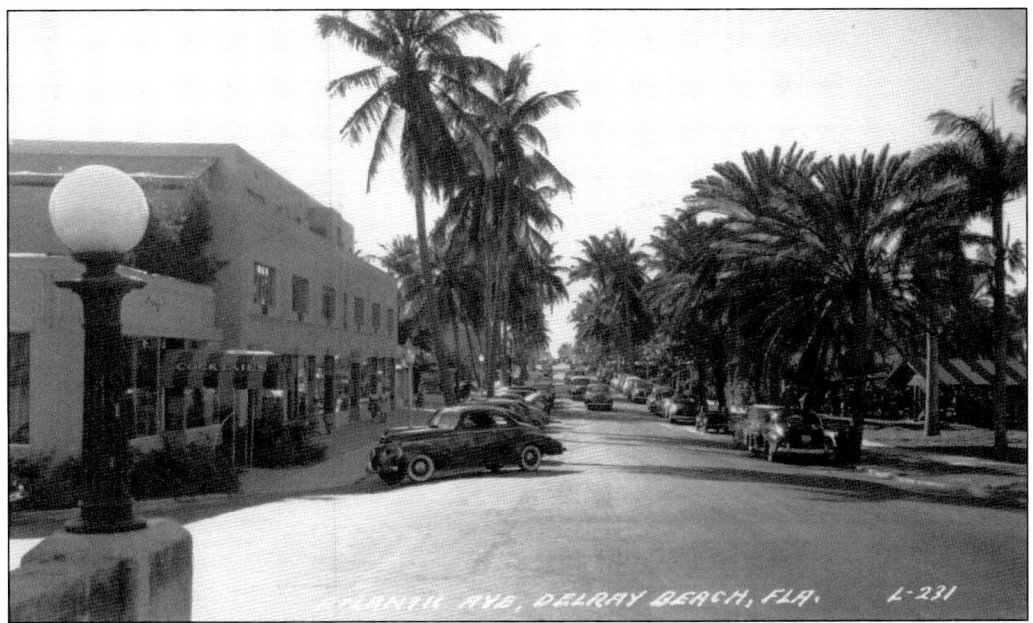

THE BOYD BUILDING. Looking west from the Atlantic Avenue bridge, this view shows the palm-lined 800 block with the Boyd Building on the left. The word "Cocktails" marks the original location of long-running Delray Beach restaurant Erny's. On the right is the shuffleboard court area with the striped roof. (Henry Higgins.)

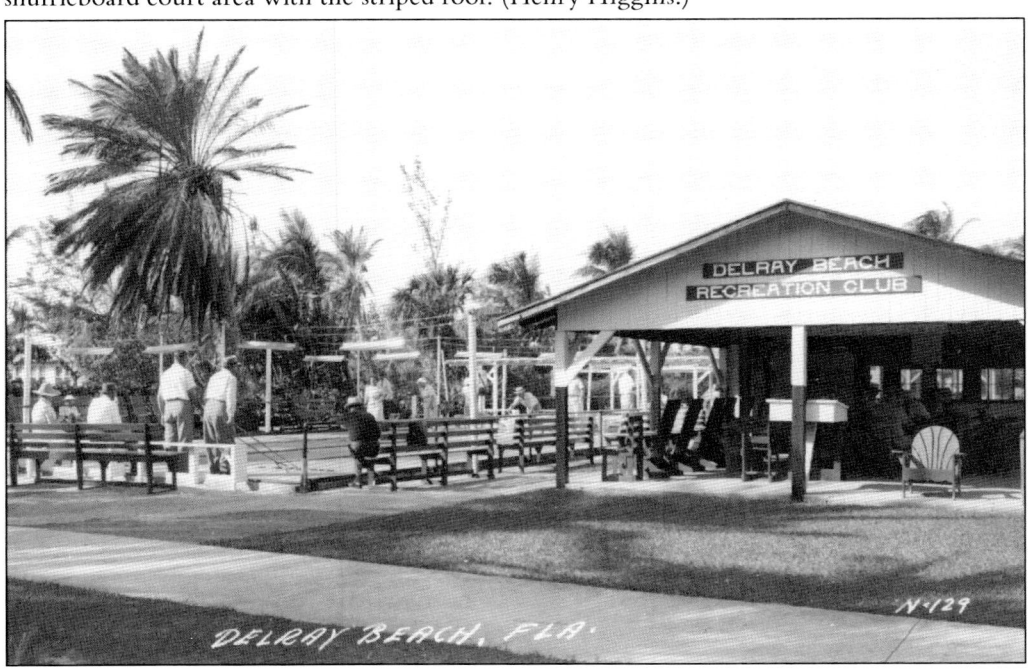

DELRAY BEACH RECREATION CLUB. This postcard provides a close-up view of the shuffleboard courts at 821 East Atlantic Avenue. Shuffleboard is an old English game, although it has features in common with similar games in other European countries. Physical fitness requirements for playing shuffleboard are comparatively low. (Henry Higgins.)

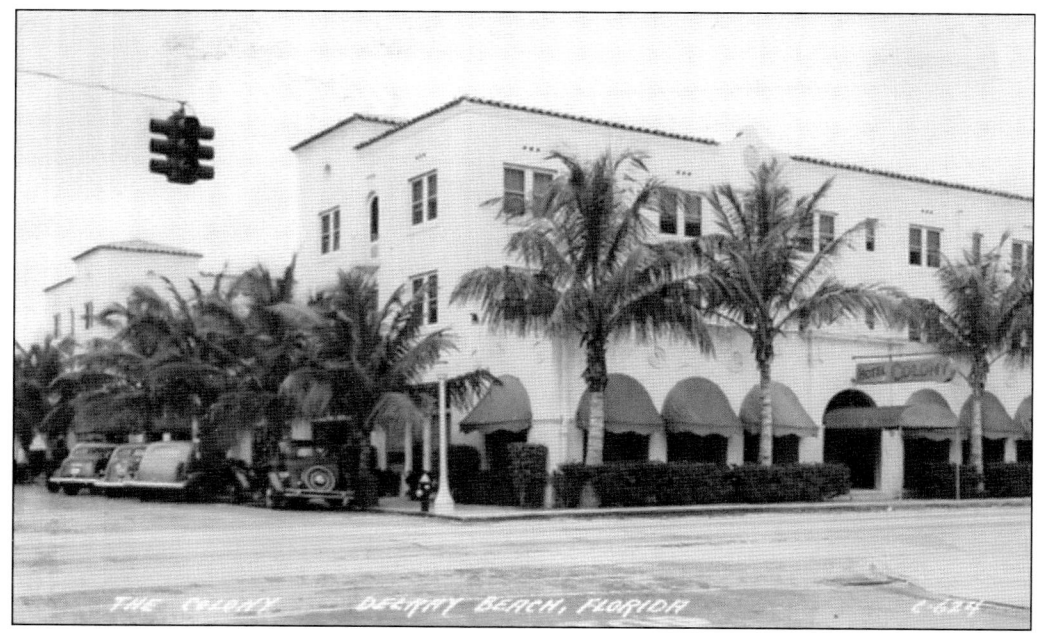

THE COLONY, c. 1935. This photograph was taken soon after the Colony was purchased by the Boughton family in the mid-1930s. Located at 527 East Atlantic Avenue, the hotel was and still is a favorite of winter visitors to Delray Beach—though in recent years it has been open year-round. The card was published by the L. L. Cook Company. (Henry Higgins.)

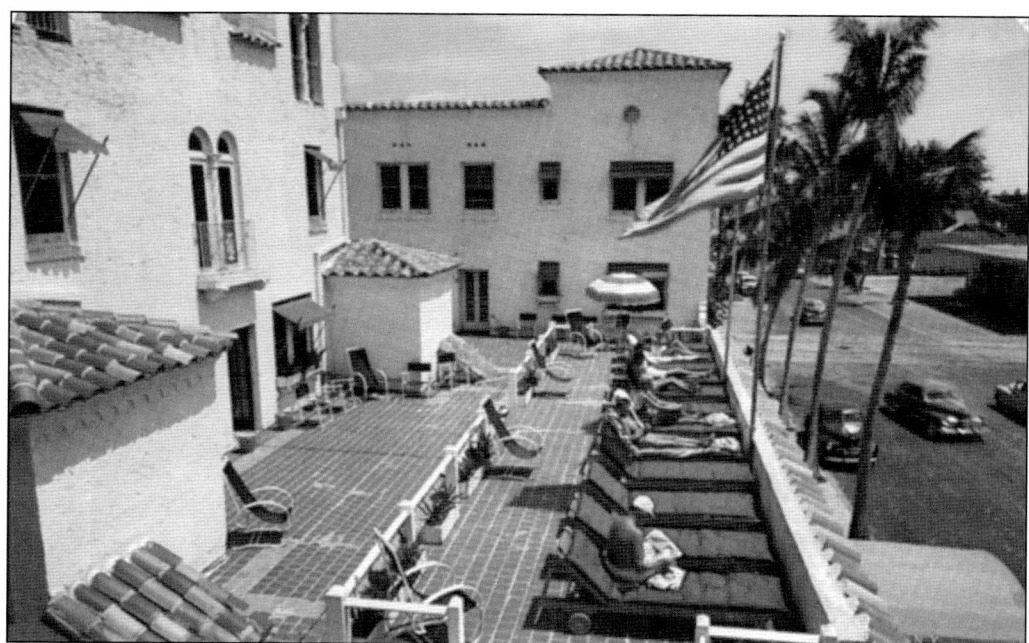

COLONY, c. 1950s. Hotel guests enjoy the rooftop terrace in this close-up view. The Dextone card was published by Edward Hipple of Riviera Beach, Florida. On the reverse is the hotel's slogan: "Warm Winters." "Boughton ownership and management" is printed under the name. (Henry Higgins.)

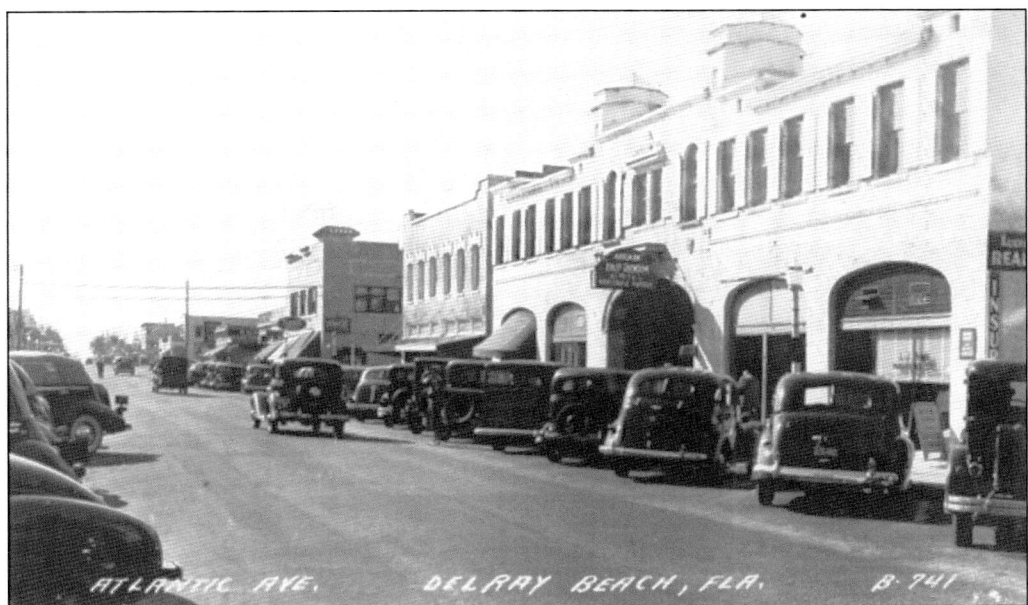

THE ARCADE. In this late-1930s photograph, the sign over the Tap Room entrance reads, "Arcade Tap Room, Grill, Package Store." The offices on each side included the following, among others: C. Y. Byrd, attorney; Sam Ogren Sr., architect; A. W. Miller, dentist; Gulf Stream Engineers; and Matt Gracey and Lucile J. Nichols, real estate. Cartoonists Fontaine Fox, Herb Roth, and H. T. Webster and writer Hugh McNair Kahler had studios upstairs.

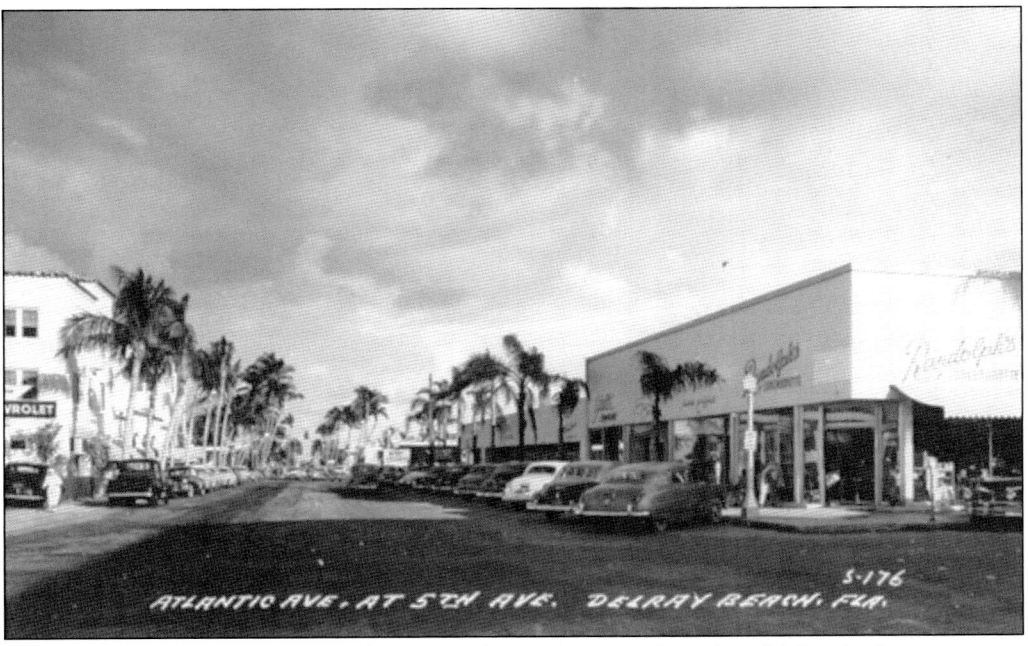

RANDOLPH'S. This view from the 1950s shows the opposite side of Atlantic Avenue across from the Colony. Randolph's Luncheonette is on the corner. In the background, on the same side of the street, a large sign is visible for Rosella's Pastry and Delicatessen at number 614. (Henry Higgins.)

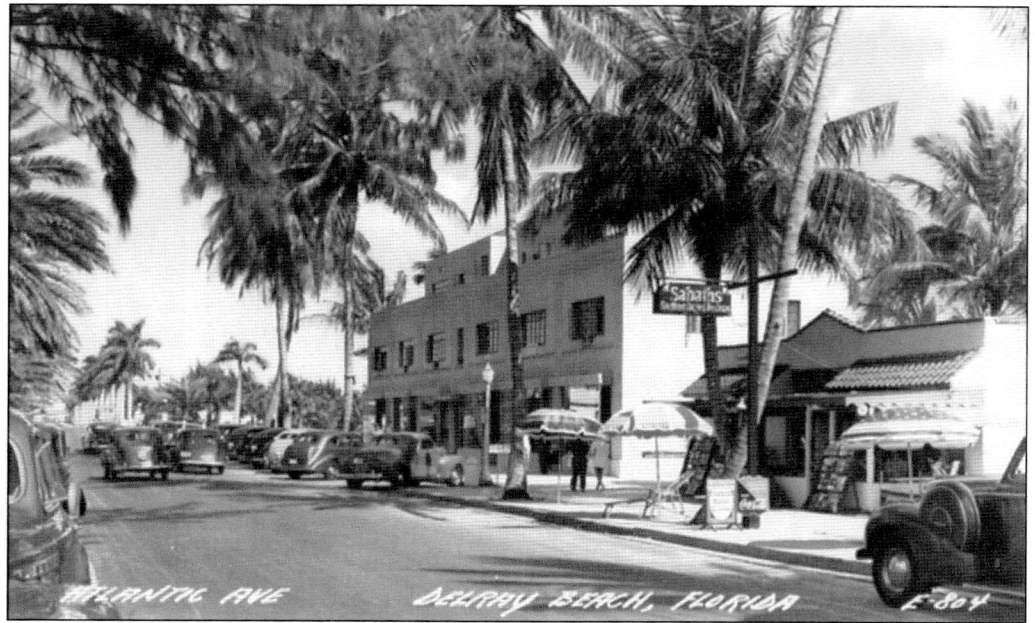

SABATH'S. This 1940s view looks east down a palm-studded Atlantic Avenue. Sabath's, the store on the right, carried beach equipment and catered to beachgoers. The store also sold magazines, Southern Dairies ice cream, and soft drinks. (Henry Higgins.)

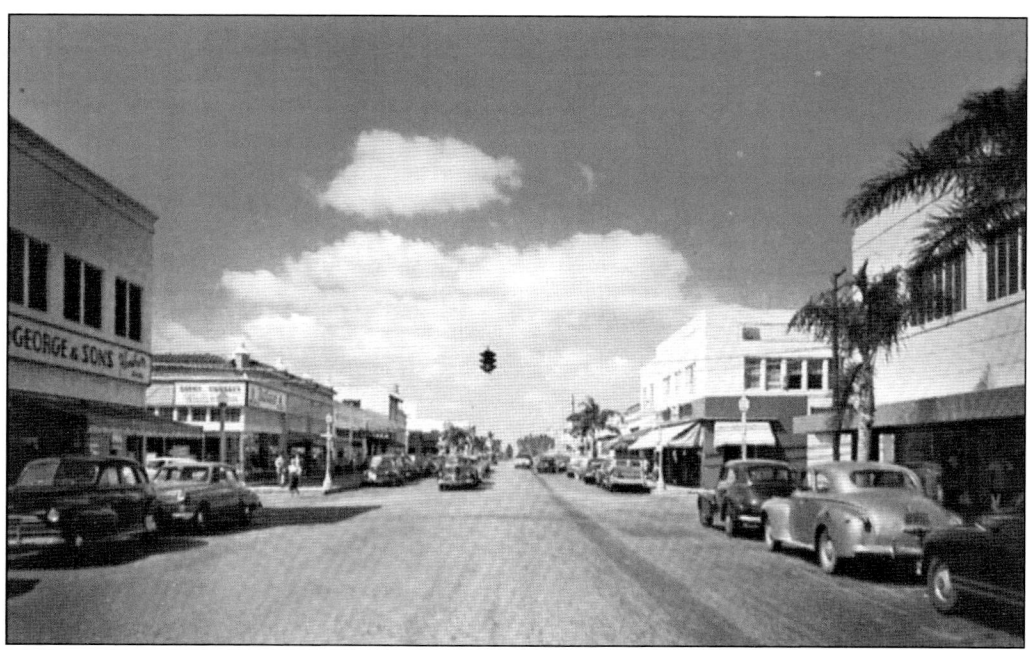

A. GEORGE & SONS. This retail clothing store was for many years an Atlantic Avenue institution at 402 East Atlantic Avenue. Abraham George founded the business in 1911, and the family operated the business until 1997 from the same location. This Kodachrome reproduction from the L. L. Cook Company shows the street as it looked in the 1950s. (Henry Higgins.)

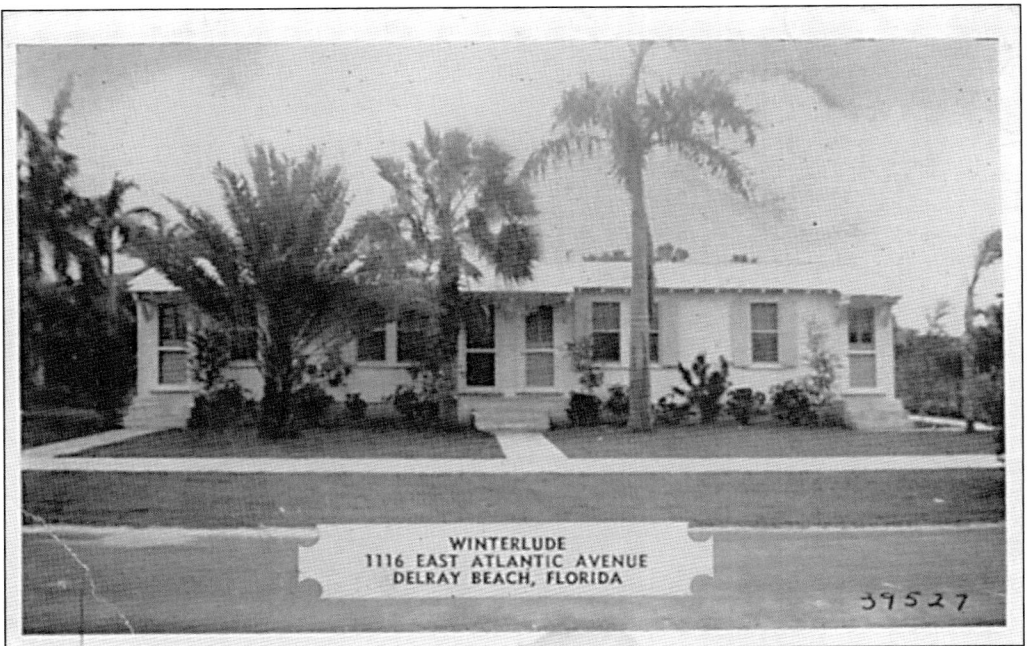

WINTERLUDE. Two blocks from the beach, Winterlude offered rooms and efficiency apartments for rent at 116 East Atlantic Avenue. Each unit had a separate entrance. In the 1950s, the rentals were managed by Carolyn Thomas, who worked at Montgomery and Adams Realty.

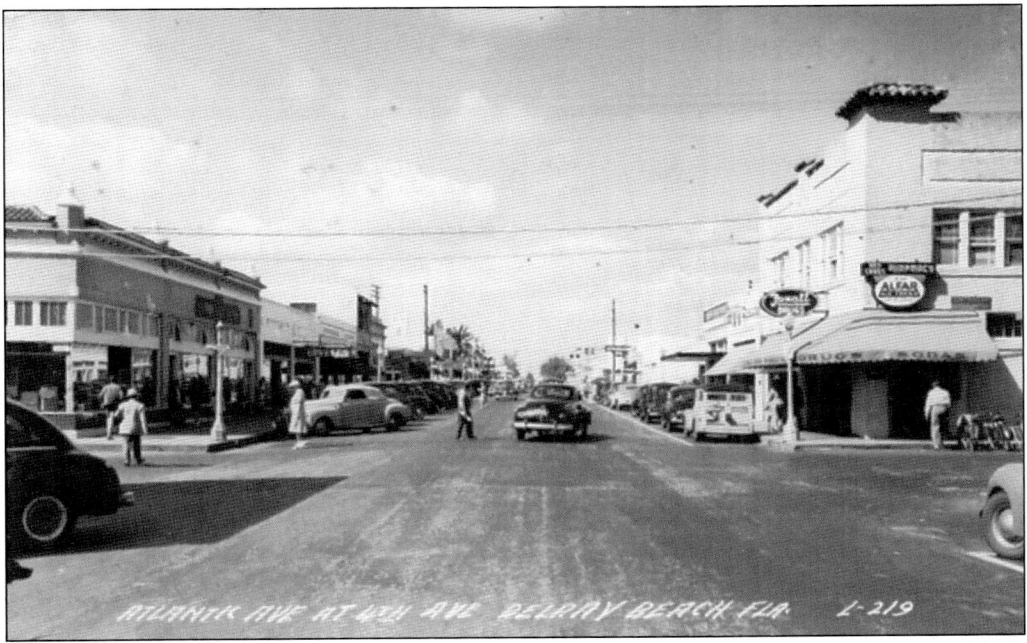

ALFAR ICE CREAM. Lots of cars and people are seen in this westward view of the 300 block from the late 1940s. Signs on the Love Building advertise Rexall Drugs, Red Cross Pharmacy, and Alfar Ice Cream. In the distance, the signal for the Florida East Coast Railway tracks and the Barwick Building can be seen.

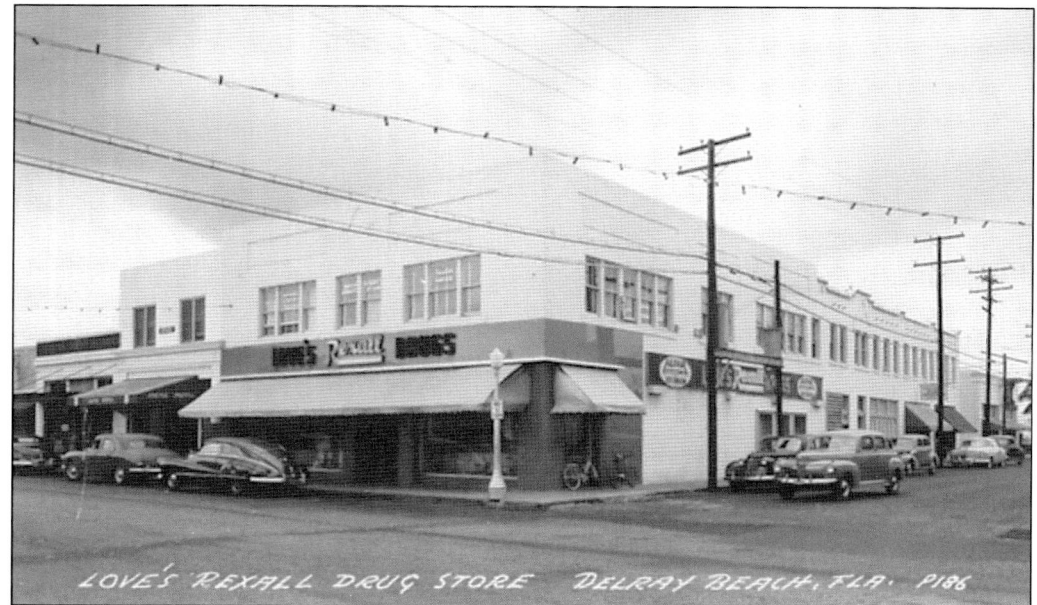

STREAMLINED BUILDING. Pharmacist James L. Love Sr. opened his first drugstore on Atlantic Avenue in 1912. This postcard shows the Love's Rexall Drugs location at 329 East Atlantic Avenue. In the 1950s, the building underwent a makeover. Its faux bell towers were removed so that the building presented a facade with clean, straight lines. James L. Love and his son operated Love's Drugstores in Delray for over 80 years.

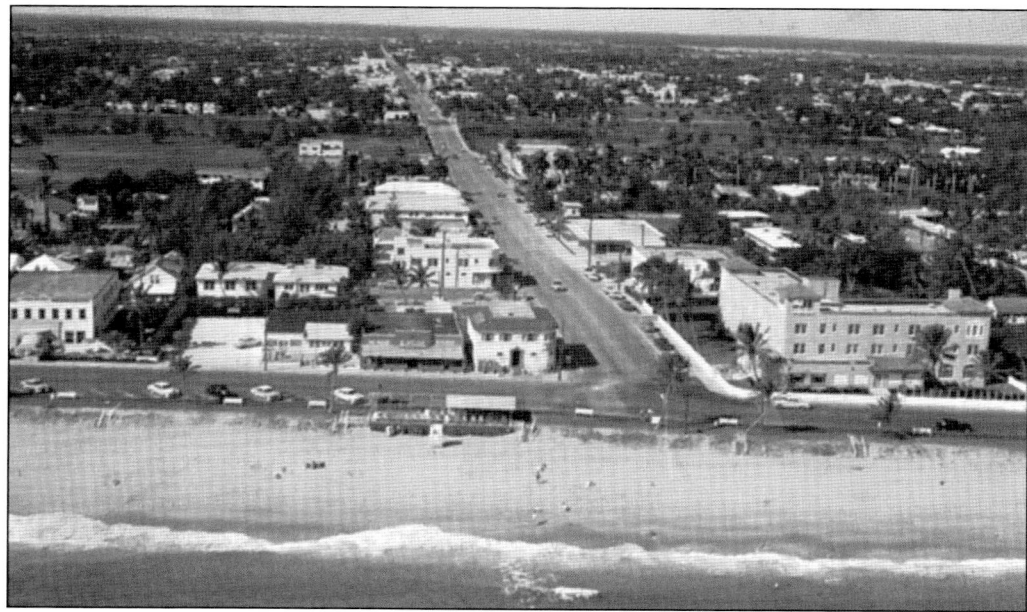

AERIAL VIEW. This postcard, purchased in 1961, is included to show the length of Atlantic Avenue as it stretches from the ocean across the Intracoastal Waterway and disappears into the distance. Here the road is anchored by the Seacrest Hotel on the north and the city casino and pool on the south. Next to the casino is the Rip Tide Restaurant, and on the south edge is the Hotel Casa Las Olas.

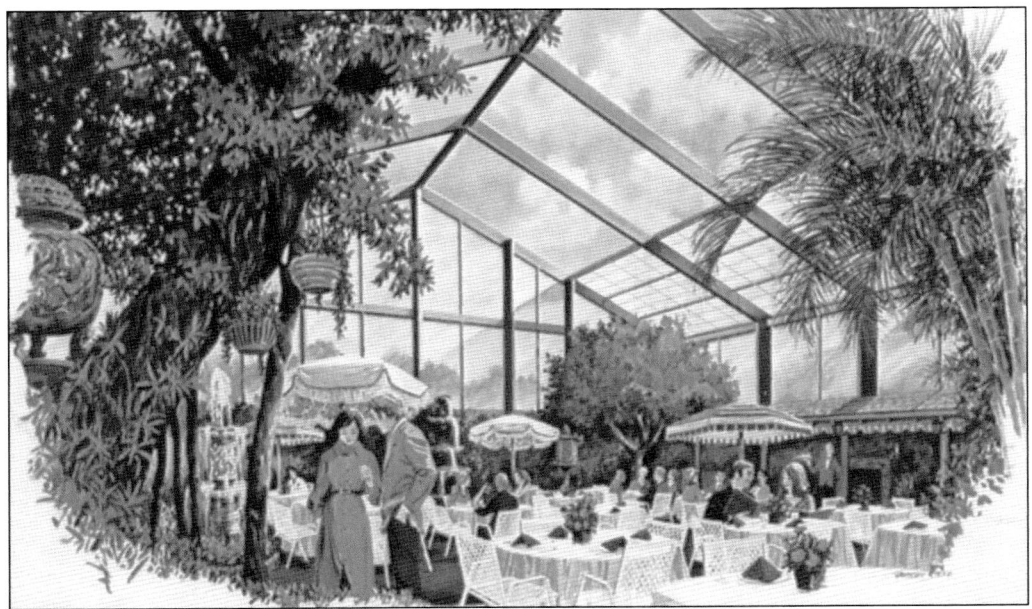

PATIO DELRAY. Published in Boca Raton, this Creative Photographers card is an artist's concept of a restaurant at 714 East Atlantic Avenue that was for decades one of the favorite spots for winter colony dining. The Patio billed itself as "The Only Real Florida Restaurant." It was established in the late 1930s by Henry Ostro, the golf pro at the Delray Beach Country Club. The closed building burned in 1989.

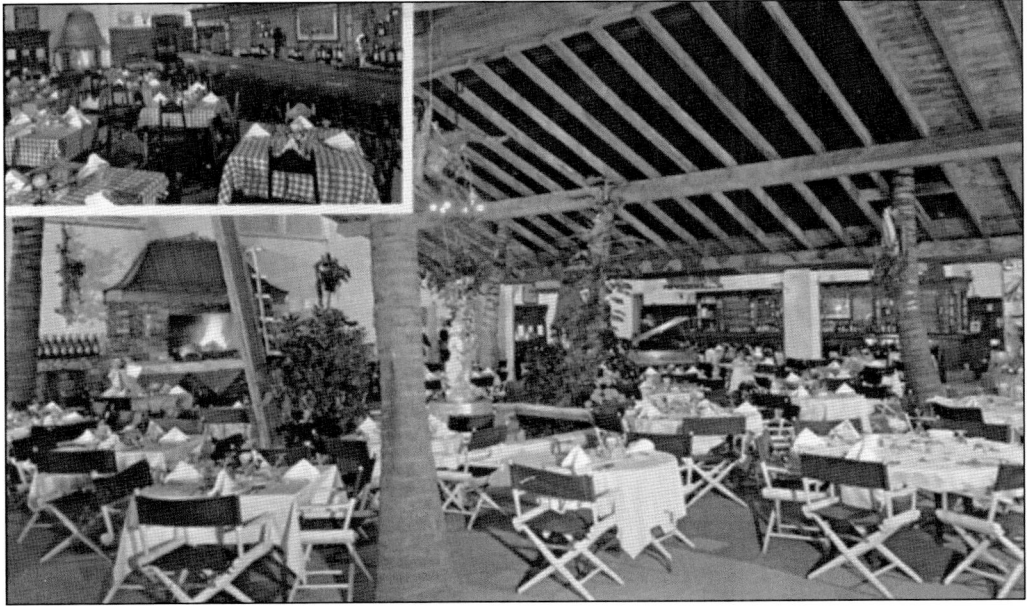

ARCADE TAP ROOM. The other Atlantic Avenue landmark frequented by winter colony guests and locals alike was the Arcade Tap Room at 411 East Atlantic Avenue. An advertisement in a 1935 Directory and Tourists Guide contains nothing about food or beverages; rather, it begins, "For a feast of reason and a flow of soul." The restaurant was established by Bill Krauss in 1933. This card, published by Stan Sheets Photography, depicts a later period in the 1970s.

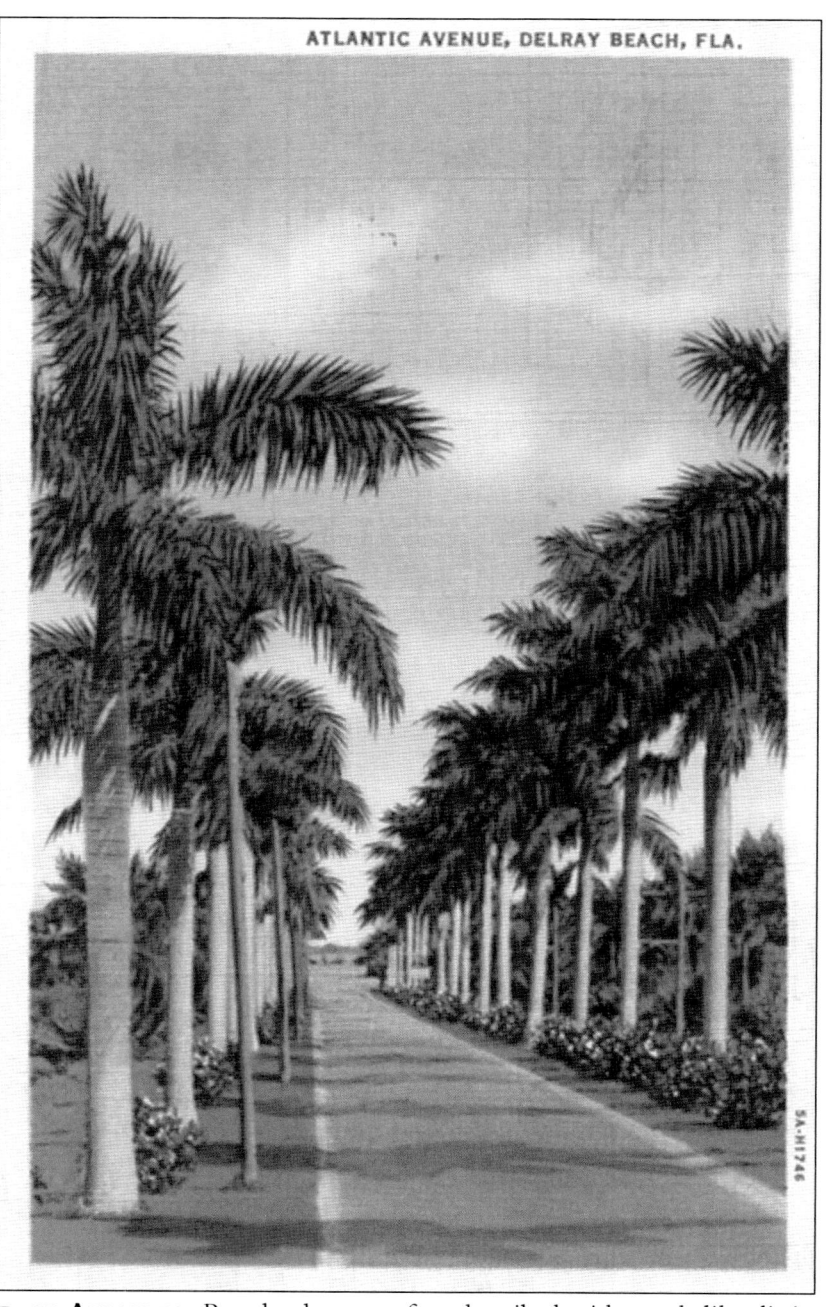

East End of Atlantic. Royal palms are often described with words like distinctive and sophisticated. The trunks look as if they have been cast from concrete. Florida royal palms (*Roystona elata*) are native to South Florida cypress swamps and can tolerate occasional flooding. They are not particular about soil and are salt tolerant. Cuban royal palms (*Roystona regia*) have been imported in great numbers. Their trunks are curvier than the straight, simple lines of the Florida natives, and the seeds are also shaped differently. Here East Atlantic Avenue is lined with tall royal palms and rows of blooming hibiscus underneath. The beach pavilion is framed at the end of the palm tree colonnade. This card was mailed on March 29, 1936. (Henry Higgins.)

Seven

MILE-LONG MUNICIPAL BEACH

In addition to being a beautiful attraction for tourists and residents alike, Delray's beach is unusual for a couple of reasons. When the map was drawn for the town of Linton, all the land east of the platted building lots near the ocean was dedicated to the people of the town. When W. S. Linton defaulted, the mortgage was foreclosed in favor of the previous owners. Sara Gleason and the heirs of William Hunt—Belle G. (Dimick) Reese and Ella M. (Dimick) Potter—again dedicated the area east of the ocean beach lots, known as the "ocean road," to the public in 1899.

This is the basis for the title to the city's present municipal beach. After 1927, when the town of Delray Beach merged with the city of Delray and was incorporated as the city of Delray Beach, the Gleason and Hunt heirs quit-claimed any reversionary interest to the city. John Ross Adams, a local attorney who researched beach property abstracts for the historical society in 1968, has said that the strip of land between Beach Drive and Causarina Road was the only portion of A1A between Jacksonville and Key West for which there was no state-owned right-of-way. Another characteristic, unlike many Florida beaches, is that most of the three miles of city beachfront lies opposite low-rise homes and condominiums. Although there are hotels and seasonal rentals across the street from the beach, less than a block of the property west of State Road A1A is home to restaurants or commercial retail establishments.

Beginning in the 1920s, postcards of the beach show that the natural dunes were leveled. In the 1960s and 1970s, a series of projects was started to halt erosion. Restoration of the dunes was successful in later years. The dunes are now covered with native plants.

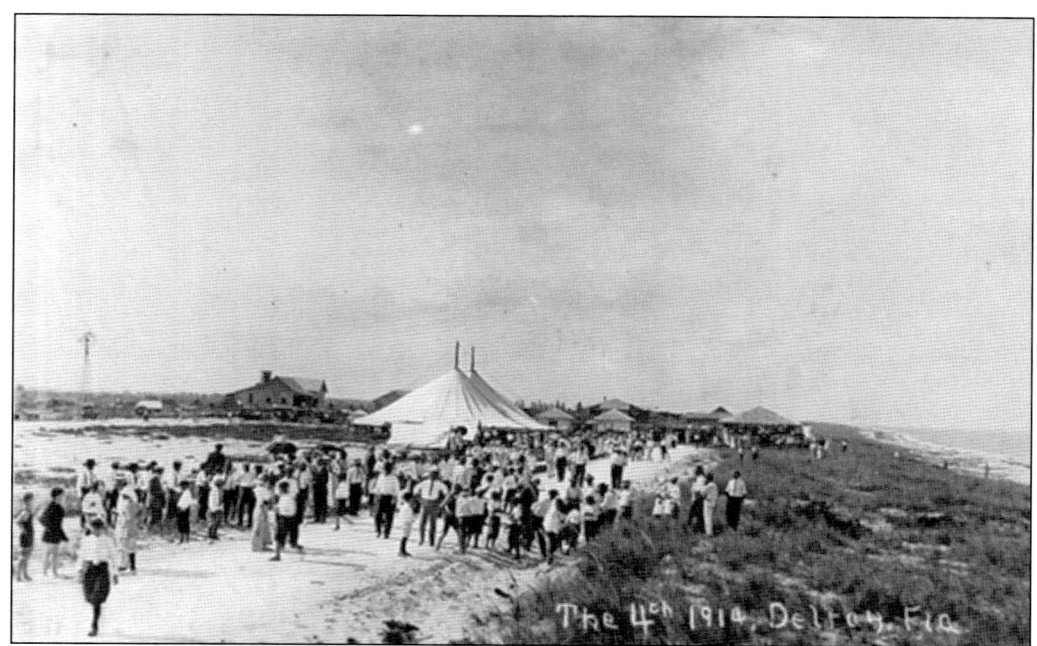

UNDER TENTS. A crowd gathers at the beach for a big Independence Day celebration after the 1914 parade. Based on this photograph, the dune area and beach grasses were still in place then. Notice the two large, white tents. The beach pavilion is overflowing with people. Someone has written on the back, "This is where they served free dinner. Most of the people are down by the pavilion."

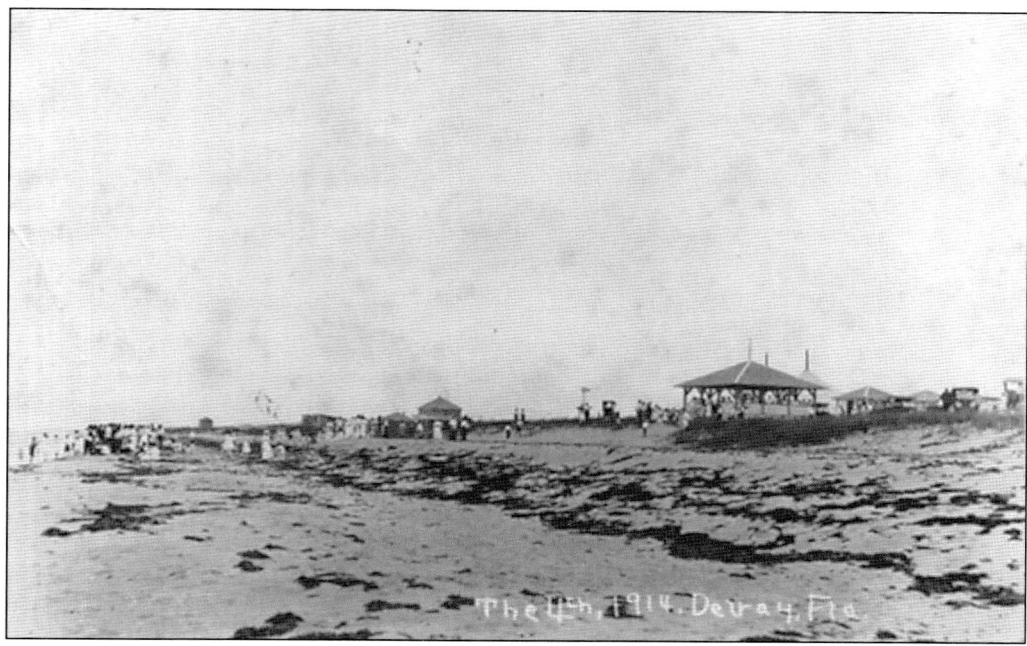

BEACH PAVILION. This photograph is another in the series taken on Independence Day in 1914. Here we see what is in the background above. At least two bathhouses were located near the pavilion, the larger building on the right.

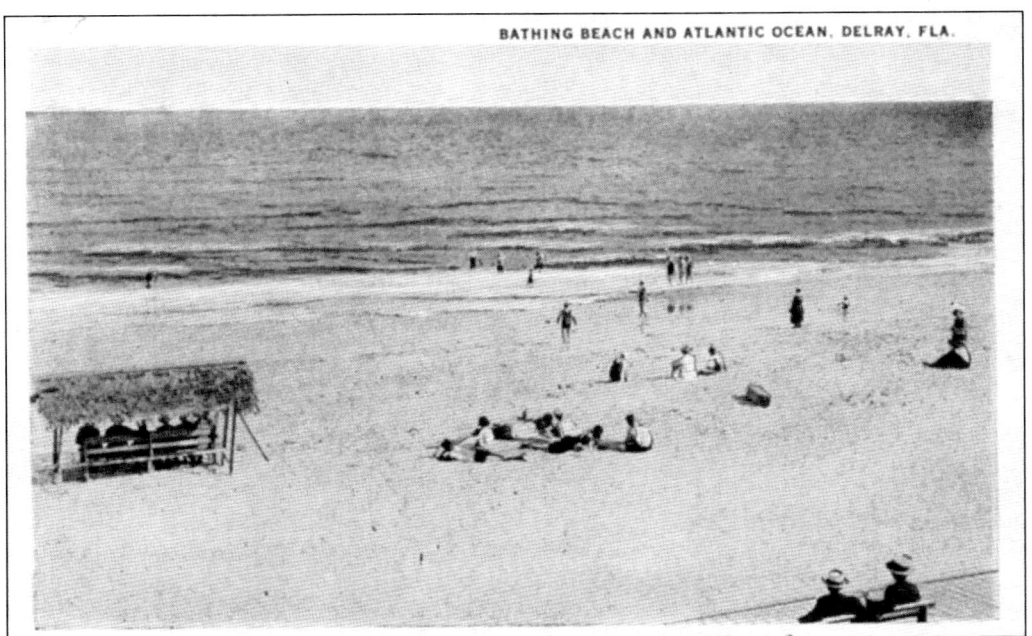

THE WIDE BEACH. This Beautiful Florida Series postcard was likely produced in the late 1920s. The two men in the right corner sit on the boardwalk wearing what appear to be suit coats. A group sits under a palm thatch shelter. Palm fronds were used for shade on the beach in those years.

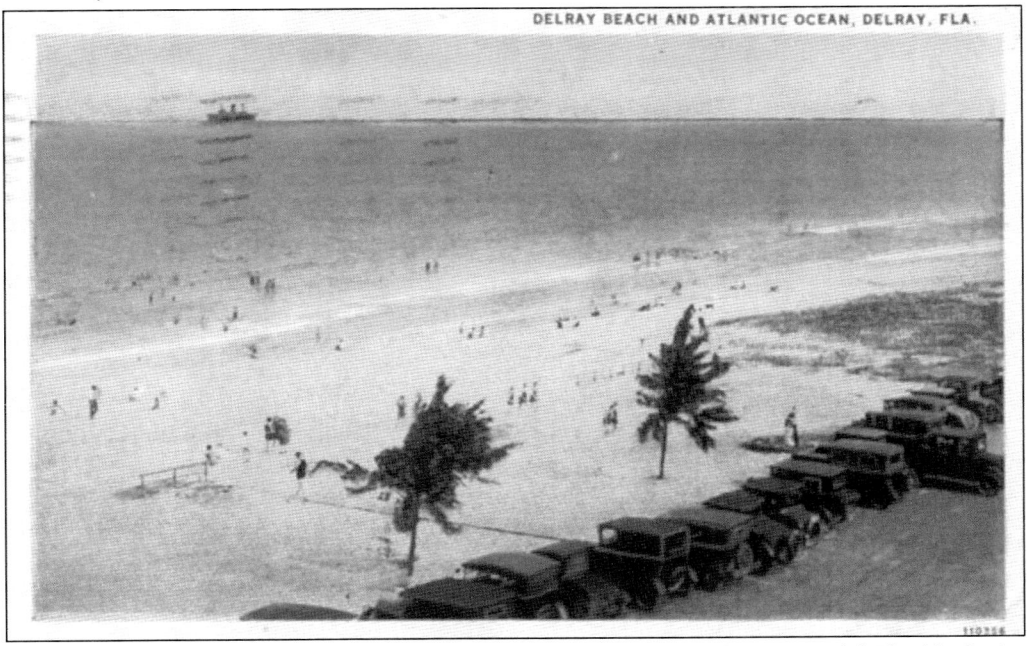

FLORIDA TRIP. Cars are lined up at the edge of the beach in this Beautiful Florida Series postcard. A few Australian pines have been planted. The card was mailed to Kennebunk, Maine, on February 13, 1930. The sender remarks that he has driven 2,000 miles so far on the trip and that fashionable Palm Beach is expensive. (Henry Higgins.)

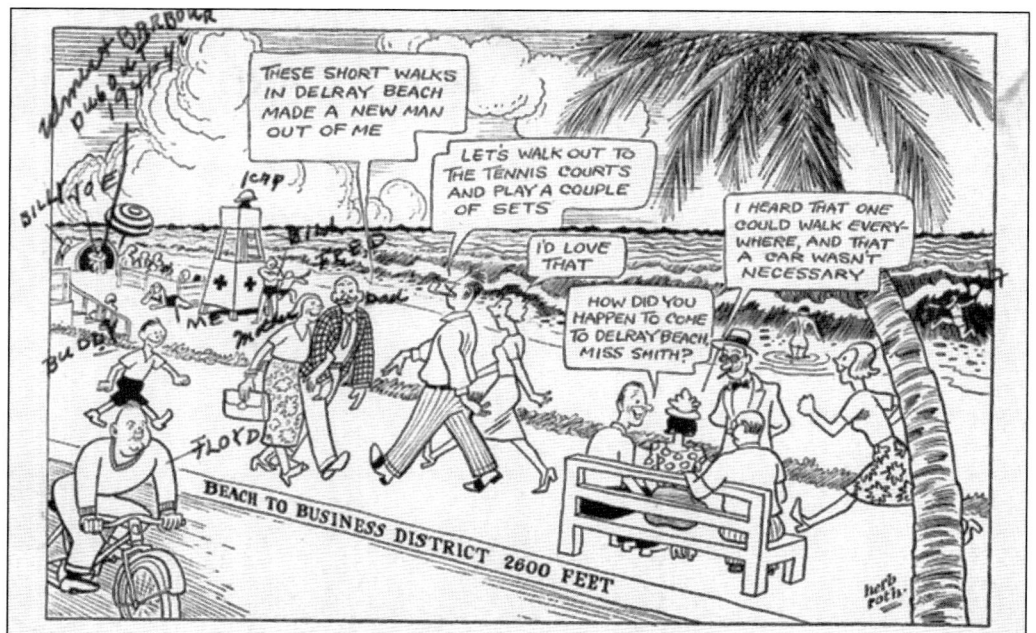

CARTOON CARD. Herb Roth's cartoons were published as a postcard series in the 1940s by the *Delray Beach News*. Roth documented the World War II years in Delray Beach through cartoons that were many times on the front page of the paper under the headline. He shared a studio with fellow artist H. T. Webster, whose cartoons usually appeared on the editorial page of the same paper.

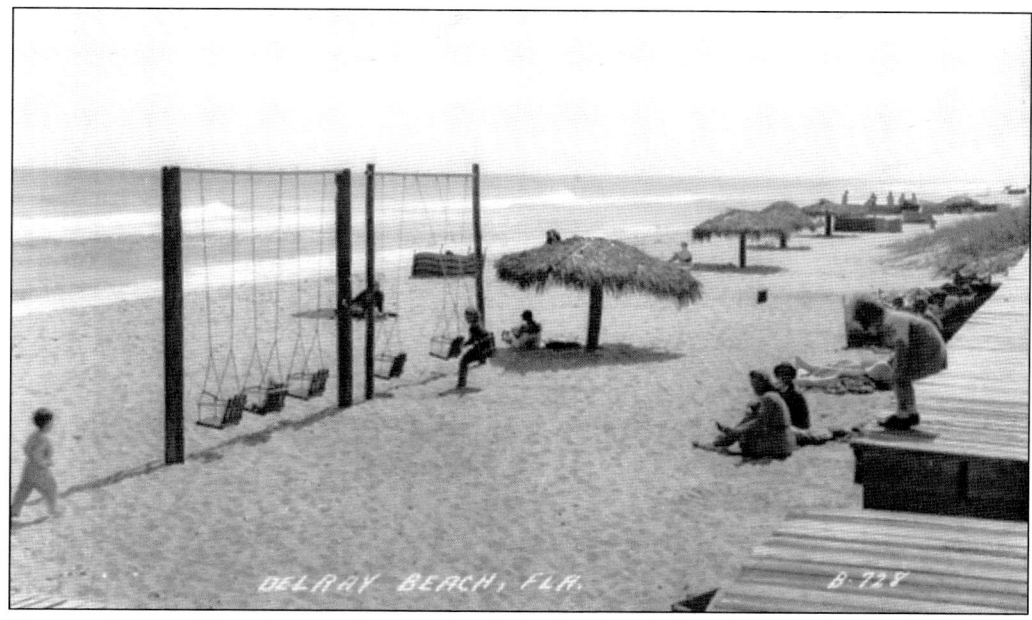

BEACH SCENE. Here is a good example of the handmade beach umbrellas populating the sand in the 1920s, 1930s, and 1940s. The umbrellas were made from dried saw palmetto, a predominant local native plant at the time. The boardwalk is visible in the right corner. (Henry Higgins.)

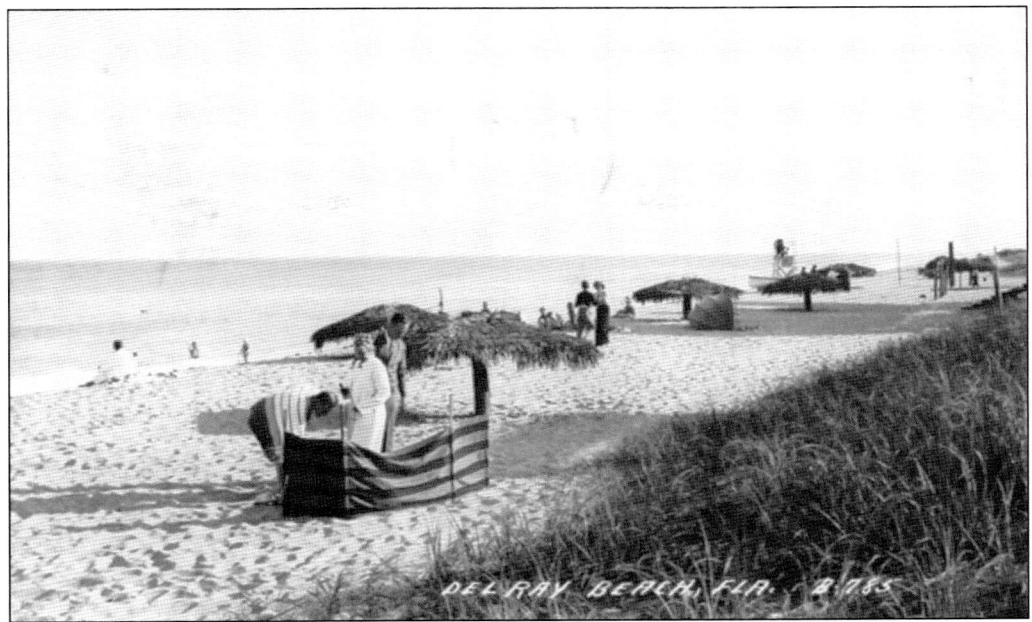

COOL BEACH. Beachgoers are dressed for a cool day in this postcard view, sent in February 1940. During that time, the big beach news in the local paper was that dogs living across the street had been stealing sunbathers' picnic lunches. (Henry Higgins.)

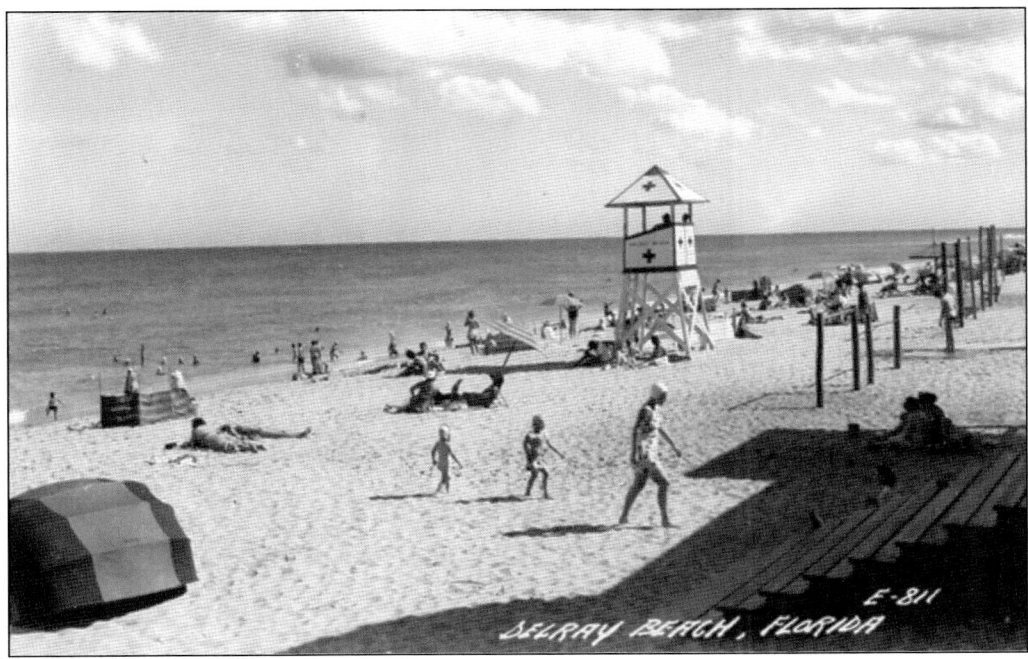

LIFEGUARD STAND. This undated postcard shows beachgoers around a lifeguard stand. The scene is believed to be from the 1940s. In 1948, two local firms paid the city $1,500 each for the privilege of renting auto-top, collapsible canvas wind breaks on the municipal beach. One such top is seen in the left corner. (Henry Higgins.)

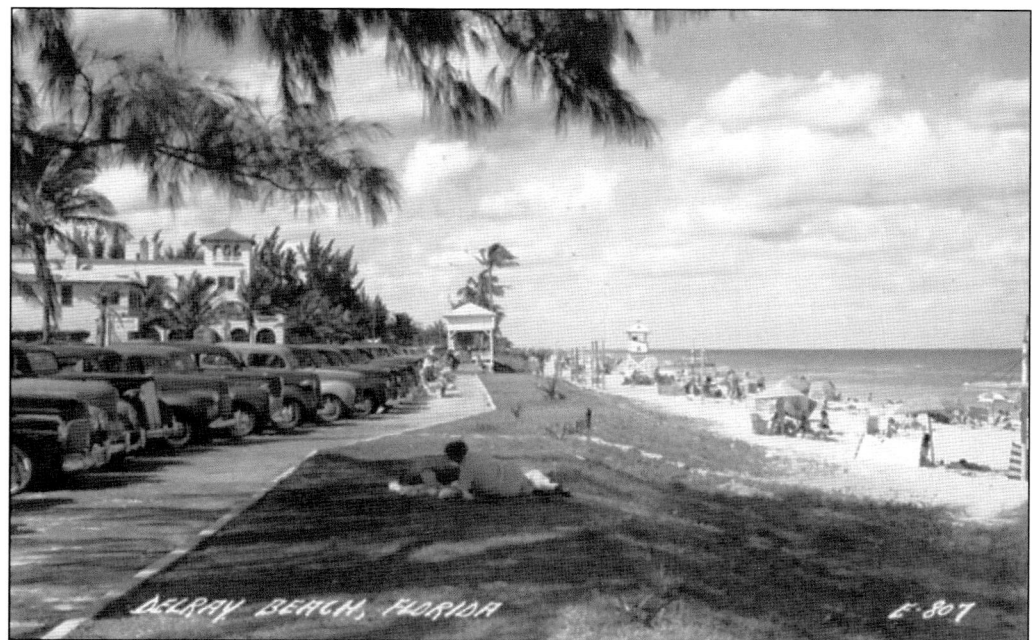

A DAY AT THE BEACH. This tranquil beach scene near the Seacrest Hotel in 1943 is a favorite photograph of people in town. Beachgoers crowd the sand. The message begins, "Dear Ma & Pa, I was in Delray today. It's a small city just 8 miles from Boca Raton," and ends, "Take care of yourselves, Irene."

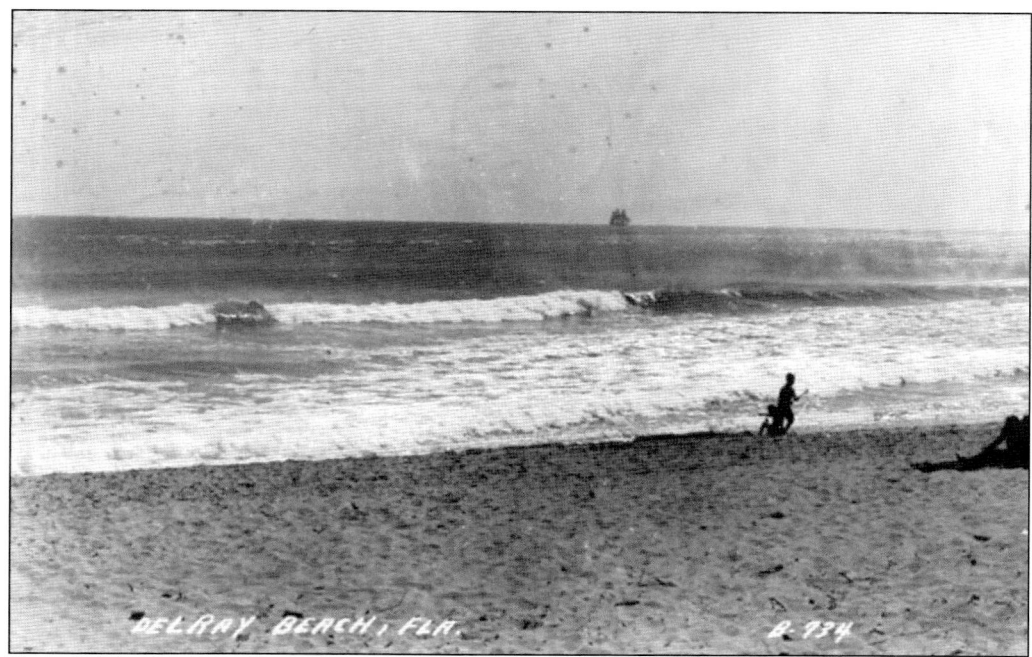

BEAUTIFUL BEACH. On this 1946 card, the sender writes, "Yes, this is still here and as beautiful as ever. Really is good to see my friends here once again. The children have grown so much and the old people look older." (Henry Higgins.)

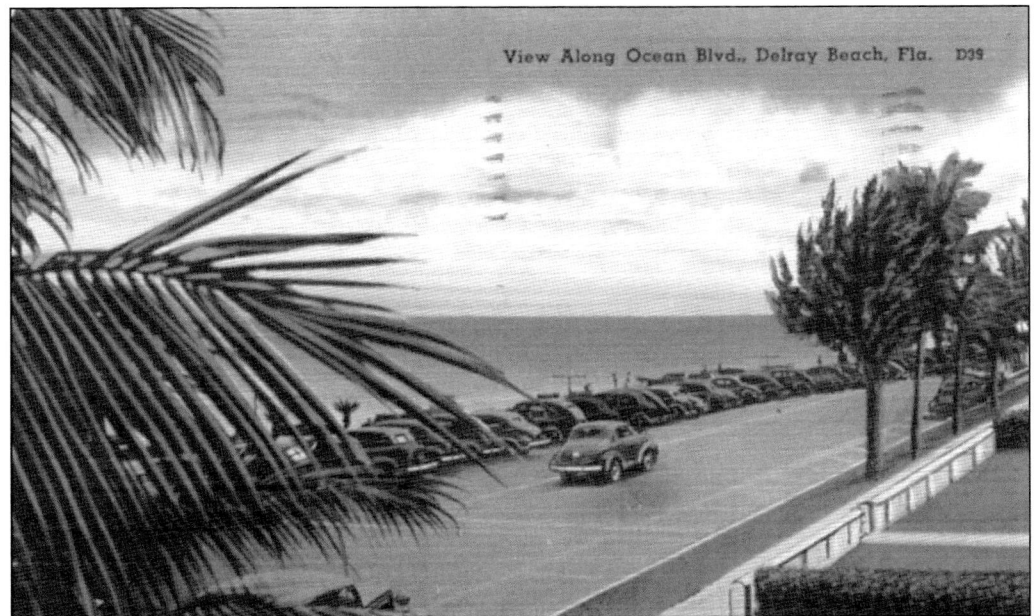

OCEAN BOULEVARD. In 1945, Randall Davis of Delray Beach, who was then living in Washington, D.C., received this postcard from his mother. It was published by the Eli Witt Tobacco Company of West Palm Beach.

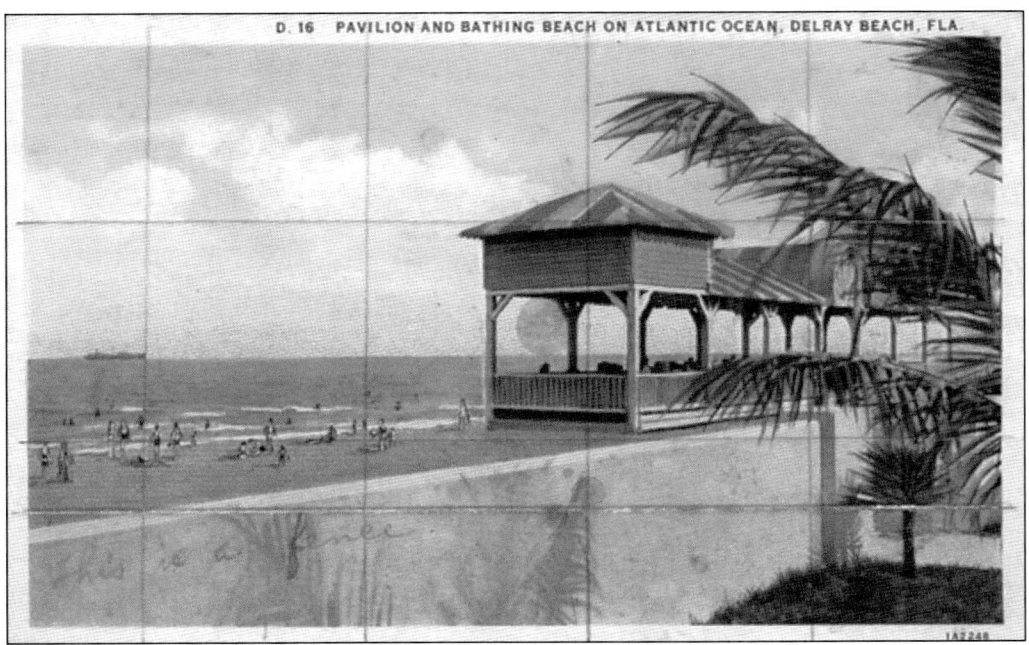

PAVILION AND BATHING BEACH. This postcard from the Beautiful Florida Series presents a good view of the appealing beach pavilion that existed between 1928 and 1947. The pavilion was constructed by respected Delray Beach builder Irwin J. Sinks. Unfortunately, it was washed away in the 1947 hurricane. Someone has written, "This is a fence." It is actually a wall in front of the Seacrest Hotel. (Henry Higgins.)

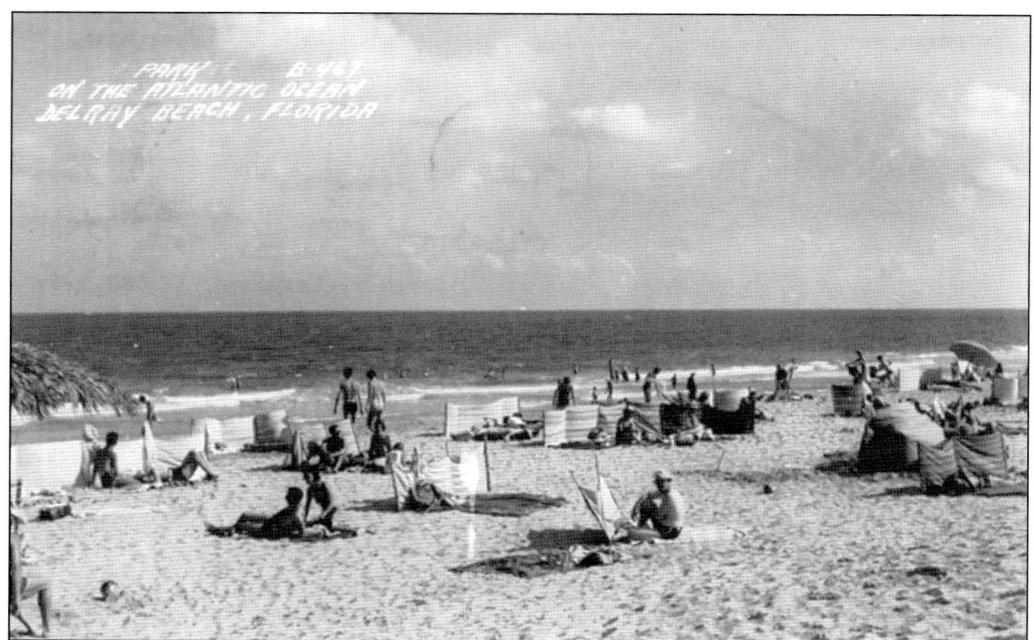

SUNNING AT THE BEACH. The sender, writing beautifully in purple ink, penned this formal message: "Your letter is received. I shall reply and furnish the material you requested in a few days." The postcard was sent from Delray Beach on March 22, 1941. (Henry Higgins.)

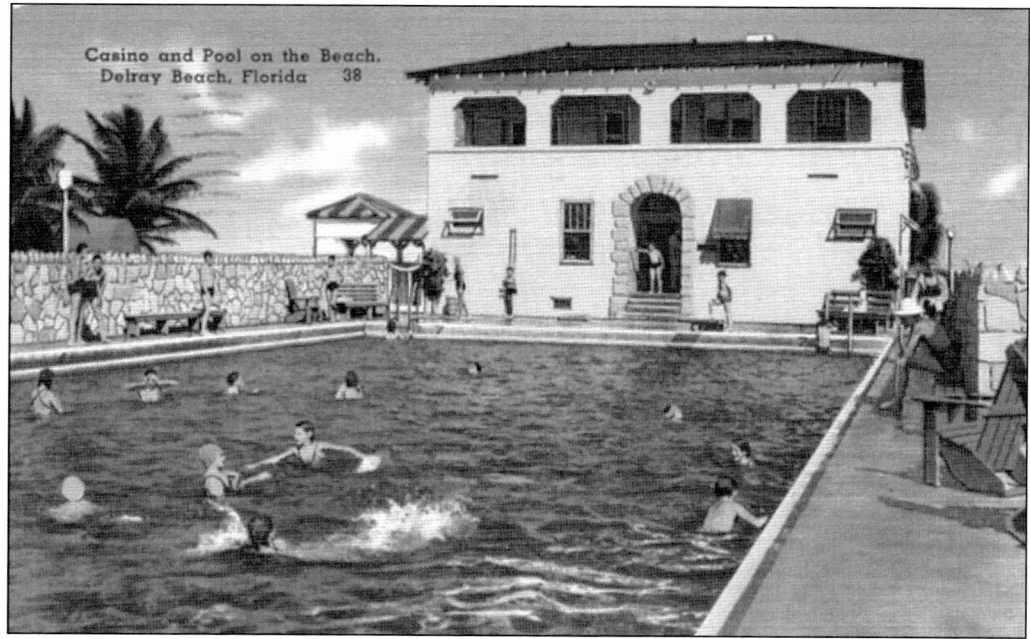

CASINO AND POOL. Postmarked March 12, 1940, this card shows the casino and pool. Construction on the casino began in 1934 through a project federally funded by the WPA during the Franklin D. Roosevelt presidency. After completion in 1935, the first lifeguard and the first pool manager were hired. That same year, the Delray Seahawks competitive swim team was formed. (Henry Higgins.)

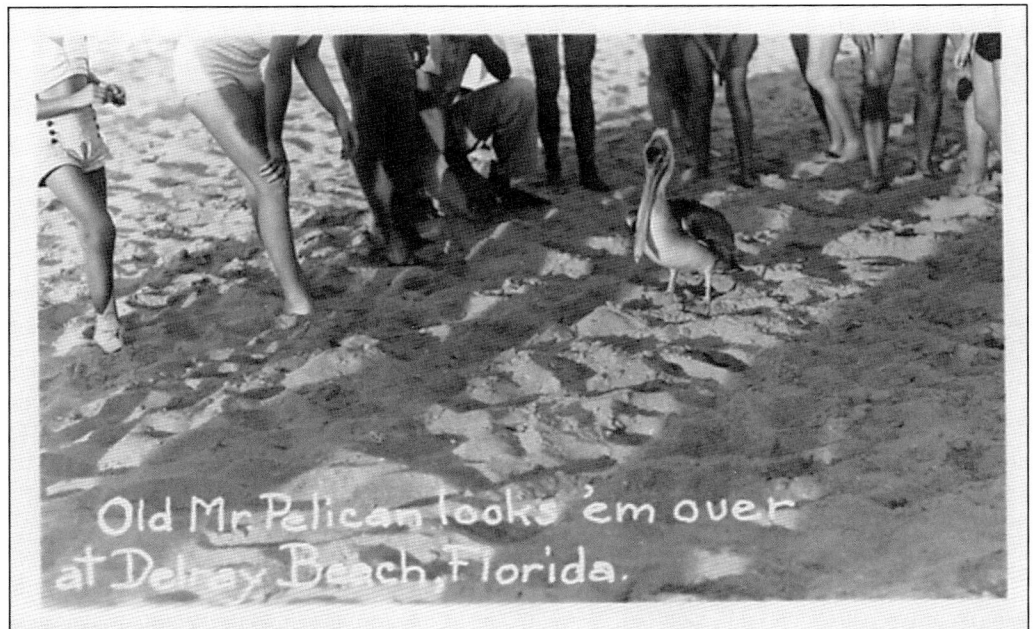

OLD MR. PELICAN. Bathers pose with a pelican around 1948. In 1943, a law was passed stipulating that bathing suit clad pedestrians were not allowed west of the Intracoastal Waterway. In 1947, lifeguards rescued 75 newly hatched turtles that were headed toward the street rather than the ocean. (Henry Higgins.)

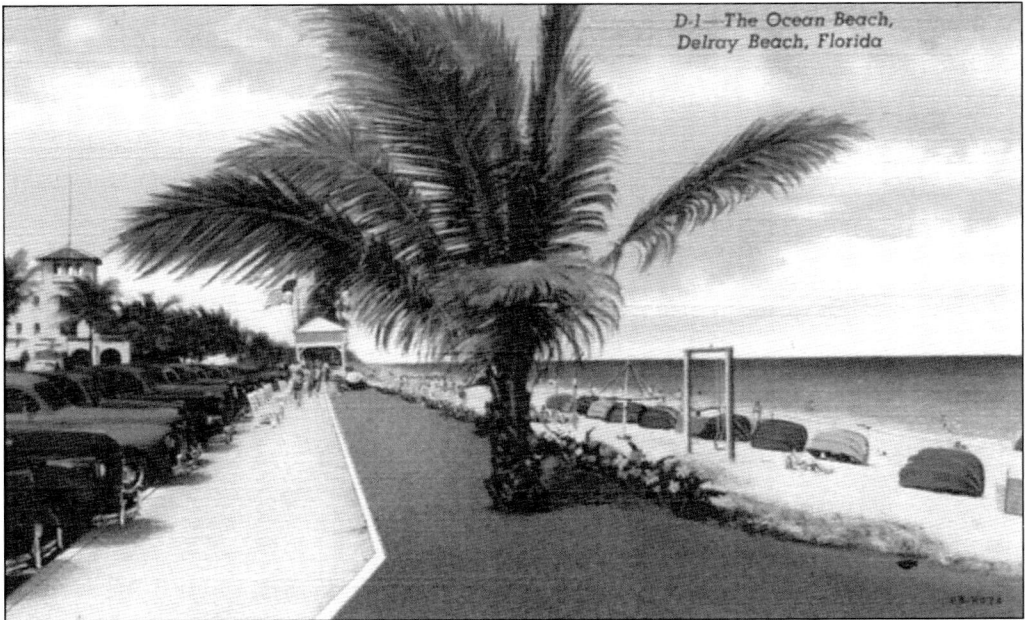

THE OCEAN BEACH. This hand-tinted linen card, produced by the FEC News Company, provides a long view of the municipal beach before 1947. Here the thatched umbrellas have been replaced by colorful auto-top wind breaks.

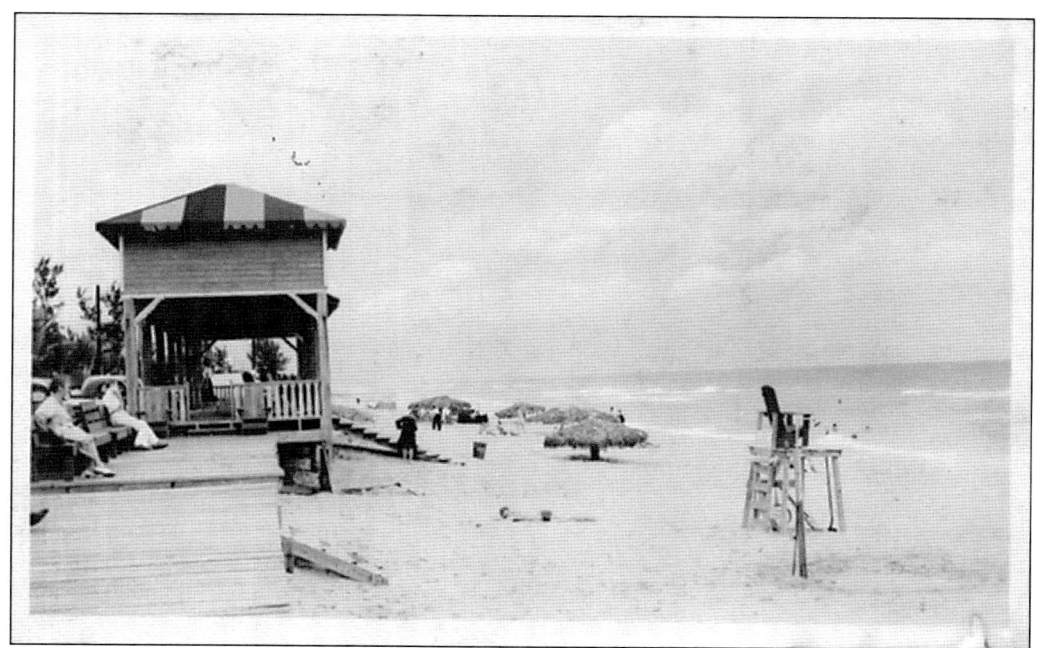

LIFEGUARD STAND. This view gives one last look at the pavilion from the south end. Since there were no lifeguards before 1935 and this lifeguard stand looks as if it is an early one—just a simple stand with a chair on top—the date is estimated to be the late 1930s.

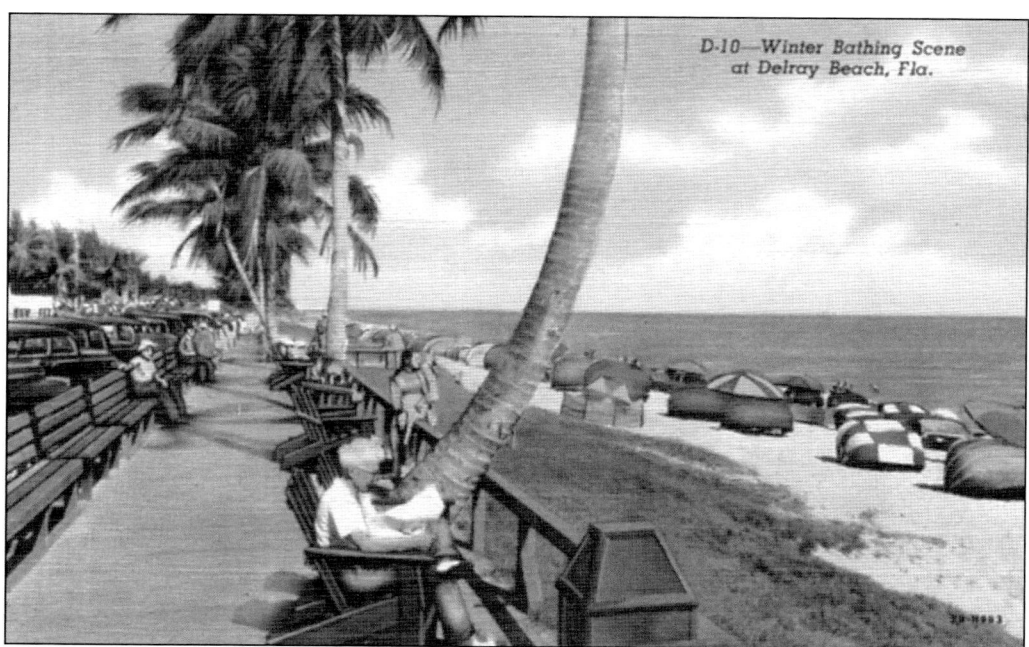

BOARD WALK. Delray's beach boardwalk is depicted in this pretty, hand-tinted linen card from the FEC News Company. The beautiful municipal beach was threatened by the September 19, 1947, hurricane when the pavilion and dunes washed away. The sea consumed one half of Ocean Boulevard, necessitating the rebuilding of the road.

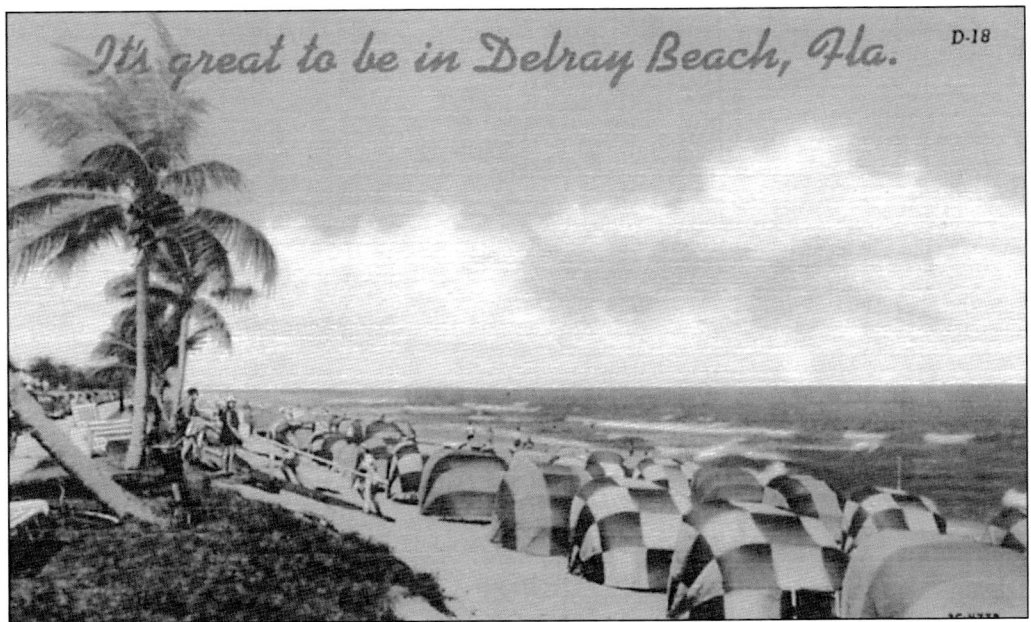

IT'S GREAT. A closer view of the army of colorful wind breaks is provided on this hand-tinted linen card, also produced by the FEC News Company of West Palm Beach. In order to reduce crowding, the city council voted in 1945 that any privately owned structures on the beach would be removed. Concessionaires were banned from the beach in 1947.

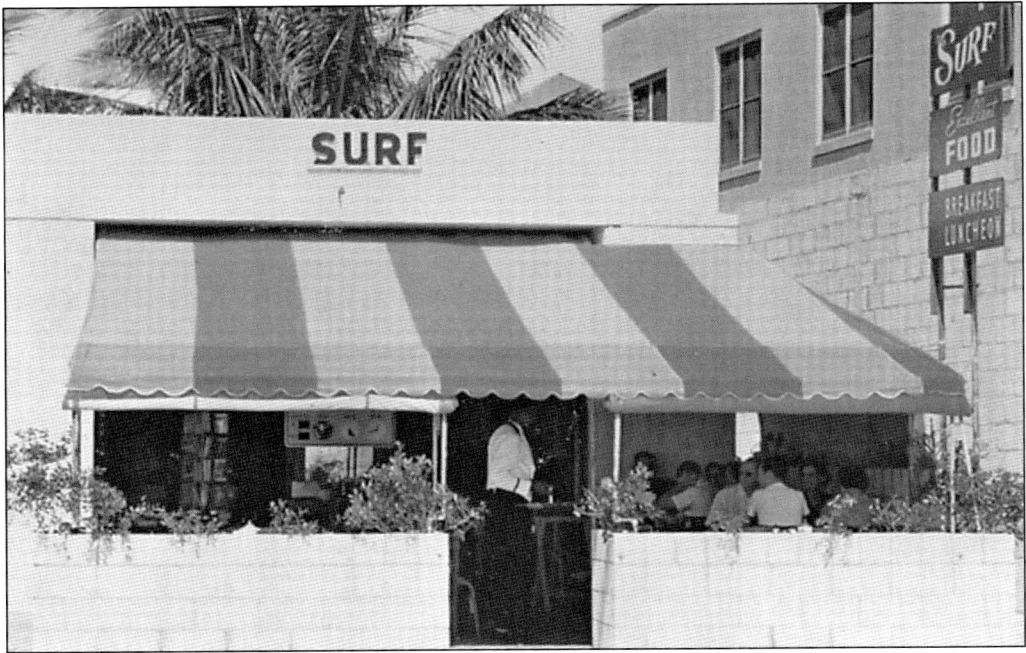

THE SURF. This pleasant beachside restaurant was located in the first block south of Atlantic Avenue on Ocean Boulevard. The management encouraged patrons to enjoy the patio overlooking the ocean. The Surf was known for its excellent food and outstanding service. This print was created by Helen O'Brien of O'Brien Studios in Boca Raton. (Henry Higgins.)

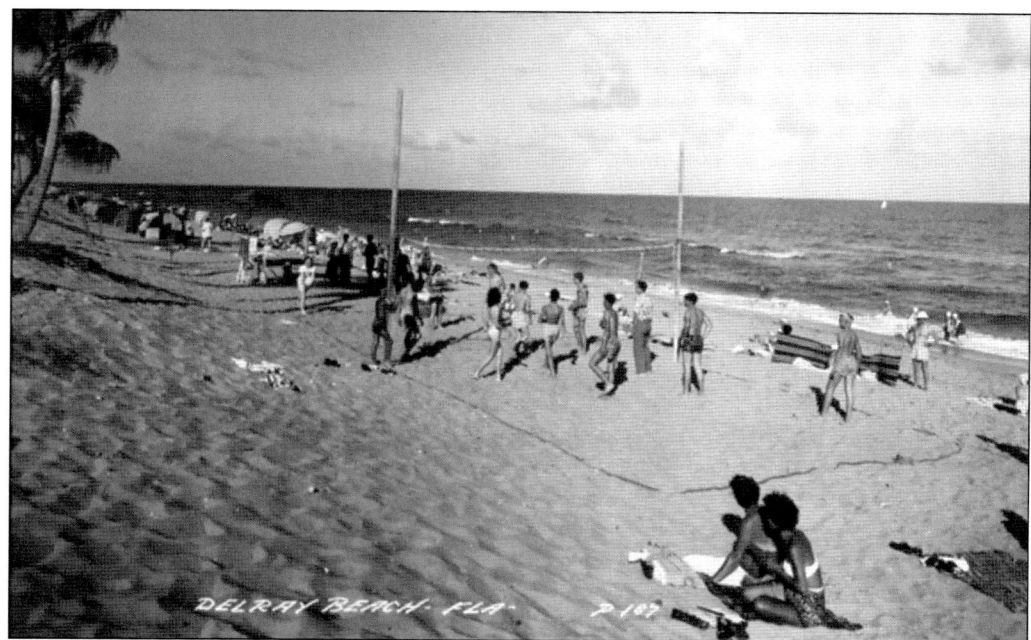

VOLLEY BALL. A group plays volleyball at the beach in an idyllic scene. The tall wooden posts seen on this and other cards were used to hold volleyball nets, swings, and other beach games. The first such beach equipment was furnished by the city in 1939. (Henry Higgins.)

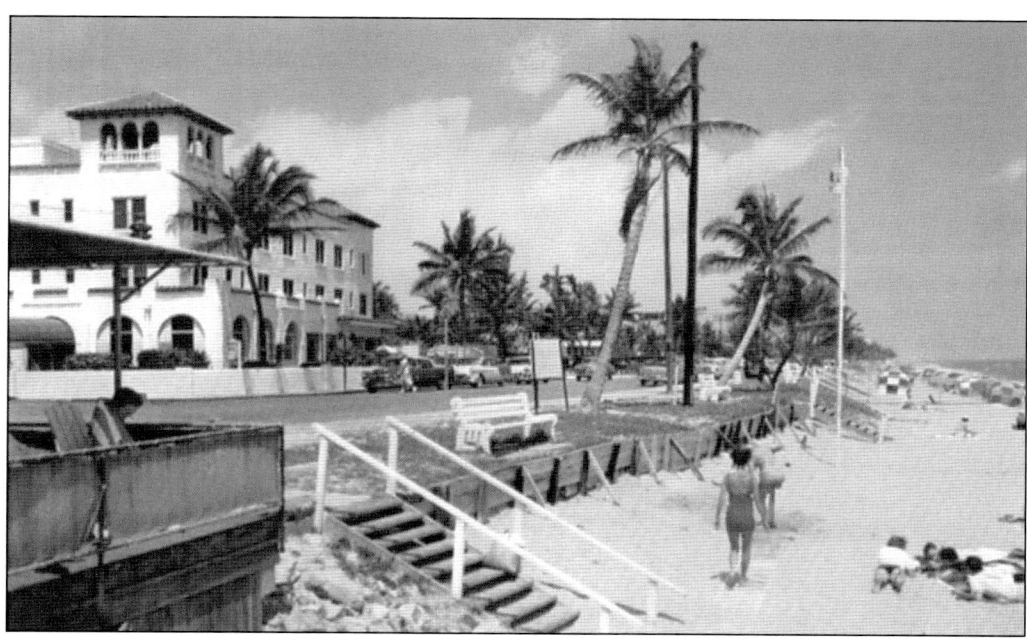

SUN BATHED SANDS. In this September 29, 1956, view, one can see the replacement for the pavilion destroyed by the 1947 hurricane. The temporary-looking structure was built of wood, metal, and canvas. Cars are lined up in front of the Seacrest Hotel. Note the wood seawall; the beach seems to have washed closer to A1A. The beach would continue to erode until alleviated by restoration projects in the 1980s.

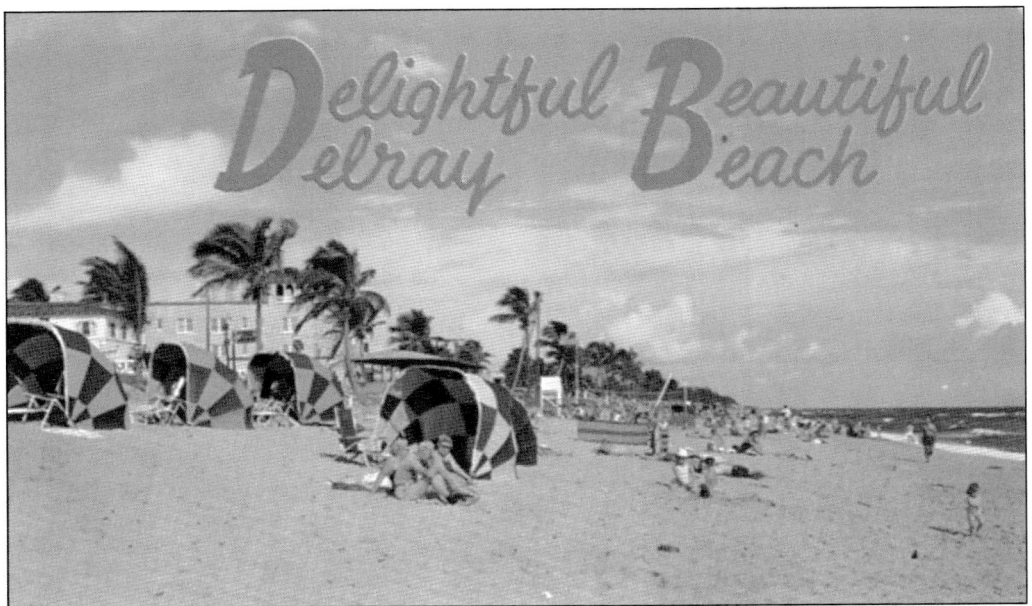

DELIGHTFUL DELRAY. Wind breaks are in place for the sunbathers. The Seacrest Hotel appears in the distance, along with a lifeguard stand and a volleyball net. An American flag flaps in the breeze from the southeast. The postcard text reads, "The beach at Delray Beach, Florida—Surf bathing at its very best." (Henry Higgins.)

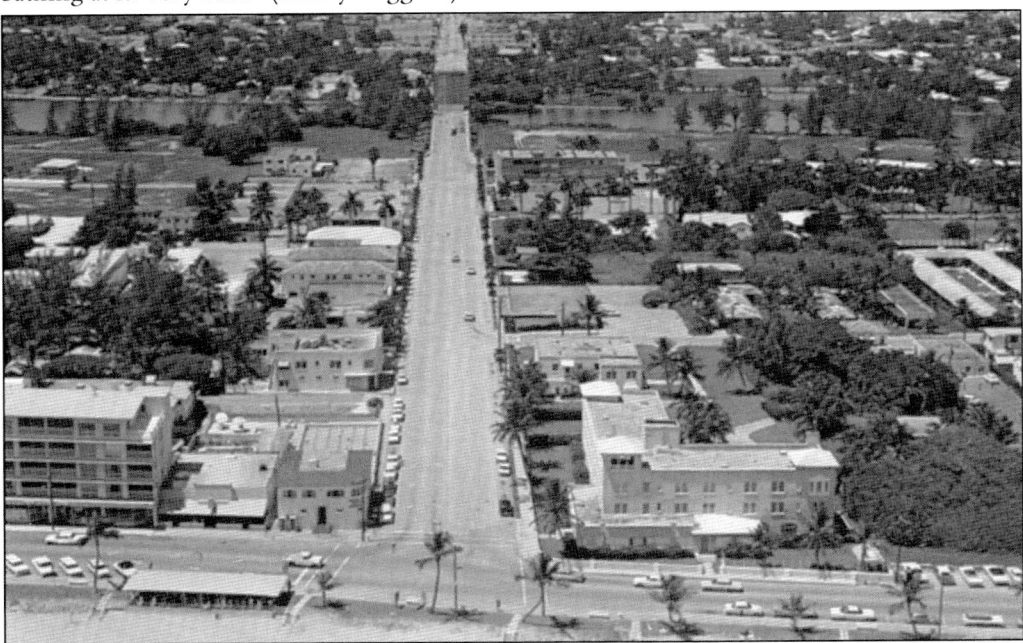

AERIAL VIEW. This photograph, taken by Larry Witt, was published as a card by the D&M Post Cards and Records Company of West Palm Beach. Although the card is undated, it is possible to fix an approximate date from the buildings. At the left edge are the Monmouth Co-op Apartments, built at 6–8 South Ocean Boulevard in the early 1960s. The adjacent municipal casino and pool, at 2 South Ocean Boulevard, were demolished in the mid-1970s.

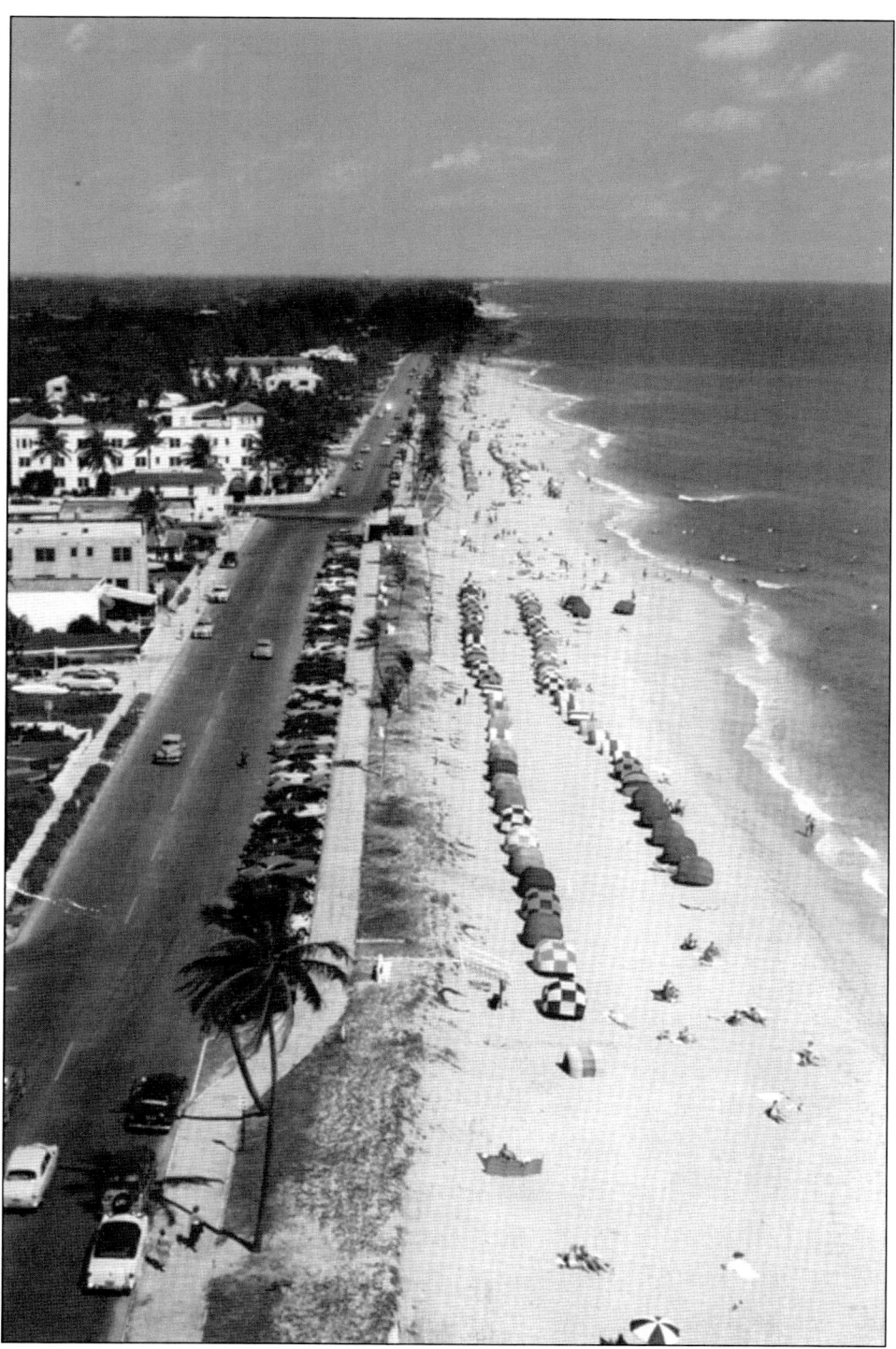

OVERSIZE HELICOPTER VIEW. This oversized postcard of Delray's municipal beach in the 1950s was mailed to the historical society by Jim and Flo Nowlin on June 30, 2007. An Ektechrome card, it was published by the FEC News Company of West Palm Beach.

Eight

MID-CENTURY YEARS
1941–1971

The World War II years and the ambiguous 1950s brought increasing and continuing change and growth. Boca Raton Airfield, a secret radar training center, was quickly built by the federal government on the land south of Delray that had been the site of a Japanese farming colony since 1904. Delray, a larger town than Boca Raton at the time, had attracted Japanese colonists in the past just as it would later lure military personnel from the airfield. They came to Delray Beach looking for houses and rooms to rent, as well as entertainment in the restaurants, theaters, USO clubs, and the bowling arcade.

Some of those who became acquainted with Delray Beach when in military service returned to live in town permanently. African Americans coming home from the war had little tolerance for the old segregation laws and continued to work toward equal rights. The 1950s and 1960s saw civil rights struggles for equal pay for teachers, access to the municipal beach, and the integration of schools and the city golf course and pool. At the beginning of the 1969–1970 school year, Seacrest High School, established in 1949 after the old Delray High School was closed, and George Washington Carver High School officially began the transition into the integrated Atlantic High School. During this period, building designs were changing to the clean lines of the Streamline Moderne style favored by many architects and builders. By 1970, the official census population of Delray Beach was 19,915.

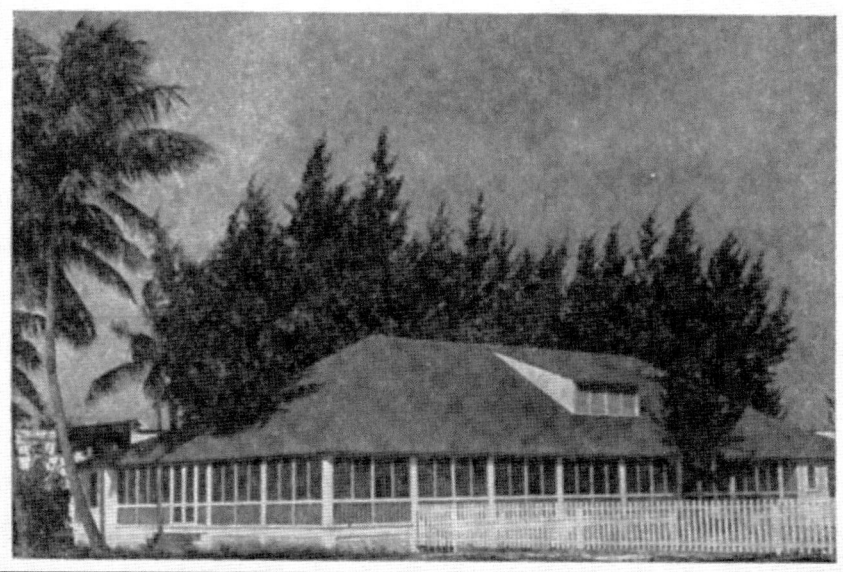

U. S. O. CLUB, DELRAY BEACH, FLORIDA

THE USO. During World War II, the USO Club was wholeheartedly adopted by the citizens of Delray Beach. The local USO was established in 1942—first using the facilities of the Woman's Club and American Legion Hall before moving to the old Booster Hall in 1943. Almost 98,000 hours were donated by 483 volunteers to operate the club.

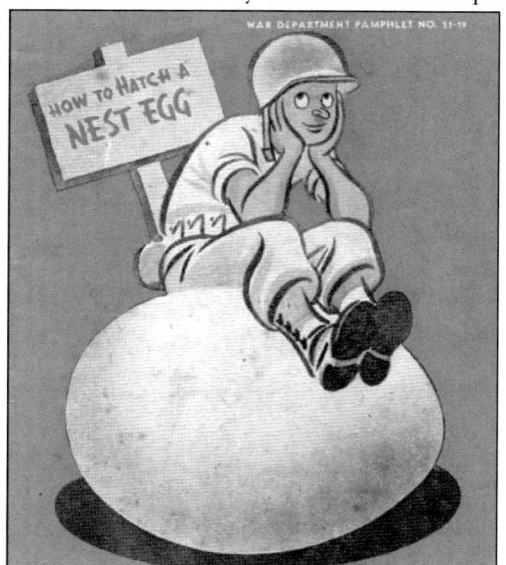
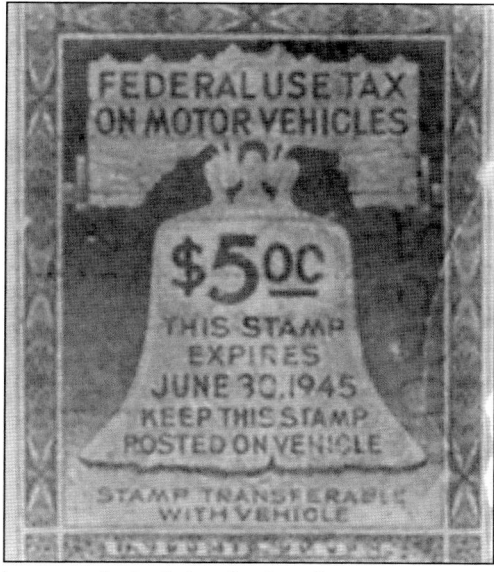

NEST EGG. This little booklet on the left offering practical advice for handling money was distributed to service personnel by the War Department. Each section is illustrated by a cartoon-like drawing. According to the booklet, interest paid on a Soldiers' Deposit savings plan was four percent. Readers are advised to buy war bonds, and different classes of allotments are explained. The booklet employs the usual jokes about liquid assets and warnings against gambling and "Allotment Annies." **TAX STAMP.** The $5 Federal Use Tax on motor vehicles was transferable with each vehicle. This stamp, pictured on the right, expired on June 30, 1945.

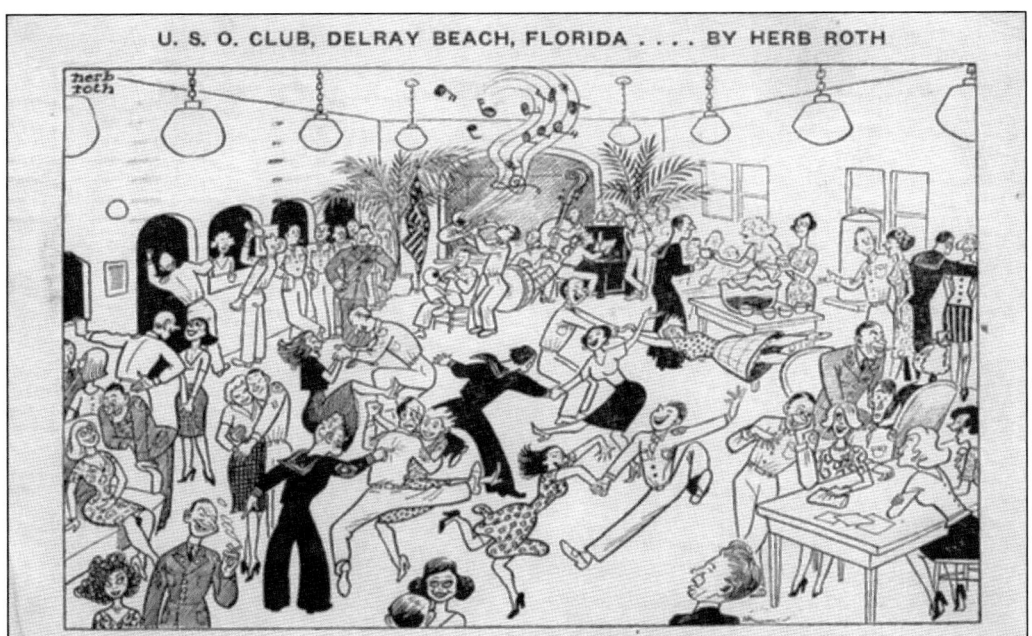

USO Club Dance. This lively cartoon depicts a dance at the club, complete with a live band, punch bowl, and the jitterbug. Herb Roth, a favorite seasonal resident, was lively himself and likable with a wicked sense of humor. Many times this excellent illustrator drew himself into the cartoons. (Henry Higgins.)

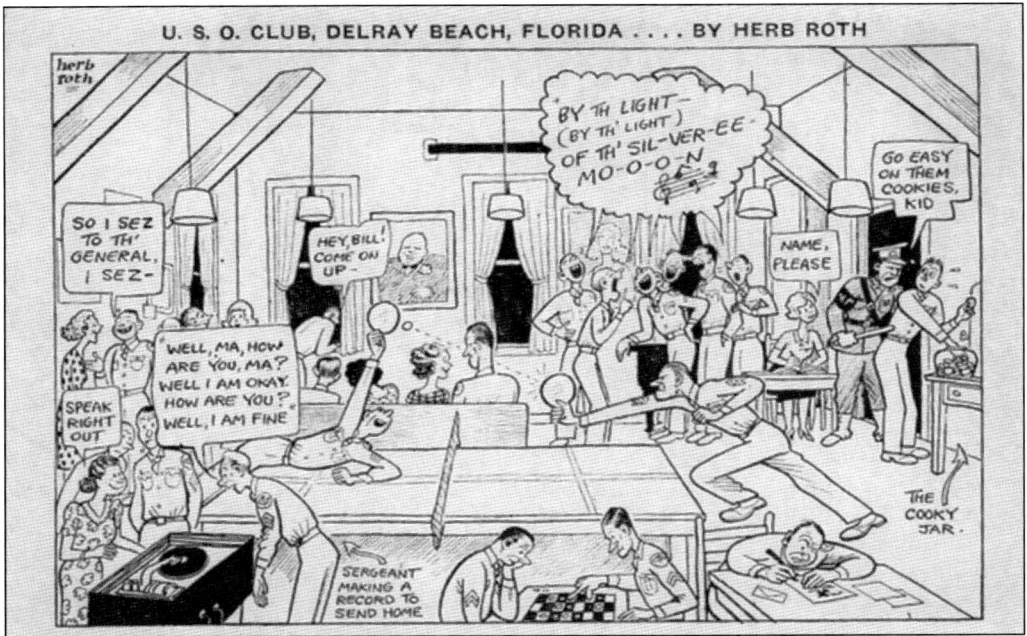

USO Cartoon. Herb Roth got it right in his cartoon. There were all kinds of activities at the USO Club during the World War II years, including chatting with the hostesses, playing games like ping pong and checkers, and eating snacks. (Henry Higgins.)

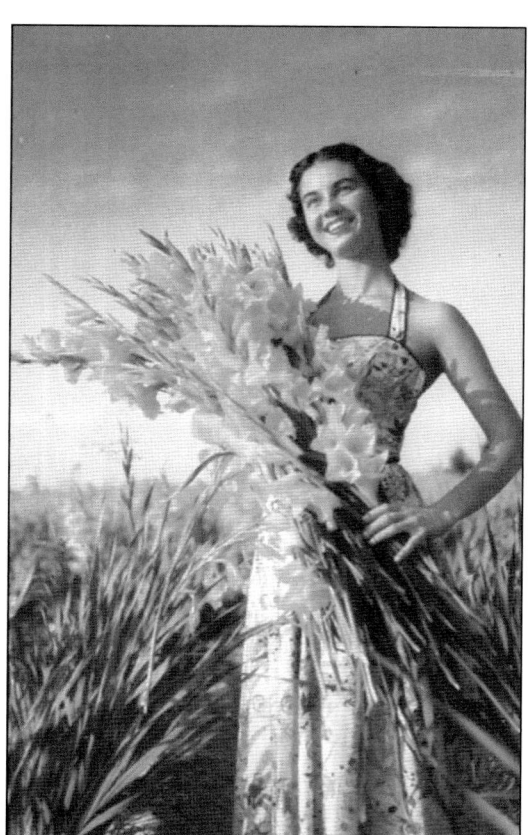

GLADIOLI FESTIVAL. Shirley Craige was crowned queen of the South Florida Gladioli Festival in 1953. This "Mardi Gras of Flowers" was held in Delray Beach from 1947 to 1953, when it abruptly ended in spite of seeming popularity and success. This photograph was taken in the fields of flowers surrounding Delray Beach. Hank Cohen's Press Bureau published the card to advertise the 1954 festival.

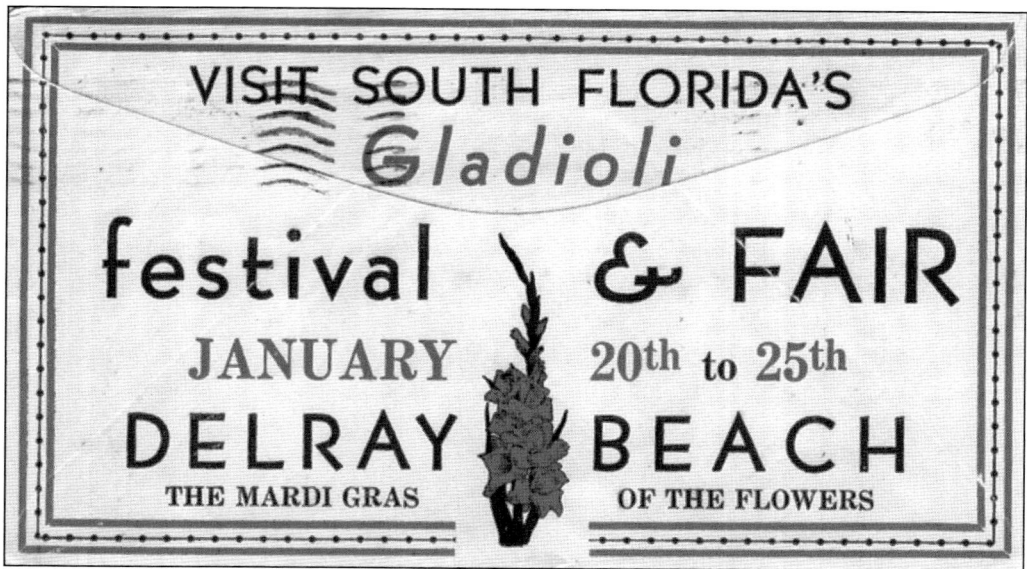

FESTIVAL ADVERTISEMENT. This attractive envelope was mailed on January 2, 1947, to Henry J. Sterling in West Palm Beach, Florida, as a clever way to advertise the festival and fair. When the festival was discontinued, townspeople missed it so much that a successor called the Delray Affair was started several years later. (Henry Higgins.)

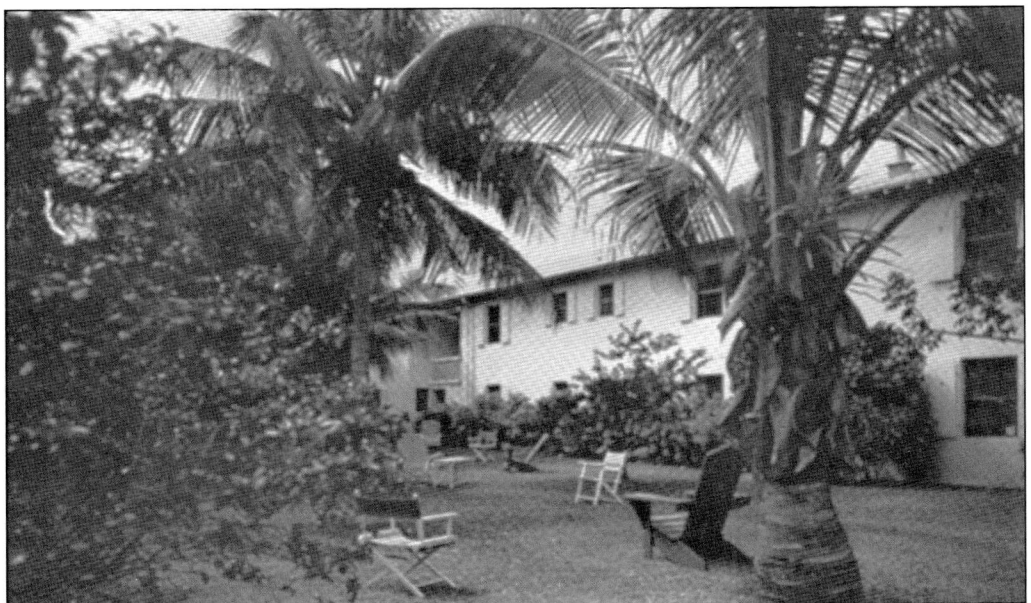

SUNDY APARTMENTS. For many years, two daughters of Delray's first mayor, Addie and Sadie Sundy, managed the Sundy Apartments in back of their home. This Press Bureau photograph provides a view of the gardens. The Sundy home is now a charming restaurant. The apartments have been renovated into an inn, and a nonprofit botanical garden has been established on the grounds.

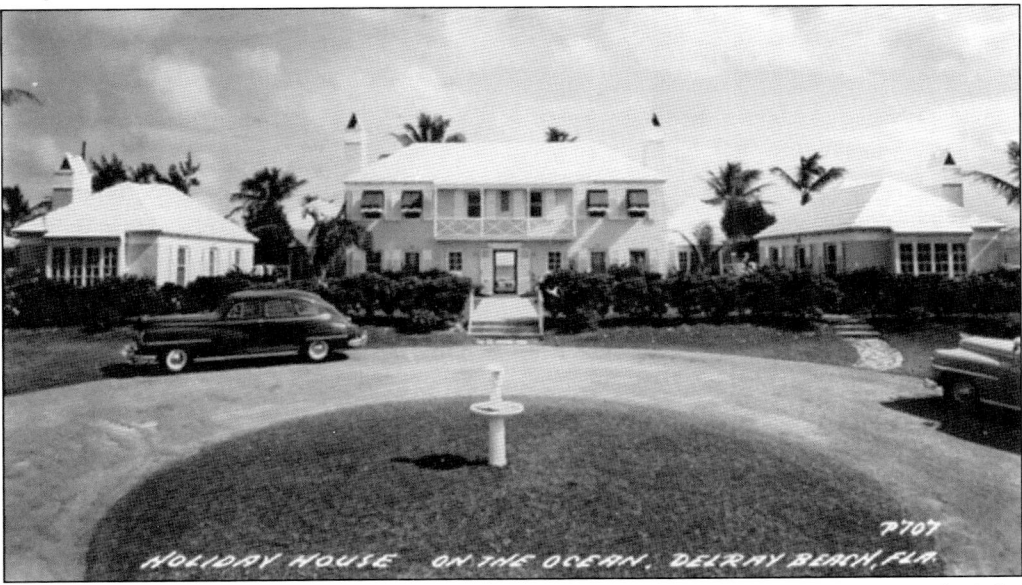

HOLIDAY HOUSE. The architecture and setting of the handsome Holiday House evoked the ambience of upscale Caribbean islands. The small resort was located south of Delray Beach at 2575 South Ocean Boulevard (Highway A1A). Josephine Johnson served as the manager. Holiday House was built before the 1949 town incorporation of Highland Beach. The town is now predominantly a high-density condominium community. This card is postmarked 1953. (Henry Higgins.)

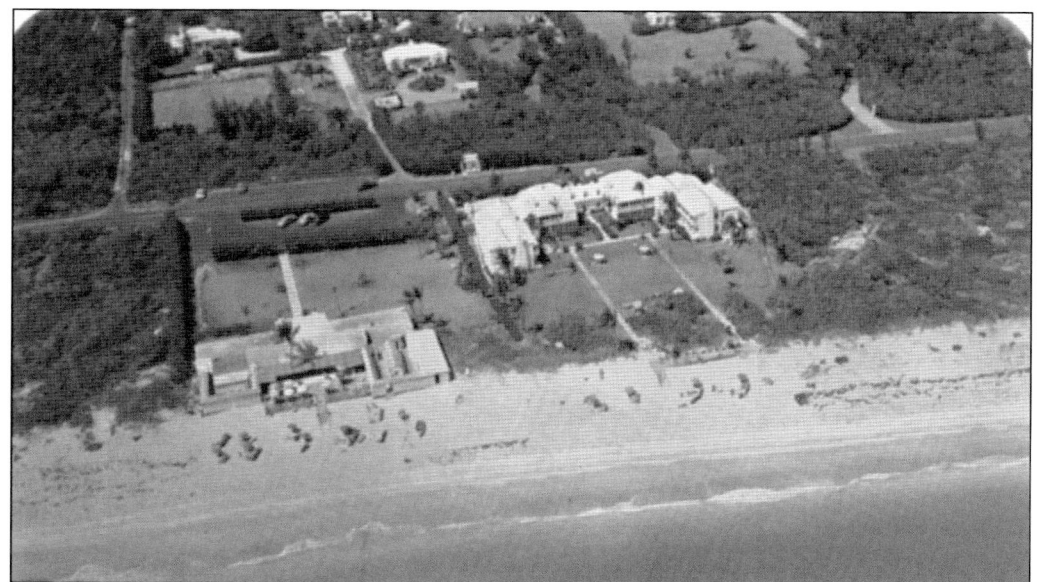

JAMAICA SQUARE. Jamaica Square and Gulf Stream Bath and Tennis Club at Gulf Stream, Florida, were photographed from the air for this postcard. The text describes, "A unique colony of residences. . . . Completely furnished. Daily maid service. . . . W. T. Jebb, owner-manager." Built in 1939, Jamaica Square was the first rental property in Gulf Stream. Well-known architect Howard Major designed the buildings in a British Colonial or West Indies style. (Henry Higgins.)

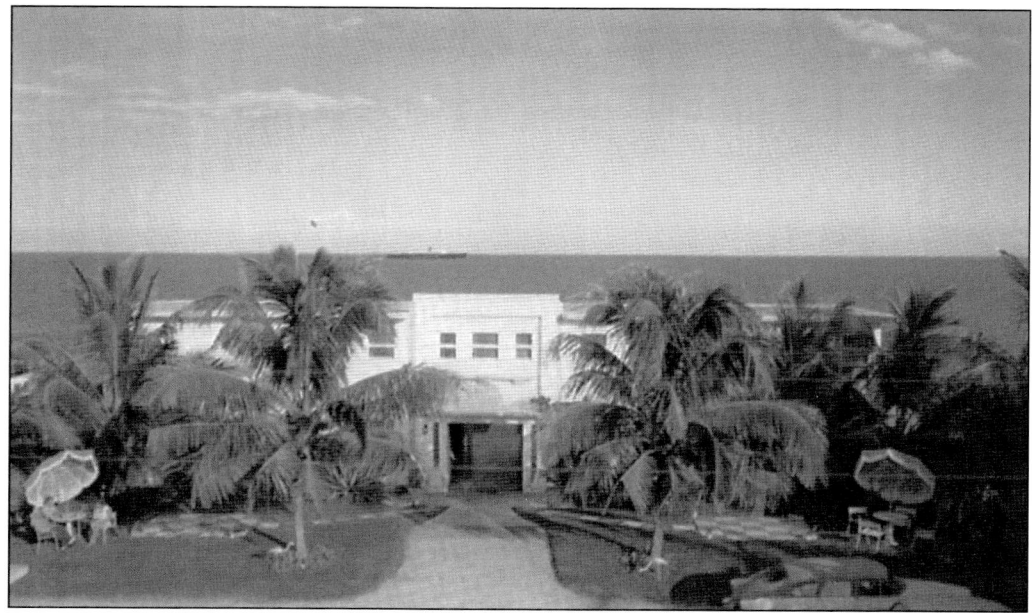

DREAM HOUSE APARTMENTS. This beautiful setting was located at 4217 South Ocean Boulevard in Highland Beach, just south of Delray Beach. As the population of Delray and the surrounding area grew, the resort life spread south of Delray to Highland Beach and north into Gulf Stream, Ocean Ridge, and Briny Breezes. At one time, some of these areas had Delray Beach postal addresses. (Janet DeVries.)

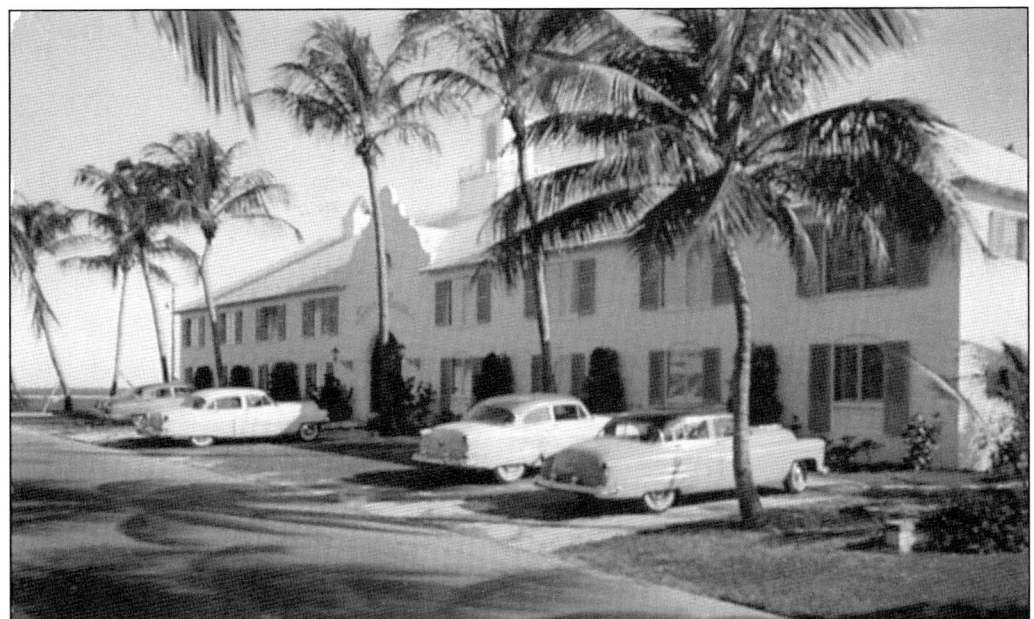

DOVER HOUSE. At the corner of South Ocean Boulevard and Miramar Drive, the Dover House displays architecture of a pleasing Resort Revival style. This card is postmarked Palm Beach, February 14, 1957. The sender requests information from a friend about "a climbing rose that blooms all summer." (Henry Higgins.)

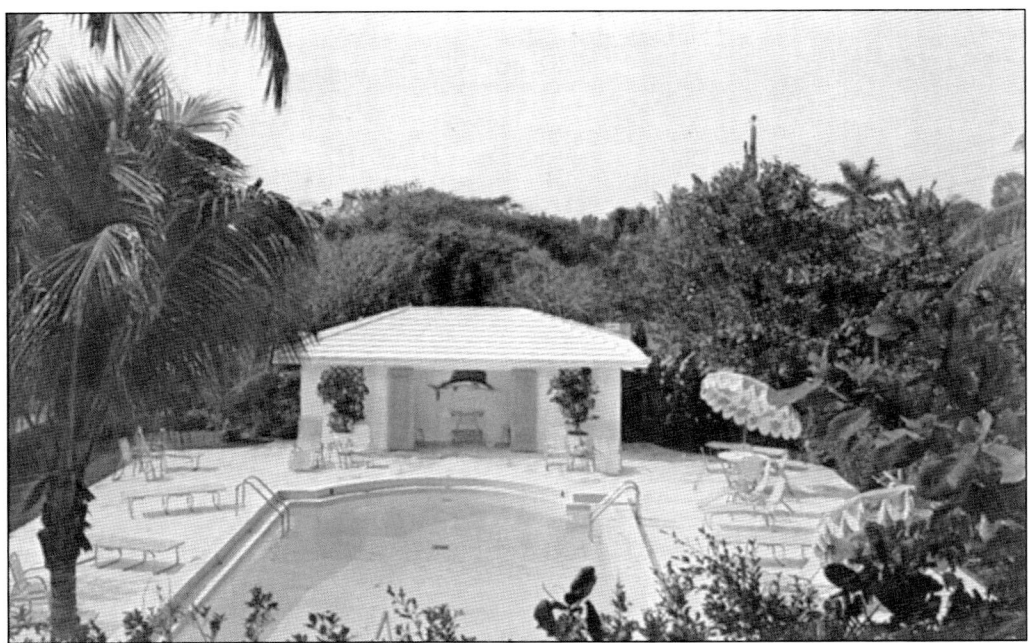

THE DOVER HOUSE POOL. In the message, Fred and Flo complain that the weather has been cloudy and windy for 14 straight days. January 14, 1966, is the postmark date. The stamp price has gone up to 4¢. (Henry Higgins.)

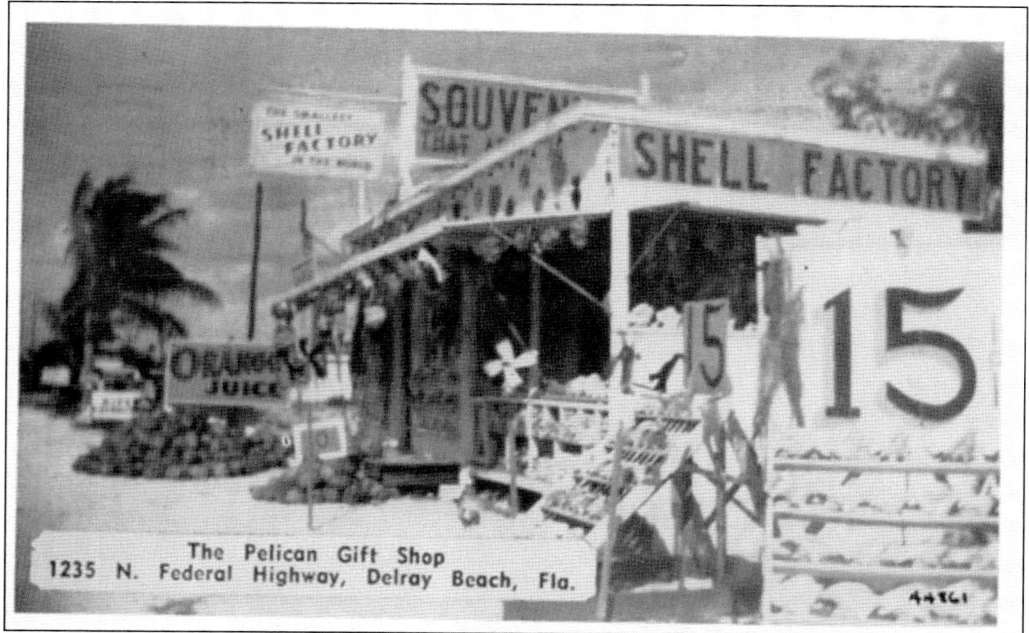

PELICAN GIFT SHOP. The Pelican Gift Shop, located on U.S. Highway 1, advertises that it is the "smallest shell factory in the world specializing in shell lamps and carved coconut heads." Florida tourist souvenirs of this type were popular in 1950, the postmark year. At the time, stamps were still 1¢. (Henry Higgins.)

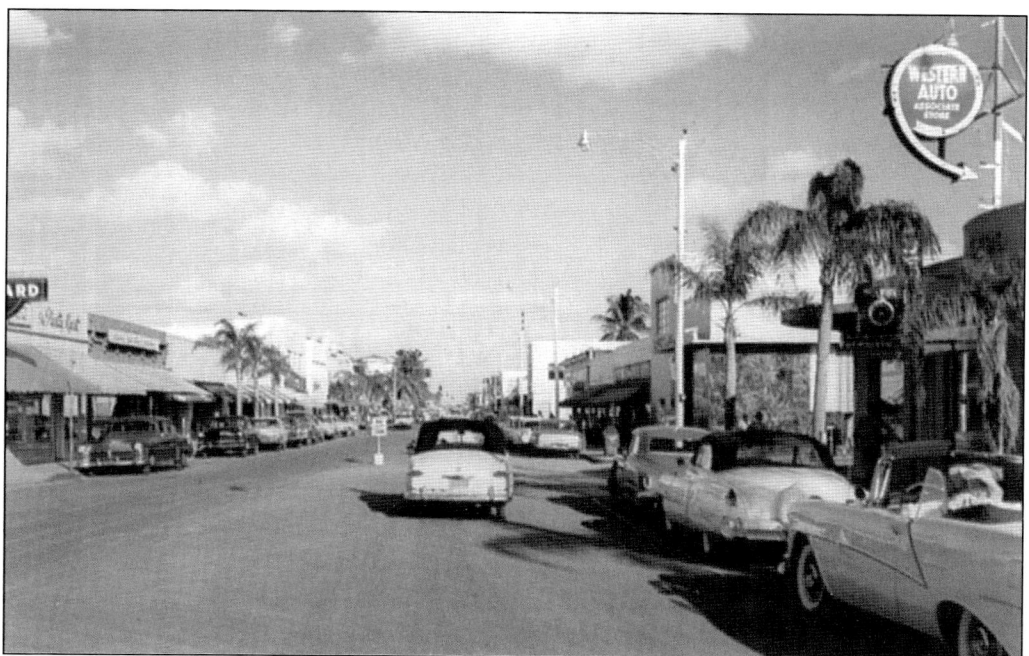

ATLANTIC AVENUE. A woman in a wide-brimmed hat waits in the convertible parked next to the Western Auto Associates store at 228 East Atlantic Avenue. This 1955 view looks to the east.

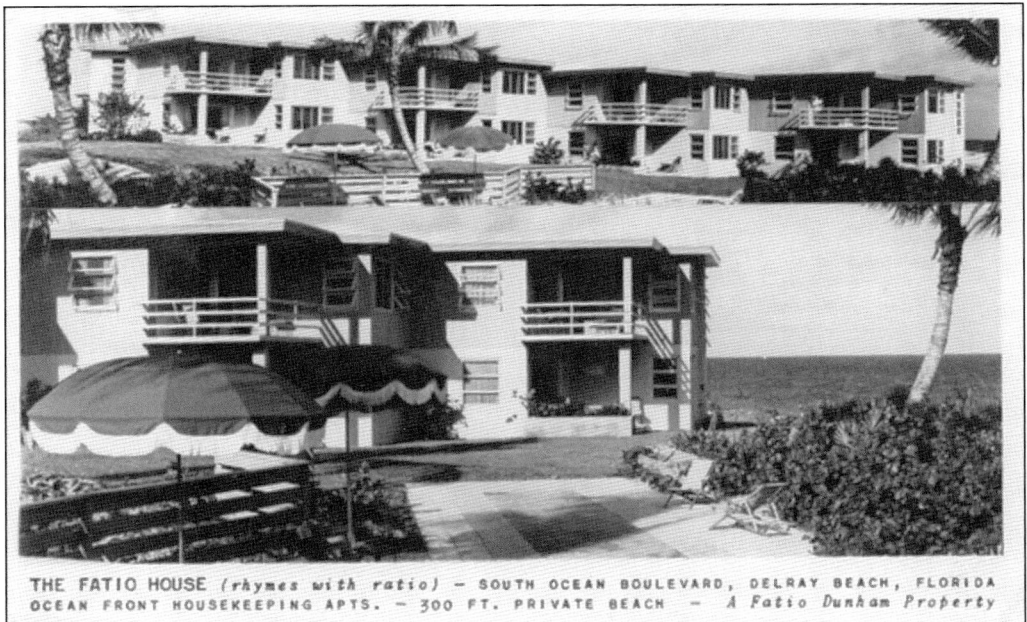

FATIO RHYMES WITH RATIO. A guest at the Fatio House on South Ocean Boulevard writes, "Dear Aunt Clara, This is a new apartment right on the beach, and most attractively furnished." The card is postmarked Palm Beach, July 24, 1952, when a stamp cost 2¢. (Henry Higgins.)

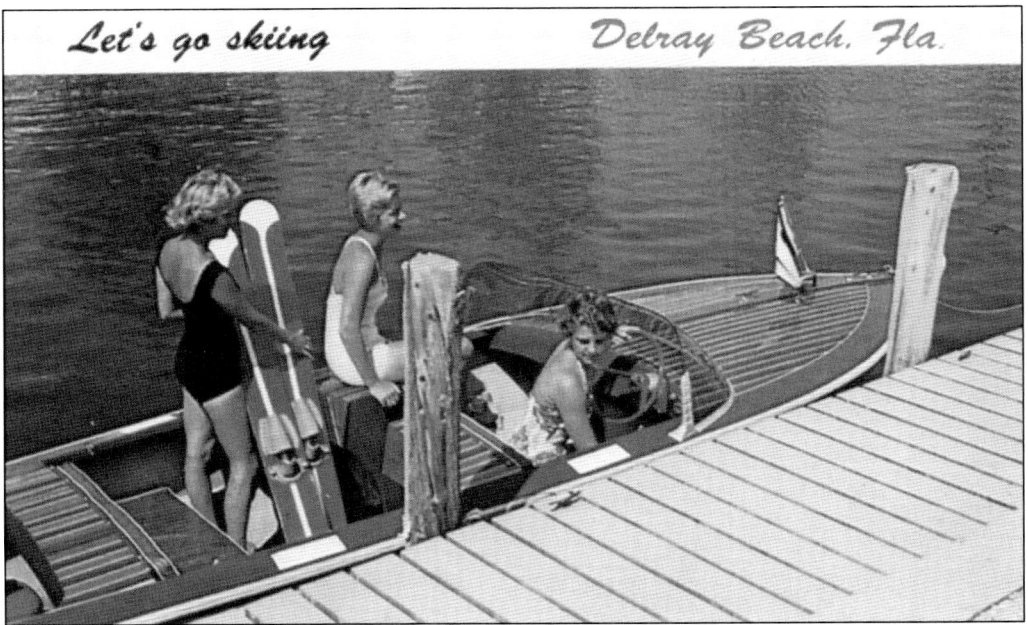

LET'S GO SKIING. A young woman visiting Delray Beach sent this card to her family in Baltimore on June 2, 1960. Waterskiing was invented in Minnesota in 1922 and became an official competitive sport in 1939. The sport's popularity paralleled the growth of family boating. This postcard was published by the Parlin Color Company of Boynton Beach. (Henry Higgins.)

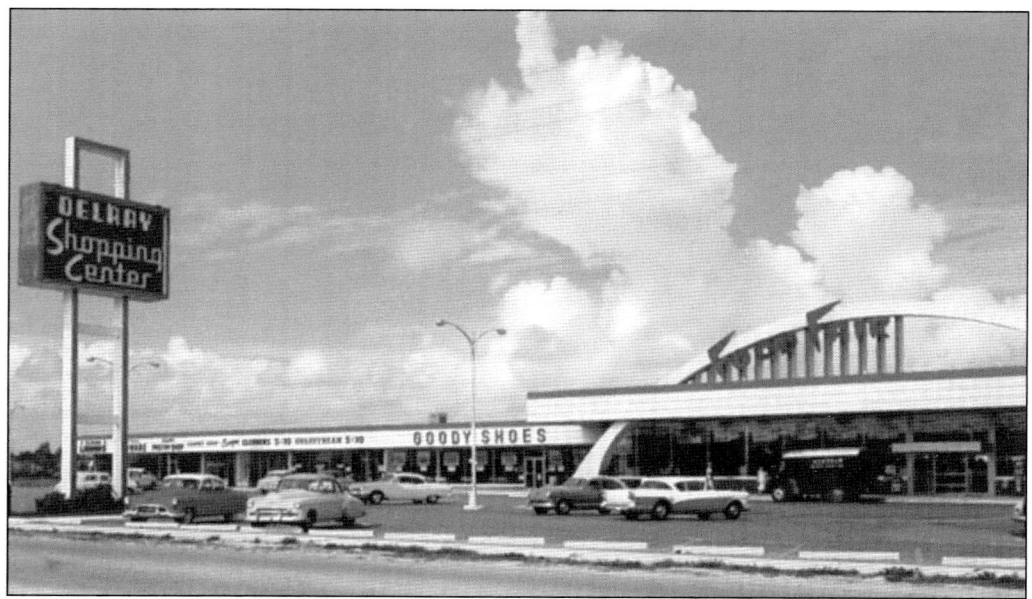

FOOD FAIR. The Delray Shopping Center is located on North Federal Highway (U.S. 1). This postcard, revealing a view of the beautiful sky, was mailed in March 1966. In addition to Food Fair, the streamlined strip shopping center with the distinctive arch contained several other businesses, including Goody's Shoes and the Gulfstream 5&10. The arch always had verticals halfway, as pictured here.

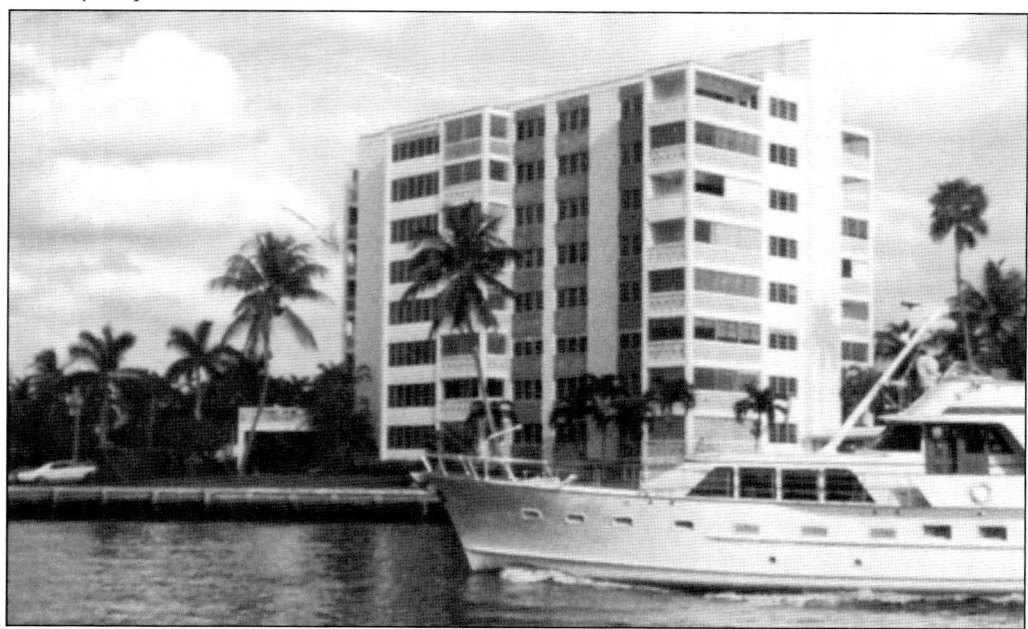

DELRAY SUMMIT. The Delray Summit Apartments were constructed at 1000 Lowry Street in 1965. With eight stories, the Summit was said to be the tallest building in Delray Beach at the time. This postcard was written and delivered locally in 1977 by a seasonal resident with family ties in Delray Beach. The photographer was William Crapo, a resident of the Summit. (Henry Higgins.)

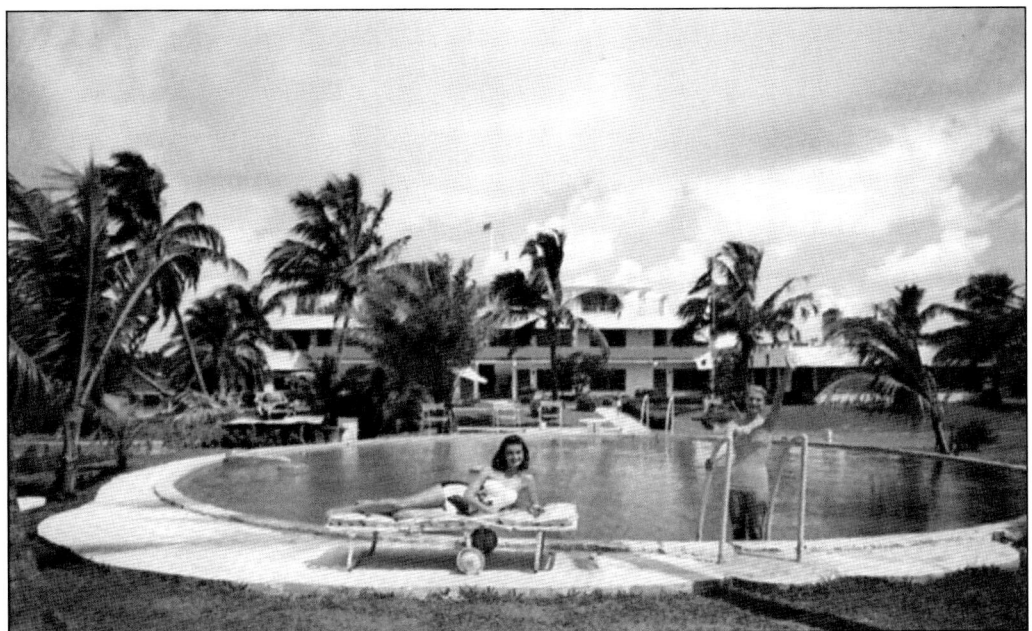

NAUTICAL AIRE POOL. The oval pool at the Nautical Aire Apartments looks inviting. The streamlined Nautical Aire building stands next to the Intracoastal Waterway at 917 Bucida Road. Management advertised that the apartments had a "private yacht basin" and a "private pool." The postcard text stated, "Open all year. References exchanged." (Henry Higgins.)

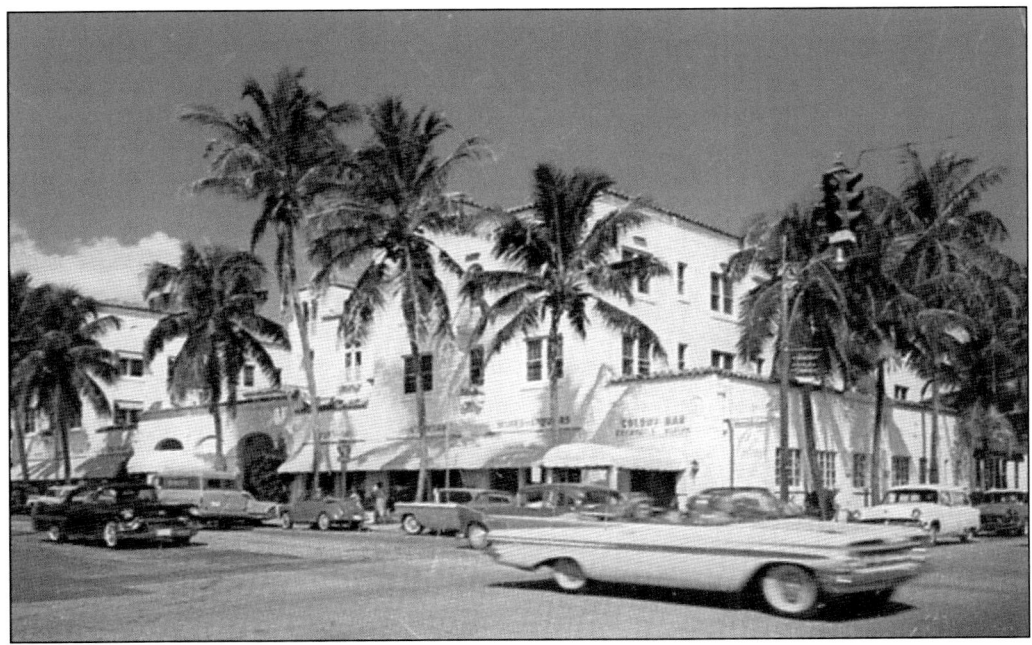

CONVERTIBLE ON THE AVENUE. A convertible streaks past the Colony Hotel on Atlantic Avenue, perhaps heading for the beach. This postcard was produced as an advertisement for the Colony Hotel in 1959. (Henry Higgins.)

Discover Thousands of Local History Books Featuring Millions of Vintage Images

Arcadia Publishing, the leading local history publisher in the United States, is committed to making history accessible and meaningful through publishing books that celebrate and preserve the heritage of America's people and places.

Find more books like this at
www.arcadiapublishing.com

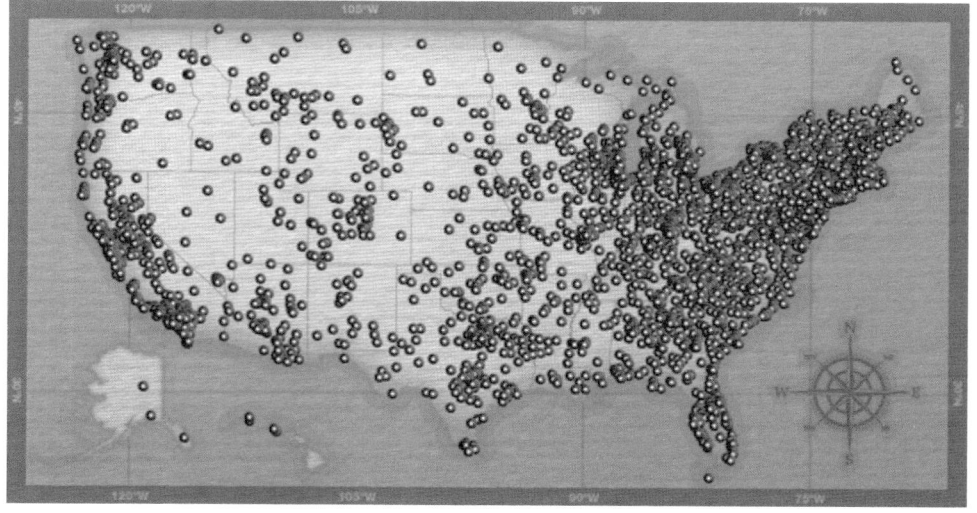

Search for your hometown history, your old stomping grounds, and even your favorite sports team.

Consistent with our mission to preserve history on a local level, this book was printed in South Carolina on American-made paper and manufactured entirely in the United States. Products carrying the accredited Forest Stewardship Council (FSC) label are printed on 100 percent FSC-certified paper.

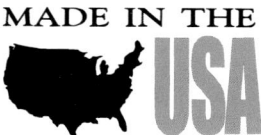